Also sprach Zarathustra

TABLE OF CONTENTS

DEDICATION

I dedicate this guide to Warren Milner, for his strength, humor, and the unique joy he brought to our family. He will be remembered with warmth.

Also sprach Zarathustra

Xenosaga III is a fight for the survival of the human race. Dangerous creatures called the Gnosis have invaded the universe and are killing anything they touch. These monsters have been seen here and there for many ages. Now, they come in immense numbers, summoned for reasons that few understand. Their presence may mean that the entire human race may one day disappear from all the worlds.

Even worse, the Gnosis aren't the only enemy. Elements within several planetary governments and covert organizations have chosen sides. Within every conspiracy seems to be layers of truth and deception, and the technology used by these groups far surpasses that of even some of the strongest planets. How are these entities connected to the Gnosis? What can be done to stop this seemingly infinite army of monsters and those who won't strive to fight against them?

As you investigate the Gnosis and deeper connections to the problem, many enemies will stand in your way. Your party members will learn more about themselves and become stronger. There is much to be found along the path and understanding how to use the materials scavenged from your enemies will make for a fairer fight. This book is available to even the odds, providing insight into many things about the game.

Maps, hidden items, character strategies, battle tactics, peripheral missions, and a full background on the Xenosaga experience are found within. For returning players, this guide offers a thorough explanation of all that has changed between the last episode and **Xenosaga III.** For newer players, the book gets you up to speed on the extremely-developed plot of the series while explaining combat basics to get you started comfortably.

INTRODUCTION

ARCHIVES

CHARACTERS

TACTICAL FILES

EQUIPMENT

THREAT ASSESSMENT

REGIONAL ANALYSIS

SUPPLEMENTAL DATA

ARCHIVES

The future is what you make of it. However, those who do not study the past are doomed to repeat it. Within the archives is all the history since time was time. To keep your reading light, they have been sorted and only the files pertaining to the current dilemma are listed.

GENERAL INFORMATION AND TERMS

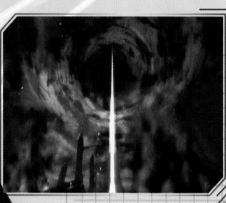

ABEL'S ARK

Abel's Ark is seen as a Gnosis the size of an entire star system. Several planets can be seen fused with the Gnosis, including an Earth-like planet.

ABYSS

The Abyss has two uses. The most common and least accurate is a synonym for hell.

The less common and far more descriptive is the pair of massive black holes located near where Old Miltia once was. The binary gravitational forces make travel through the area impossible without the Y-Data locked within MOMO's subconscious.

A.G.W.S.

Pronounced "eggs" by many people, the Anti-Gnosis Weapon System mechs are significantly smaller than the A.M.W.S. This is to allow them to maneuver within a starship or space station.

The A.G.W.S. cannot function without the power feed from the ship to which they are assigned. To keep their size small, they do not have any onboard fuel or power generation.

There are several weapon and equipment configurations for A.G.W.S. used by the various organizations, but only a few are able to purchase the combat models created by Vector Industries.

A.M.W.S.

The Assault Maneuver Weapon Systems, pronounced "aims," mechs are much larger and more powerful than the A.G.W.S. units. While more deadly than A.G.W.S., the A.M.W.S. are not nearly as powerful as the E.S. Units.

ANIMA RELIC

The primary difference in construction of an A.M.W.S. and an E.S. unit is the Anima Relic, or Vessel of Anima. These are artifacts shaped like enormous human spines that were found with the original Zohar during the Lake Turkana excavation.

The Anima Relic increases the response speed between the E.S. and the pilot. This allows the mech to maneuver much faster than the slower A.M.W.S. and perform attacks that would be impossible in the standard mechs.

CATHEDRAL SHIP

While its name is deceiving, Cathedral Ship isn't a ship at all. During the Ariadne incident, it is widely believed that a giant Gnosis swallowed the planet. In truth, Ariadne was transformed into the planet sized Gnosis named Cathedral Ship.

While most of the planet has been transformed into parts of this monstrous Gnosis, there are still parts of the planet, such as parks and streets, fused with the Gnosis.

COMPASS OF ORDER

Another artifact from the Lake Turkana dig, the Compass of Order has been in Wilhelm's possession for some time now. With it, he can see events as they will transpire before they do.

DESIGNER CHILDREN

A number of parents in the galaxy have the money and want to have the perfect child. Designer Children are genetically enhanced from a very young age to excel at a task chosen by the parents.

DME ADDICTION

Consumption of Realian flesh can cause this physical and mental illness. Due to the engineering behind Realians, their flesh and brain tissue is extremely addictive. The consumed flesh causes physical mutation and complete emotional addiction.

ENCEPHALON

A virtual copy of the physical world, the Encephalon can be used to recreate locations in absolute detail. This makes it very useful for testing combat systems without the inherent danger of actual combat.

Some have noted that the Encephalon feels more like another dimension rather than simply a virtual world. They have reported meeting odd characters within the Encephalon.

INTRODUCTION

ARCHIVES

CHARACTERS

TACTICAL FILES

EQUIPMENT

THREAT ASSESSMENT

REGIONAL ANALYSIS

SUPPLEMENTAL DATA

E.S.

Each named after a child of Jacob, as they appear in the book of Genesis, the E.S. units are A.M.W.S. units equipped with Anima Relics. This gives them faster response time and special abilities. These abilities can range from being able to enter hyperspace without contacting the U.M.N. to allowing the pilot use of Ether Skills.

ETHER

Especial Theory of Rudimentary has been shortened to "ether" by most people as the proper name is far too long for civilized conversation. Ether uses nanomachines to create effects that are seen as magic by many.

The effects of Ether abilities vary as widely as people do. Whether by contact with U-DO, genetic manipulation or mutation, or archaic skills, the powers granted by Ether can range from energy emission to psychic powers.

FIFTH JERUSALEM

Though the original home world has been lost, humans have managed to flourish in the galaxy. Fifth Jerusalem is the capital of the known universe and home to the Galaxy Federation Army.

GNOSIS

These creatures began their attack shortly after the incident on Miltia. 'Gnosis' refers to the army of creatures attacking the known universe and can also be used to describe a single type of creature within the army.

The Gnosis exist in imaginary space and, as such, are not affected by either the laws of physics or ordinary weapons. The only way to destroy a Gnosis is to first bridge the gap between imaginary space and real space. When pulled into real space, Gnosis are comprised almost entirely of salt.

Though there seem to be many different types of Gnosis, they have never been seen disagreeing or communicating at all. They work together with brutal efficiency. Gnosis have existed throughout time, but until the Miltian Conflict, the sightings have been seldom and far between. The use of the Song of Nephilim, during the Miltian Conflict, began the mass invasion of the known universe.

HILBERT EFFECT

Named after the scientist that first discovered it, the Hilbert Effect is a limited perception field that can connect real space to imaginary space for a short time.

The KOS-MOS unit is capable of sustaining a field of 300,000 kilometers and can expand that, for short periods, to several million astronomical units. 100-Series Observational Units can also create a field up to 100 kilometers in size using a special amplifier. Without the amplifier, however, they can only create fields up to a few hundred meters in size.

LABYRINTHOS

The main headquarters of U-TIC during the Miltian conflict, Labyrinthos was used by Dr. Mizrahi for his Zohar research. The massive structure housed the original Zohar, the Song of Nephilim, and U-DO. At the end of the Miltian conflict, Labyrinthos vanished into the Abyss along with the rest of the planet. It was not seen again until Ormus and Albedo caused its reappearance. It didn't last long and soon became the center of the planet wide transformation into the Omega System.

LAKE TURKANA

The large body of water, in northern Kenya, where the Zohar and Anima Relics were found.

LOST JERUSALEM

It's been over 4,000 years since Earth was removed from the star maps and renamed "Lost Jerusalem." Mankind was forced to flee into space shortly after a large metal plate was found in an archaeological dig near Lake Turkana, in northern Kenya. The "Zohar" as it has become known was at the center of the disturbance that resulted in the absolute disappearance of mankind's home world.

MILTIAN CONFLICT

While the outcome of the Miltian Conflict is well known, the actual events that transpired and the motivations behind them are known to very few.

The planet Miltia was plunged into conflict when the U-TIC Organization made a play for power. The Galaxy Federation deployed its Third Descent operation against Labyrinthos, the headquarters of U-TIC. Officially, these U.R.T.V.s were sent to sever the connection between the U-TIC A.M.W.S. units and the Zohar, their power source.

In an attempt to counter the U.R.T.V.s sent by the Federation, U-TIC activated the Song of Nephilim. The Song caused mass panic and confusion as soldiers and Realians alike went mad. Only a few soldiers and Realians seemed to be resistant to the Song of Nephilim and a special unit made its way through to chaos to Labyrinthos.

The U.R.T.V.s made it to the Zohar and prepared to use their anti-existence waves to destroy U-DO, which was though to be part of the control mechanism for the Zohar. There was dissent in the U.R.T.V. ranks and, as a result, most of the U.R.T.V.s were affected by U-DO.

During the disarray, the Zohar went berserk and created a space-time anomaly. The entire planet of Miltia was pulled into the Abyss and anyone still on it was lost. The end result of the conflict was the mass invasion of the Gnosis.

M.W.S.

Designed by Miyuki Itsumi, the Multiple Weapon System is a device that attaches to the user's arm. Equipped with a weapon for every occasion, the M.W.S. made a name for itself when Shion tested the prototype.

PROTO MERKABAH

Built by Joachim Mizrahi, the station's public function was to research and develop Realians. However, the true function is far more complex.

This enormous space station was designed as one of three pieces to discover the truth of the universe. When docked with the Song of Nephilim and the original Zohar, the Proto Merkabah was to use the Gnosis summoned by the Song as an energy source to tap into the Zohar, an even greater source of power.

Proto Merkabah was instead used as a weapon by Albedo during the battle over Second Miltia. With the power of the summoned Gnosis, Albedo was able to destroy the Federation forces around Second Miltia entirely. He was, thankfully, stopped before he could destroy Second Miltia and the station was broken apart and allowed to disintegrate while entering Second Miltia's atmosphere.

PROTO OMEGA

Found in Labyrinthos, Proto Omega was originally a weapon designed to destroy the Gnosis. With its U.M.N. Phase Transfer Cannon, it could attack any target anywhere in known space. Using the original Zohar as its power source, the Proto Omega had few matches in the universe.

REALIAN

With the construction and perfection of Realians, androids and cyborgs became largely obsolete. Originally seen as property and equipment, Realians had their emotions suppressed to make them more docile and less prone to disobey commands. Shortly after the Miltian Conflict, Realians were granted basic human rights and, aside from military or other dangerous occupational Realians, tampering with their emotions was made illegal.

While all Realians have the same basic programming, created by Vector, most of their skills and capabilities are tailored to the job they will be performing.

RENNES-LE-CHÂTEAU

Originally thought to be an asteroid, close inspection reveals this to be a piece of a planet that still has an atmosphere. Floating in the middle of space, the chunk of rock has forests and a set of ruins. Gnosis seem abnormally drawn to the area.

RHINE MAIDEN

When all three flagships and the corporate headquarters of Vector Industries activate the Rhine Maiden in the proper configuration, the Rhine Maiden's effect is awesome. It's an anti-Gnosis sonic weapon that is harmless to humans, but breaks down all Gnosis into their base element: salt.

Only when the Woglinde II, Wellgunde, and Floβhilde are in formation with the Dämmerung, can the effect be produced. This is, however, the only requirement as the cannon can even be fired while in hyperspace.

SONG OF NEPHILIM

Designed to combine with the Proto Merkabah, the Song of Nephilim was a pyramid-shaped space station. Its primary weapon was a psychic wavelength that was broadcast in all directions. The wavelength can only be heard by a few special people and is said to sound like a female voice.

While only a few can hear the song, nearly everyone contacted by it is affected. Realians are the most affected with humans only slightly less prone to fall into madness. The primary function of the wavelength is the mass summoning of Gnosis to the area. This played a major role in the Miltian Conflict, but is thought to have been destroyed when the Proto Merkabah, to which it was docked, disintegrated in the atmosphere of Second Miltia during the Kukai Foundation incident 14 years later.

T.C.

The acronym used in the current dating system. It stands for Transcend Christ and the calendars were changed in 2510 A.D.

U-DO

U-DO is linked to nearly every major event in recent years. Shortened from Unus-Mundus Drive Operation system, U-DO was originally described by Dmitri Yuriev as an artificial consciousness that had linked with the U.M.N. that was carrying some kind of dangerous waves.

This statement was completely false and issued to cover up Dmitri's complete lack of understanding of U-DO. U-DO is a wave consciousness from a higher realm. It manifests itself as a huge cloud of red gas with long tendrils.

The U.R.T.V.s were originally designed by Dmitri Yuriev to counter U-DO. Their anti-waves were designed to resist U-DO, but there was a major flaw in the design. The waves did not neutralize each other. This opened the possibility of a waveform collision that would release immense thermal energy and destroy anything in the area.

During the Miltian Conflict, the U.R.T.V.s were preparing to attack U-DO, which was part of a Zohar control system at the time, when Rubedo had a vision of the entire planet being destroyed by their actions. Rubedo severed the psychic link with the other U.R.T.V.s, but this left them vulnerable to U-DO, which killed all but Nigredo, Rubedo, and Albedo.

U.M.N.

The Unus Mundus Network, U.M.N. for short, is a network spanning known space that deals with space warps and faster than light communications. While the network is overseen by the U.M.N. Management Agency, meaning they control nearly all information within the Galaxy Federation, Vector Industries provides almost all of the resources and facilities.

To use travel through hyperspace, ships contact the U.M.N. in a Column Area and transmit a flight plan. When the plan has been approved and the fee paid, the ship can gate into hyperspace.

U.R.T.V.

Biological children of Dr. Dmitri Yuriev, the U-DO Retro Virus units are a series of biological weapons whose life energy wavelength cancels that of U-DO. Though units 001-669 were created from the same embryonic culture, only 666-669 were given additional mutations to develop their unique gifts. These mutations separated them from the collective conscious shared by the other units and resulted in differing hair and eye colors; they became know as Variants.

Y-DATA

A complete log of Joachim Mizrahi's research including information regarding the Zohar, the Gnosis phenomenon, and the location of Lost Jerusalem. The access codes for the U.M.N. transfer column near Old Miltia, which have been lost since the Miltian Conflict, are also in the Y-Data.

Only two copies are known to exist. MOMO and Canaan both have encrypted copies buried within their consciousness.

ZOHAR

The original Zohar was found in an archaeological dig in Africa over four millennia ago. The object is an enormous gold-colored metallic plate. The original caused the disappearance of Earth and later Miltia. Before the disappearance, much research was done by Joachim Mizrahi, the Galaxy Federation and a scientist affiliated with Ormus, named Sellers.

While much of the Zohar seemed to remain a mystery, enough was learned to create Zohar Emulators. These emulators look identical to the original, but pale in comparison to the energy output of the original. Visually, the emulators are identical to the original save for the red Hebrew letters in place of the blue jewel.

While the emulators are far less powerful, planet Ariadne vanished as a result of an emulator's power.

Nearly every organization in the known universe is after any and all information about the Zohar. Many believe the Zohar to be the cause of the Gnosis dilemma, an unlimited source of energy, and the virtual prison of U-DO, all in one!

MAJOR ORGANIZATIONS

GALAXY FEDERATION

The Galaxy Federation Government (GFG) is an over-reaching government that spans two galaxies and nearly half a million planets. This allows each planet to keep its own government and resolve small intra-planet issues without needing to contact the GFG.

HYAMS GROUP

A massive corporation with substantial wealth, the Hyams Group has become the rival of Vector Industries. The Hyams Group has funded many organizations and institutions that compete with Vector in a variety of ways. The Yuriev Institute and U-TIC are both known recipients of Hyams money. Through these two organizations, Ormus also benefits from this corporation.

IMMIGRANT FLEET

The Immigrant Fleet is the public face of the Ormus Society. Through the use of its military branch, U-TIC, the Immigrant Fleet has declared itself the guardian of the Zohar "since time immemorable." They were at the center of the Miltian Conflict, and made another attempt at the Zohar when the path to Old Miltia was opened again. The Immigrant Fleet was largely wiped out by the Omega System.

KUKAI FOUNDATION

Originally a military force put together to destroy the remains of the U-TIC Organization, much of the Kukai Foundation's military might has been decommissioned. In an effort to avoid total decommission, and thus leave U-TIC free to reform, the Kukai Foundation expanded into several civilian sectors and has become one of the fastest rising organizations.

The center of the Kukai Foundation is an enormous space colony that is able to move by docking with the Durandal, the flagship of the foundation. Closely allied with the planet's government, the Kukai Foundation was present at the incident at Second Miltia. During the subsequent Gnosis attack, the colony took moderate damage.

ORMUS

The roots of this religious cult date back to Lost Jerusalem. They were some of the first to evacuate Earth as the Immigrant Fleet. They have created satellite organizations, including U-TIC, to change the fate of the galaxies without drawing attention to itself.

Dealt a blow when the Patriarch was killed on the Omega System when Margulis betrayed him, Ormus is now under the control of Heinlein. Though the Hyams Group funds the many organizations, Ormus is the one that pulls the strings.

SALVATOR FACTION

Secretly controlled by Dr. Dmtri Yuriev, the Salvator Faction still holds substantial power in the Galaxy Federation after his apparent death. Headed by Designer Children, the faction has a number of high-profile members such as Pierre Ruryk.

SCIENTIA

Founded over 100 years ago on the planet Michtam, Scientia is an anti-Vector underground organization. The leader, Doctus, is so secretive that an android is used to make contact with outsiders.

S.O.C.E.

Convened in 4752 to counter the Gnosis threat, the Subcommittee on Close Encounters is directly overseen by and reports to the Galaxy Federation Government. With over 2,000 members, the subcommittee is based on the orbital station of Fifth Jerusalem. While substantial in size, only seven members are considered part of the operational core. The other members are scientists from various fields, government agencies, and corporations.

INTRODUCTION

ARCHIVES

CHARACTERS

TACTICAL FILES

EQUIPMENT

THREAT ASSESSMENT

REGIONAL ANALYSIS

SUPPLEMENTAL DOSSIER

U-TIC ORGANIZATION

The Unknown Territory Interventing and Creation Organization was buried in obscurity for several years after its involvement with the Miltian Conflict. Led by Heinlein, the organization resurfaced in 4767 T.C.

As the military arm of Ormus, U-TIC has no direct allegiance to the Galaxy Federation. This causes many conflicts as U-TIC uses technology that far surpasses that of the Galaxy Federation.

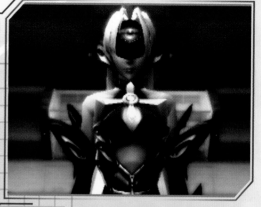

VECTOR INDUSTRIES

Almost everything made in the Galaxy Federation can be traced in some way back to Vector Industries. This conglomerate has facilities on every planet and manufactures everything from military weapons to food.

The current CEO, and founder of Vector Industries, is Wilhelm. This seems odd as the company was founded in the Lost Jerusalem era.

The most noteworthy of the many divisions are the First, Second, and Third R&D Divisions. Shion Uzuki was employed by Vector Industries until recently.

YURIEV INSTITUTE

Dr. Dmtri Yuriev created the U.R.T.V. units to counter U-DO, and the Yuriev Institute on Planet Vartas to train the U.R.T.V. units. While the goal of countering U-DO seems to have remained unchanged, the institute has been maintained by the Salvator Faction until Dr. Yuriev can return to control.

ZIGGURAT INDUSTRIES

Once specializing in the Life Recycling Cyborgs, Ziggurat Industries has changed its focus to nanotechnology. This change was primarily due to the repeal of the Life Recycling Act, which allowed cybernetic enhancement to be used without the consent of soldiers who had been wounded on the battlefield, by the Species Preservation Act.

PERSONS OF NOTE

INTRODUCTION

ARCHIVES

CHARACTERS

TACTICAL FILES

EQUIPMENT

THREAT ASSESSMENT

REGIONAL ANALYSIS

SUPPLEMENTAL DATA

ALBEDO

Originally called U.R.T.V. 667, Albedo was one of the final four U.R.T.V. units and was subjected to additional mutation to bring his powers to full flourish. Albedo was close friends with units 666 (Jr.), whom is Albedo's conjoined twin, and 669 (Gaignun Kukai).

During the Miltian Conflict, Albedo was left undefended against U-DO and was driven insane by the contact. He joins Ormus until his death at the hands of Jr. Albedo is resurrected as the White Testament.

ALLEN RIDGELEY

After graduating from Bormeo University, Allen joined Vector's First R&D Division and was put on the KOS-MOS project under Kevin Winnicot. After Kevin's death, and the promotion of Shion Uzuki, Allen is promoted to Junior Chief Engineer.

Allen is swept along with Shion during the events from the Woglinde disaster through the incident at Second Miltia. Allen is later promoted to Chief Engineer of the KOS-MOS project when Shion resigns from Vector.

CHAOS

There is very little data on the one called chaos.

A jack of all trades, chaos works aboard the Elsa in nearly every capacity. He met Shion Uzuki, Allen Ridgeley, and KOS-MOS while working on the Elsa.

DMTRI YURIEV

The genetic father of the U.R.T.V. units, Dmtri is obsessed with the destruction of U-DO. He has used life-enhancing technology to extend his life-span so he may accomplish this driving goal. He created the Yuriev Institute to train the U.R.T.V. units and is the primary force behind the Salvator Faction.

He was thought killed when Nigredo shot him, however, he discovered a way to transfer his consciousness into Nigredo and further extend his life.

ERICH WEBER

More commonly known as the cyber terrorist "Voyager," Erich killed the wife and stepson of counterterrorism agent Jan Sauer. He was later resurrected by Wilhelm and became the Black, and first, Testament.

HEINLEIN

Though no one has seen Heinlein, many have seen his machinations. As head of U-TIC, and now Ormus as well, he wields a great deal of influence and commands both Margulis and Sellers. The three conspired to kill the Patriarch and clear the way for Heinlein to take command of Ormus. As if he didn't have enough power, Heinlein is also the CEO of the Hyams Group, the main competitor of Vector Industries.

JAN SAUER

See "Ziggy."

JIN UZUKI

Jin Uzuki was a Captain in the Galaxy Federation's Special Forces Intelligence Division during the Miltian Conflict. Margulis was his direct commander. He discovered that Margulis was working as a double agent and tried to steal the Y-Data to uncover him, but Margulis confronted him. Jin Uzuki was able to steal the Y-Data from Margulis, but during the battle with Margulis, Jin gives Margulis a large scar on his face. He retired after the Miltian Conflict and opened an antique bookstore on Second Miltia. Jin is the older brother of Shion Uzuki.

JR.

Gaignun Kukai, Jr. goes by many names. Originally called U.R.T.V. 666, Rubedo tried to save Miltia during the Miltian Conflict by breaking the link with the other U.R.T.V. units. Many of them were killed with only two others surviving. Jr. joined the Kukai Foundation and masquerades as Gaignun Kukai's son, though Jr. is Gaignun's older brother. Now second in command of the Foundation, and in direct command of the Durandal, many of those working beneath him call him "Little Master."

KEVIN WINNICOT

Graduating from Bormeo University at the age of 14, Kevin Winnicot became employed by Vector Industries and developed KOS-MOS. Kevin and Shion Uzuki met and became lovers while working on the KOS-MOS project at Vector. Kevin, then engaged to Shion, was killed when the Archetype KOS-MOS was activated prematurely and went on a rampage. He was later resurrected and became the Red Testament.

KOS-MOS

Developed primarily by Kevin Winnicot, KOS-MOS is an anti-Gnosis combat android. With Kevin's death, Shion Uzuki took over Vector's KOS-MOS project. Containing a Hilbert Effect projector more powerful than some space ships and having more processing power than Observational Realians, there is some question as to whether Kevin Winnicot was the only genius behind the project.

LUIS VIRGIL

Lt. Virgil was a soldier in the Galaxy Federation with a few problems. His violent hatred of Realians was known to many, but his DME addiction was lesser known. When the Gnosis attacked the Woglinde, Lt. Virgil was killed by KOS-MOS as a necessary loss to guarantee Shion's survival. He was later resurrected by Wilhelm and became the Blue Testament.

MARGULIS

Margulis is a Lieutenant Commander in U-TIC. He reports directly to Heinlein and was part of the conspiracy that removed the Patriarch from the living and allowed Heinlein to become the leader of Ormus. During the Miltian Conflict, he was a double agent serving as a Colonel in the Federation Military. Jin Uzuki learned of his treachery and attempted to uncover it. During the fight that ensued, Jin was able to steal the Y-Data and leave a scar across Margulis' face.

MOMO

A 100-Series Observational Realian, MOMO was created by Joachim Mizrahi to link Sakura Mizrahi, his severely autistic daughter, to the real world. When Sakura died, Joachim Mizrahi attempted to meld her consciousness with MOMO's.

This failed and after the Miltian Conflict, MOMO was sent to Fifth Jerusalem to live with Juli Mizrahi, Joachim's wife. As the carrier of the Y-Data, MOMO has been kidnapped and attacked several times. Ziggy, at the request of the S.O.C.E., rescued her from Margulis.

Albedo tried several times before he was able to pull the Y-Data from MOMO's mind.

PATRIARCH SERGIUS

Sergius XVII was the leader of the Immigrant Fleet and Ormus until his death at the hands of the Testaments. Generally referred to as the "Patriarch," Sergius used Ormus' dummy corporations and contacts to open the way to Old Miltia and the original Zohar. Upon obtaining the Zohar and the Proto Omega, the Patriarch had plans to subjugate the entire universe, but was betrayed by Margulis, Sellers, and Heinlein. With no one to protect him, the Patriarch was easily killed.

INTRODUCTION

ARCHIVES

CHARACTERS

TACTICAL FILES

EQUIPMENT

THREAT ASSESSMENT

REGIONAL ANALYSIS

SUPPLEMENTAL DATA

PELLEGRI

Pellegri is Margulis' direct subordinate and with him during the events of Pleroma and Ariadne. She is an accomplished A.M.W.S. pilot and is in possession of the E.S. Issachar. She and her wingmen, Herman and Richard, were thwarted in their attempt to capture MOMO by Canaan in the E.S. Asher.

ROTH MANTEL

No information is available on the head of the T-elos project.

SELLERS

Confined to a hover chair, Sellers is still a prominent figure in both Ormus and the Hyams Group. He conspired with Margulis and Heinlein to betray the Patriarch during the events at Old Miltia. He ordered the destruction of the Pleroma station and is a scientist interested in the Zohar.

SHION UZUKI

Shion joined Vector's First R&D Division at the early age of 18. She was assigned to the KOS-MOS project under Kevin Winnicot. At the death of Kevin, who had become Shion's fiancé, she was promoted to Chief Engineer of the KOS-MOS project.

Shion came into contact with the Kukai Foundation's ship, the Elsa, after the Vector ship Woglinde was attacked by Gnosis while it was transporting a Zohar Emulator. During the attack, Shion was touched by a Gnosis, but was not turned into sodium chloride. She can hear the Song of Nephilim and frequently has visions of a girl named Nephilim.

After the events surrounding the Omega System, Shion resigned from Vector and made contact with Scientia.

T-ELOS

Built by the mysterious Roth Mantel, T-elos is an android almost identical to KOS-MOS. The visual differences are only color, but the tactical capabilities are quite different. T-elos appears to be a more powerful and advanced version of KOS-MOS.

TESTAMENTS

The Testaments are the vanguard of Wilhelm's forces. They are his closest assistants and servants. While granted power and immortality by Wilhelm, the Testaments have retained much of their personalities.

TESTAMENTS		
NAME	ALIAS	TESTAMENT
ERICH WEBER	VOYAGER	BLACK
KEVIN WINNICOT	ROTH MANTEL	RED
LUIS VIRGIL		BLUE
ALBEDO	U.R.T.V. 667	WHITE

WILHELM

The founder and current CEO of Vector Industries, Wilhelm has been around for many years. As Vector Industries began during the Lost Jerusalem era, he is likely to be over 4,000 years old. Wilhelm is often seen using the Compass of Order to see how events will play out.

He has resurrected the dead Erich Weber, Kevin Winnicot, Luis Virgil, and Albedo Piazolla and given them powers beyond that of mortals. They joined as the Black, Red, Blue, and White (respectively) Testaments.

ZIGGY

Born Jan Sauer and employed as a Federation counter-terrorism agent, Ziggy's life changed forever when his wife and stepson were murdered by the cyber terrorist Voyager, Erich Weber.

Jan Sauer committed suicide. Due to the Life Recycling Act, Ziggurat Industries used his body to create a new cyborg. Ziggurat 8 was the eighth, and final, of the cyborgs as the Life Recycling Act was repealed. As cyborgs have no human rights, Ziggy was at the whim of his superiors until being sent to rescue MOMO, whom he now accompanies as a guardian.

EVENTS OF PREVIOUS EPISODES

INTRODUCTION

ARCHIVES

CHARACTERS

TACTICAL FILES

EQUIPMENT

THREAT ASSESSMENT

REGIONAL ANALYSIS

SUPPLEMENTAL DATA

XENOSAGA I

The Woglinde, flagship of the 117th Marine Division of the Galaxy Federation Army, investigated the disappearance of planet Ariadne.

An object, thought to be a Zohar, was found in the area and stored in the Woglinde.

During a Gnosis attack, in which Shion was nearly killed, KOS-MOS auto-started and defeated the Gnosis (KOS-MOS killed Virgil during the fight).

The escape pod, with Shion and Allen inside, was picked up by the Elsa. Matthews, the captain of the ship, agreed to take them to Second Miltia. On the way, chaos' power over the Gnosis was seen by Shion.

Ziggy was given a mission to rescue MOMO from the U-TIC organization (interested in the Y-Data in MOMO's subconscious), which was a success. During their escape, they were saved by the Elsa and joined the crew.

The Elsa met with the Durandal, which was investigating the U-TIC organization at the time. A Federation fleet attempted to arrest the party by surrounding the Kukai Foundation (thanks to Margulis's schemes), but their innocence was proven by the battle data recorded by KOS-MOS.

The Song of Nephilim, invented by Joachim Mizrahi, appeared over Second Miltia and summoned a swarm of Gnosis. With the help of KOS-MOS's phase cannon, to force the Song of Nephilim to appear in real space, the group entered and saved the captured MOMO. During the fight, Proto Merkabah, an enormous factory/weapon, was summoned to Second Miltia. When the reactor was destroyed before it could fire on the planet, Albedo set it to collide with the planet below. KOS-MOS was able to initiate a dismantling sequence and the enormous fortress fell to pieces, which were obliterated while entering the atmosphere.

XENOSAGA II

Shion returns to Vector's Second R&D Division to turn over KOS-MOS. Jr. and the others head to the U.M.N. Control Center to analyze the Y-Data within MOMO.

Pellegri, with a mobile weapon team, attacked MOMO once more. The attackers were only repelled by the appearance of Canaan in the E.S. Asher.

Shion is reunited with her brother.

During analysis of the Y-Data with the help of the crew of the Durandal, watched by Juli (the mother of the girl whom MOMO was modeled after. MOMO considers this woman her mother) from the Contact Subcommittee, Albedo springs a trap and begins stealing the Y-Data.

To keep the data from being leaked completely, MOMO shatters her mind and severs the link. MOMO's functions shut down entirely and only through the work of Juli was her body saved.

Shion and Allen joined the group and dove into MOMO's subconscious to find her mind and awaken her. Many trials about Jr.'s past and an attack by Albedo caused MOMO to resonate with Sakura (the daughter of Joachim and Juli who she was modeled after and possessed memories of) and awoke. Upon MOMO's waking, Albedo was able to finally steal the Y-Data and restore the passage to Old Miltia.

With the path to Old Miltia restored, the Immigrant Fleet and the Galaxy Federation Government began invasion operations to recover the original Zohar from Miltia.

With such disarray in Miltian space, Second Miltian Government Representative Helmer asked the Kukai Foundation to guard the Zohar. Jr. and the others headed to Old Miltia aboard the Elsa.

Shion was called back to Vector's headquarters, but after a vision with Nephilim reminding her of her promise to Febronia, she and Allen stole the spacecraft Dinah and headed for Miltia. KOS-MOS self-started once again and defended the Dinah until they could join with the Elsa.

Trying to stop the activation of the Zohar, Shion ordered KOS-MOS to destroy the control system and Febronia's sisters Cathe and Cecily (who were trapped as part of the system). The desperate move failed and the Patriarch was able to revive Proto Omega.

With the Omega system under his control, the Patriarch destroys Miltia, and then wipes out the Galaxy Federation fleet. Shion and the others board the Omega system on the Elsa and face off against the Patriarch at the center. Before they could do anything, the Patriarch killed Albedo.

The Proto Omega shut down before the Patriarch could destroy Second Miltia as well. The Testaments appeared, killed the Patriarch, destroyed the Proto Omega, retrieved the Zohar, and revived Albedo.

Albedo was able to fulfill his deepest wish and make contact with U-DO. A space-time anomaly, created by this contact, swallowed Miltian Space and was continuing to spread. Jr. entered the anomaly, killed Albedo, and the anomaly vanished. The original Zohar was drifting in space until a giant Gnosis (Abel's Ark) swallowed it.

U-TIC fought against the party at every turn, but they arrived at Labyrinthos and found the Zohar and U-DO (the control system).

CHARACTERS

There are many characters involved in the story of Xenosaga. Some of them are under your direct control and some operate from the shadows. This section is compilation of information on the most pertinent individuals. Study it well, since it may mean the difference between victory and defeat.

CHAOS

chaos is a rather mysterious figure. He's seen during several points in history, but how he got there is somewhat of a mystery. He was involved with saving Rubedo and Nigredo during the Miltian Conflict and has been part of the Elsa's crew since then.

Perhaps it's no wonder that so little is known about him. He's very soft spoken and rarely takes the lead. Preferring to support others, chaos tends to vanish into the walls when not watched.

BIOGRAPHICAL INFORMATION

HEIGHT:	169CM (5'7")
WEIGHT:	53KG (117 LBS)
HAIR:	SILVER
EYES:	BLUE

STRENGTHS

chaos is very versatile and can do nearly everything, but there are a few things he does extremely well. He starts with a very high ether point level and this persists throughout the game. This allows him to stay in the fight at full power much longer than others. Combined later with his HP Vamp, EP Vamp, Recover HP, and Recover EP ethers, chaos is undaunted by lengthy fights.

Early in the game, chaos can gain the ability to use all four elemental ether types, break techniques, recovery ethers, and debuff ethers and techniques. Such an array of abilities allows chaos to be effective in nearly every engagement.

He also has impressive skills that can cripple enemies with debuffs while increasing the power of other party members. Fist Down, Soul Down, Defensive, and Balance can create a situation where your party will take very little damage from the enemy without hindering the ability to do damage. Mind Down, Skin Down, Offensive, and Quick are the other side of the coin and increase the amount of damage your party puts out and the damage the enemy takes.

INTRODUCTION

ARCHIVES

CHARACTERS

TACTICAL FILES

EQUIPMENT

THREAT ASSESSMENT

REGIONAL ANALYSIS

SUPPLEMENTAL DATA

WEAKNESSES

chaos can do many things, but his abilities overlap with many other characters who are a bit more specialized. Every character has this weakness, but there are only a couple areas where chaos is substantially lacking.

chaos is not a large man. He is neither physically impressive, combat trained, nor a cyborg. His physical damage is much lower than other party members and, against enemies that have a high resistance to physical damage, his abilities are better used elsewhere. He gets very few strength bonuses and does not get any of the criticals, doubles, or counters until very late in the skill lines.

chaos isn't very good at taking damage either. He simply does not have as much vitality, ether defense, and evasion bonuses that other characters have.

TRAINING

There are many important abilities that chaos has, so don't be lax about spending his skill points. Be sure to take his four starting skills, since these give him ether damage as well as physical damage and debuffs.

Choose the Break Heal option and ether point bonus next. Once you get the EX Skill Key I and open the first four extra skill blocks will have much more spending to do. Analyze and Rare Steal are not must have skills, but strongly consider getting them. Knowing an enemy's strengths and weaknesses and taking their items is important...and fun!

Round chaos out by grabbing the many buff and debuff ethers, as well as the fire and beam ethers (since you have ice and lightning ethers already). Chaos achieves his first break technique when he gains level eight, so watch for the upgrades to Spirit Strike.

This ability is the core of chaos and you can reach this technique before long. However, there are a couple of choices to make as you proceed with his training. To make him more versatile, grab the vitality, hitpoints, and ether defense to shore up his survivability. If you're looking to increase his damage, aim for the ether attack and keep grabbing new ethers and techniques as they become available.

EQUIPMENT

Weapon upgrades for chaos are available periodically throughout the game. There isn't any real choice about what you get, since it is very clear which weapon is better. The real choice comes when choosing armor: chaos and Jr. share many of the same armors, so these characters have more variety to choose from. The higher strength and vitality armor helps to shore up some of the weaknesses that chaos has, while the ether attack and ether defense armor should make him more potent when dealing damage.

Beyond weapons and armor, accessories can be used to make chaos either much more powerful or allow him to survive a conflict longer. Items that increase his hit points and decrease the damage he takes from attack types increase his staying power in a damage based party that heals between fights. For longer engagements, equip items that increase his ether points. chaos can heal himself and others, so he only really needs enough hit points to survive a single enemy attack.

COMBAT

How you use chaos in battle may depend on the type of encounter you face. He has many tools that you can use to your advantage, so it is a rare occasion when he is left without anything useful to do.

In small fights against weaker opponents, concentrate on using his area of effect ether attacks (Blizzard, Lightning, Inferno, and Satellite) to weaken enemies without killing them. This adds to your Boost significantly and paves the way for another party member to use special attacks and gain a Finishing Strike. Since chaos doesn't get a powerful area of effect special attack until later than the other party members, he's more suited for prepping enemies that other characters can take down.

If any enemies start throwing out enough damage to worry you, but are just hanging around with low HP, use your most damaging attack and kill them as quickly as possible. If you're in trouble and the enemies are still at high health, use a large heal on a wounded party member (or a heal all if everyone is wounded). Once your party is back in good shape, resume damage dealing.

He has much more to do in longer fights. Usually only bosses warrant the use of the full range of his abilities. Start the fight by casting defensive buffs on your party (Defensive and Balance). Use Refresh to keep status effects off of your allies and Disengage (available at later levels) to keep any buffs off the enemy.

Use either Skin Down or Mind Down to make the enemy more vulnerable to your party if you have more physical or ether damage dealers. Fist Down and Soul Down can keep your party from taking as much damage, but sooner or later the enemy will tire of the debuffs and clear them. Only stack on the most important debuff attacks and move chaos on to other duties.

Later in levels, you'll gain access to Recover EP, HP, and BL. These are single target spells and they take far too long to cast on everyone. Cast Recover EP and BL on the primary breaker in your party and EP on the primary healer. This will make destroying your party much more difficult for enemies.

Once all the chores are done, it's time for the real work. Use low cost break attacks to bring enemies to the brink, and then switch to low cost ether attacks. It's important to keep your ether points high in case you need to do emergency healing. Use your break heals if any party member's limit is getting close. Remember that you can't help someone once they are already broken.

SKILLS

CORE SKILLS, TECHNIQUES, AND SPECIAL ATTACKS

LEVELING SKILLS

LEVEL	NAME	LEVEL	NAME
1	PHOENIX STRIKE	26	MEDICA M ALL
3	MEDICA S	29	MEDICA L
5	BREAK HEAL S	34	IMPERIAL JUDGMENT
8	SPIRIT STRIKE I	41	MEDICA L ALL
16	MEDICA S ALL	45	BEST ALLY
18	ANGEL WINGS I	47	TWIN IMPACT I
20	MEDICA M	50	BELOVED GOSPEL
23	REVERT M		

TECHNIQUES

NAME	TARGETS	RANGE	TYPE	EFFECT	EP COST
SPIRIT STRIKE I	SINGLE ENEMY	SHORT	PHYSICAL	SMALL BREAK ATTACK	8
ANGEL WINGS I	SINGLE ENEMY	SHORT	PHYSICAL	MEDIUM ATTACK	4
TWIN IMPACT I	SINGLE ENEMY	SHORT	PHYSICAL	MEDIUM ATTACK	10

ETHERS

NAME	TARGETS	TYPE	EFFECT	EP COST
MEDICA S	SINGLE ALLY	HEAL	RECOVER SMALL AMOUNT OF HP	4
BREAK HEAL S	SINGLE ALLY	HEAL	RECOVER SMALL AMOUNT OF BREAK DAMAGE	4
MEDICA S ALL	ALL ALLIES	HEAL	RECOVER SMALL AMOUNT OF HP	12
MEDICA M	SINGLE ALLY	HEAL	RECOVER MEDIUM AMOUNT OF HP	10
REVERT M	SINGLE ALLY	REVIVE	REVIVE AND RECOVER MEDIUM AMOUNT OF HP	20
MEDICA M ALL	ALL ALLIES	HEAL	RECOVER MEDIUM AMOUNT OF HP	22
MEDICA L	SINGLE ALLY	HEAL	RECOVER LARGE AMOUNT OF HP	18
MEDICA L ALL	ALL ALLIES	HEAL	RECOVER LARGE AMOUNT OF HP	32
BEST ALLY	SINGLE ALLY	REVIVE	REVIVE AFTER DEATH WITH FULL HP	60

SPECIAL ATTACKS

NAME	TARGETS	TYPE	EFFECT	BOOST COST
PHOENIX STRIKE	SINGLE ENEMY	PHYSICAL	LARGE BREAK ATTACK + ABSORB SOUL IF FINISH STRIKE (GNOSIS ONLY)	2
IMPERIAL JUDGMENT	ALL ENEMIES	ICE	MEDIUM ATTACK (+ SOUL FOR HIGHER POWER)	2
BELOVED GOSPEL	ALL ALLIES	REVIVE	AUTO REVIVE ALL ALLIES WITH MAXIMUM HP (1 TIME)	3

BASIC SKILLS

SKILLS

NAME	SP COST
DECAYING SUN	25
DECAYING MOON	25
ICE BOLT I	25
THUNDER BOLT I	25

TECHNIQUES

NAME	TARGETS	RANGE	TYPE	EFFECT	EP COST
DECAYING SUN	SINGLE ENEMY	SHORT	PHYSICAL	SMALL ATTACK + SKIN DOWN	8
DECAYING MOON	SINGLE ENEMY	SHORT	PHYSICAL	SMALL ATTACK + MIND DOWN	8

ETHERS

NAME	TARGETS	TYPE	EFFECT	EP COST
ICE BOLT I	SINGLE ENEMY	ICE	SMALL ATTACK	6
THUNDER BOLT I	SINGLE ENEMY	LIGHTNING	SMALL ATTACK	6

INTRODUCTION

ARCHIVES

CHARACTERS

TACTICAL FILES

EQUIPMENT

THREAT ASSESSMENT

REGIONAL ANALYSIS

SUPPLEMENTAL DATA

It's important to note that while extra skills can be taken at any time (provided you have acquired the necessary item), lower level skill blocks in the primary lines must be completed before later skill blocks can be taken.

BREAKER LINE

Though his attacks might not be the most damaging, choosing the abilities in the Breaker line allow chaos to cripple an enemy and give the rest of your party the chance to eliminate it without fuss. The ability to break an enemy quickly makes tougher encounters much easier.

BREAKER SKILLS

A-2	SP COST	A-3	SP COST	A-4	SP COST	A-5	SP COST	A-6	SP COST	A-7	SP COST	MASTER	SP COST
BREAK HEAL M	35	DEFENSIVE	50	REFRESH	70	ANGEL WINGS II	100	FALLEN LEAVES II	200	ANGELIC WAVE II	300	BABYLON SEEKER	---
HP+100	35	BALANCE	50	SPIRIT STRIKE II	70	RECOVER HP	100	ANGELIC WAVE I	200	SPIRIT STRIKE III	300		
EP+10	35	FIST DOWN	50	FALLEN LEAVES I	70	RECOVER BREAK	100	BREAK HEAL L	200	TWIN IMPACT II	300		
VIT+2	35	SOUL DOWN	50	STR+2	70	EP+20	100	SHORT REVENGE	200	SHORT DOUBLE	300		

TECHNIQUES

NAME	TARGETS	RANGE	TYPE	EFFECT	EP COST
ANGEL WINGS II	SINGLE ENEMY	SHORT	PHYSICAL	HEAVY ATTACK	6
ANGELIC WAVE I	ALL ENEMIES	LONG	PHYSICAL	SMALL BREAK ATTACK	10
ANGELIC WAVE II	ALL ENEMIES	LONG	PHYSICAL	MEDIUM BREAK ATTACK	14
FALLEN LEAVES I	ALL ENEMIES	LONG	PHYSICAL	SMALL ATTACK	10
FALLEN LEAVES II	ALL ENEMIES	LONG	PHYSICAL	MEDIUM ATTACK	14
SPIRIT STRIKE II	SINGLE ENEMY	SHORT	PHYSICAL	MEDIUM BREAK ATTACK	10
SPIRIT STRIKE III	SINGLE ENEMY	SHORT	PHYSICAL	HEAVY BREAK ATTACK	12
TWIN IMPACT II	SINGLE ENEMY	SHORT	PHYSICAL	HEAVY ATTACK	12

ETHERS

NAME	TARGETS	TYPE	EFFECT	EP COST
BREAK HEAL M	SINGLE ALLY	HEAL	RECOVER MEDIUM AMOUNT OF BREAK DAMAGE	6
DEFENSIVE	ALL ALLIES	BUFF	INCREASE DEFENSE AND ETHER DEFENSE	22
BALANCE	ALL ALLIES	BUFF	INCREASE ACCURACY AND EVASION	22
FIST DOWN	ALL ENEMIES	DEBUFF	DECREASE PHYSICAL ATTACK POWER	22
SOUL DOWN	ALL ENEMIES	DEBUFF	DECREASE ETHER ATTACK POWER	22
REFRESH	ALL ALLIES	HEAL	RECOVER STATUS EFFECTS	10
RECOVER HP	SINGLE ALLY	HEAL	RECOVER SMALL AMOUNT OF HP WITH EACH TURN	12
RECOVER BREAK	SINGLE ALLY	HEAL	RECOVER SMALL AMOUNT OF BL WITH EACH TURN	10
BREAK HEAL L	SINGLE ALLY	HEAL	RECOVER LARGE AMOUNT OF BREAK DAMAGE	10
BABYLON SEEKER	SELF	BUFF	ALWAYS EXECUTE REVENGE	99

SPELL ATTACKER

While his damage still won't top the charts, the spell attacker skill line gives chaos a good bit of damage mixed with buffs and debuffs. His ability to hinder the enemy, increase your party's effectiveness, and do damage make him a useful hybrid to have in the party.

SPELL ATTACK SKILLS

B-2	SP COST	B-3	SP COST	B-4	SP COST	B-5	SP COST	B-6	SP COST	B-7	SP COST	MASTER	SP COST
HP VAMP	35	OFFENSIVE	50	BLIZZARD I	70	EP VAMP	100	ICE BOLT III	200	CURSE	300	HEAVEN'S TRACKER	---
POISON	35	QUICK	50	LIGHTNING I	70	BLIZZARD II	100	THUNDER BOLT III	200	MISTY	300		
EATK+2	35	SKIN DOWN	50	ICE BOLT II	70	LIGHTNING II	100	BLIZZARD III	200	LOCK	300		
EP+10	35	MIND DOWN	50	THUNDER BOLT II	70	RECOVER EP	100	LIGHTNING III	200	EP+20	300		

ETHERS

NAME	TARGETS	TYPE	EFFECT	EP COST
HP VAMP	SINGLE ENEMY	DRAIN	SMALL HP DAMAGE + RECOVER SMALL AMOUNT OF HP	10
POISON	SINGLE ENEMY	POISON	SMALL DAMAGE EACH ROUND	4
OFFENSIVE	ALL ALLIES	BUFF	INCREASE ATTACK POWER AND ETHER ATTACK POWER	22
QUICK	ALL ALLIES	BUFF	INCREASE SPEED	18
SKIN DOWN	ALL ENEMIES	DEBUFF	DECREASE PHYSICAL DEFENSE	22
MIND DOWN	ALL ENEMIES	DEBUFF	DECREASE ETHER DEFENSE	22
BLIZZARD I	ALL ENEMIES	ICE	SMALL ATTACK	12
LIGHTNING I	ALL ENEMIES	LIGHTNING	SMALL ATTACK	12
ICE BOLT II	SINGLE ENEMY	ICE	MEDIUM ATTACK	10
THUNDER BOLT II	SINGLE ENEMY	LIGHTNING	MEDIUM ATTACK	10
EP VAMP	SINGLE ENEMY	DRAIN	SMALL EP DAMAGE + RECOVER SMALL AMOUNT OF EP	1
BLIZZARD II	ALL ENEMIES	ICE	MEDIUM ATTACK	24
LIGHTNING II	ALL ENEMIES	LIGHTNING	MEDIUM ATTACK	24
RECOVER EP	SINGLE ALLY	HEAL	RECOVER SMALL AMOUNT OF EP WITH EACH TURN	18
ICE BOLT III	SINGLE ENEMY	ICE	HEAVY ATTACK	16
THUNDER BOLT III	SINGLE ENEMY	LIGHTNING	HEAVY ATTACK	16
BLIZZARD III	ALL ENEMIES	ICE	HEAVY ATTACK	36
LIGHTNING III	ALL ENEMIES	LIGHTNING	HEAVY ATTACK	36
CURSE	SINGLE ENEMY	DEBUFF	REFLECT INFLICTED DAMAGE	32
MISTY	SINGLE ENEMY	DEBUFF	SEAL ETHER SPELLS	26
LOCK	SINGLE ENEMY	DEBUFF	SEAL BOOST CAPABILITY	26
HEAVEN'S TRACKER	SELF	BUFF	ALWAYS EXECUTE CRITICAL ATTACKS	99

EXTRA SKILLS

These are unlocked as you collect the skill keys throughout the game. There are three keys that open the three levels of extra skills. Unlike the skill lines, skills in later blocks can be purchased at any time and you do not need to complete an earlier block first.

SKILL KEYS

SKILL KEY	SKILLS UNLOCKED	LOCATION
EX SKILL KEY I	EX-A, EX-B, EX-C, EX-D	MILTIAN FOREST: BEHIND THE WATERFALL
EX SKILL KEY II	EX-E, EX-F, EX-G, EX-H	THE MERKABAH: FIRST AREA
EX SKILL KEY III	EX-I, EX-J, EX-K, EX-L	ABEL'S ARK: JUST INSIDE

EXTRA SKILLS

EX-A	SP COST	EX-B	SP COST	EX-C	SP COST	EX-D	SP COST
ANALYZE	30	FIRE BOLT I	50	STR+2	40	HP+100	50
BALANCE DOWN	50	BEAM BOLT I	50	VIT+2	40	EP+10	50
RARE STEAL	40	INFERNO I	70	EATK+2	40	STR+2	40
SLOW	40	SATELLITE I	70	EDEF+2	40	EATK+2	40

EX-E	SP COST	EX-F	SP COST	EX-G	SP COST	EX-H	SP COST
SAFETY	150	FIRE BOLT II	100	STR+2	80	HP+100	100
DISENGAGE	100	BEAM BOLT II	100	VIT+2	80	EP+10	100
HP+100	100	INFERNO II	150	EATK+2	80	STR+2	80
EP+10	100	SATELLITE II	150	EDEF+2	80	EATK+2	80

EX-I	SP COST	EX-J	SP COST	EX-K	SP COST	EX-L	SP COST
FIRE BOLT III	300	MEDICA REST	999	TYPE-B CRITICAL	400	HP+200	300
BEAM BOLT III	300	REVERT L	300	TYPE-M CRITICAL	400	EP+10	300
INFERNO III	400	RARE HUNTER	300	SHORT COUNTER	400	STR+2	250
SATELLITE III	400	HEAT	200	LUCK+2	250	EATK+2	250

ETHERS

NAME	TARGETS	TYPE	EFFECT	EP COST
ANALYZE	SINGLE ENEMY	N/A	ANALYZE AN ENEMY'S DATA	1
BALANCE DOWN	ALL ENEMIES	DEBUFF	DECREASE ACCURACY AND EVASION	22
RARE STEAL	SINGLE ENEMY	N/A	MEDIUM CHANCE OF STEALING AN ITEM	8
SLOW	ALL ENEMIES	DEBUFF	DECREASE SPEED	18
FIRE BOLT I	SINGLE ENEMY	FIRE	SMALL ATTACK	6
BEAM BOLT I	SINGLE ENEMY	BEAM	SMALL ATTACK	6
INFERNO I	ALL ENEMIES	FIRE	SMALL ATTACK	12
SATELLITE I	ALL ENEMIES	BEAM	SMALL ATTACK	12
SAFETY	SINGLE ALLY	REVIVE	AUTO REVIVE AFTER DEATH WITH 50% OF HP	40
DISENGAGE	ALL ENEMIES	DEBUFF	REMOVE ALL BUFFS	10
FIRE BOLT II	SINGLE ENEMY	FIRE	MEDIUM ATTACK	10
BEAM BOLT II	SINGLE ENEMY	BEAM	MEDIUM ATTACK	10
INFERNO II	ALL ENEMIES	FIRE	MEDIUM ATTACK	24
SATELLITE II	ALL ENEMIES	BEAM	MEDIUM ATTACK	24
FIRE BOLT III	SINGLE ENEMY	FIRE	HEAVY ATTACK	16
BEAM BOLT III	SINGLE ENEMY	BEAM	HEAVY ATTACK	16
INFERNO III	ALL ENEMIES	FIRE	HEAVY ATTACK	36
SATELLITE III	ALL ENEMIES	BEAM	HEAVY ATTACK	36
MEDICA REST	ALL ALLIES	HEAL	RECOVER SUBSTANTIAL AMOUNT OF HP	42
REVERT L	SINGLE ALLY	REVIVE	REVIVE AND RECOVER LARGE AMOUNT OF HP	32
RARE HUNTER	SINGLE ENEMY	N/A	HIGH CHANCE OF STEALING AN ITEM	14
HEAT	ALL ENEMIES	N/A	SET THE TARGET FOR ALL ENEMIES TO SELF	8

JIN

BIOGRAPHICAL INFORMATION

HEIGHT:	183CM (6'0")
WEIGHT:	74KG (163 LBS)
HAIR:	BLACK
EYES:	BROWN

From fairly early in his life, Jin has been making hard decisions and doing what others are afraid to do. Jin spent a great deal of time on covert missions as a captain in the Galaxy Federation's Special Forces Intelligence Division,. The final mission before he left the military was during the Miltian Conflict.

It was during the conflict that he discovered the treachery of his commanding officer; Colonel Margulis. Jin stole the Y-Data to expose Margulis to the authorities. During his escape, he found Canaan and chaos searching for the U.R.T.V. units. Before the three could move, Margulis confronted them and challenged Jin to a duel. As both had learned beneath the tutelage of Jin's grandfather, they were very evenly matched. The fight ended with Jin wounded and Margulis fleeing with a wound on his face that would become a scar. Jin received an urgent transmission from an ally of his within the U-TIC organization. He uploaded the Y-Data to Canaan and sped across the city as quickly as he could. He arrived at the hospital in time to save Shion (his younger sister), but neither of their parents.

After the Miltian Conflict, Jin left the Galaxy Federation Military and opened an antique store on the outskirts of Second Miltian's capital. He took care of Shion for years until she could do so herself.

Taught martial arts by his grandfather, Jin approaches life with a rather calm and calculated demeanor. His manner has often caused trouble with Shion's much more emotive expressions and those close to Jin can see the sadness this brings him.

Regardless of the skeletons in his closet, Jin proceeds through life holding strong to his principles. He does what is right and watches over Shion as much as she will let him.

STRENGTHS

Sheer damage is Jin's primary strength. Throughout the game, Jin is likely to be one of your most damaging characters. The amount of physical damage he can dish out to single or multiple targets is quite frightening. With so much damage being done, your boost gauge raises quite quickly. Even if Jin never uses any of his special attacks, he opens to door for everyone else to.

Jin learns Skeletal Slash and Armor Pierce very early. Both of these are physical attacks that are more effective against Type-B and Type-M enemies. These two attacks are quite useful, but the best is yet to come. Obtaining Twin Dragon and Raging Sea give Jin the ability to hit multiple enemies.

Jin isn't a slacker in the dependability department either. Jin has a higher evasion than some of the other characters and this works well with his moderate vitality and hit points. Many enemies will have real trouble bringing Jin down before they die. It boils down to a damage race that isn't fair to anyone on the wrong side of Jin's blade.

WEAKNESSES

Jin is a very physical being. In an all out brawl, few can stand up to him. It's when the enemy starts using tricks that Jin has more trouble. His ether defense isn't anything to be proud of and he can take a beating from any enemy that uses ether-based attacks. He also doesn't have any way to break an enemy. He has no break techniques and using Erde Kaiser is quite painful with his limited ether points.

Enemies strong to physical attacks give Jin trouble as well. Nearly all of his attacks (aside from special attacks) are physical in nature. He can learn a number of attack ethers, but his ether attack is low enough that it's usually better to swap in another character that is better at it and save Jin for another fight.

TRAINING

Fast fights are what Jin is all about. Scooping up his basic skills give you both Skeletal Slash and Armor Pierce. These attacks ensure that anything short of Gnosis will not enjoy meeting Jin on the battlefield.

Abilities that increase his damage to kill enemies before they can even attack should be first on your list. Twin Dragon, strength bonuses, and agility bonuses make Jin devastating against anything that isn't a boss. Ether points and hit points should come next because they give him the staying power he that he needs for boss encounters. Avoid most of the ethers, since Jin spends nearly all his ether points on techniques. Rare Steal is the only one you should worry about early on.

As Jin grows, seek out other abilities that increase his damage. Short Counter, and the critical types are wonderful purchases. As everyone should have some backup recovery ethers, grab Recover HP, Recover EP, Refresh, and a break heal. These will only be used in very long encounters, but they can turn the tide. Losing a round of Jin's damage is nothing compared to losing another member or Jin getting broken.

Keep grabbing skills that increase Jin's damage and don't look back. Choosing some attack ethers can help round out his damage, but there are other characters that are far superior to him in ether attacks. Instead, once you have taken every skill that can increase Jin's damage directly, grab some buff ethers such as Quick and Offensive to increase his damage indirectly!

EQUIPMENT

Damage is Jin's primary role, so his equipment should reflect this aspect. Keep his weapon upgraded at all times and watch for weapons that also increase his luck. Armor with bonuses to strength or luck should be the ones most sought after.

Equipping accessories that protect Jin from effects that reduce his damage will keep bosses from crippling his effectiveness. Boosting his ether points will give him the staying power to plow through entire maps before needing a rest and adding an elemental effect to his weapon the enemies are weak to is devastating.

With Jin's ability to get up close and personal with deadly results, rings that increase his counter, revenge, or double or hinder the enemy's ability to counter, revenge, or evade are positively destructive to enemy units.

INTRODUCTION

ARCHIVES

CHARACTERS

TACTICAL FILES

EQUIPMENT

THREAT ASSESSMENT

REGIONAL ANALYSIS

SUPPLEMENTAL DATA

COMBAT

There are only slight differences in suggested actions depending on the battle you face. Jin is best at short fights, but nearly indispensable in longer encounters.

There are two ways to deal with large groups of weaker enemies. Jin can generally kill one each turn using either Skeletal Slash or Armor Pierce. This reduces the damage your party is taking each round considerably, but there is another route if you don't mind taking a couple hits.

Using Twin Dragon or Raging Sea damages multiple enemies considerably and increases your boost gauge. Coupled with another character's area of effect special attack, this tactic lands more finishing strikes and gives you skill points to make your characters even more powerful.

Longer engagements are to be handled a bit differently. They rarely have multiple opponents, so using Jin's area of effect attacks is a waste of ether points. Throw Recover EP on Jin (if you have it) and start the fight with your lower cost techniques. This gets the damage started, but gives your other party members time to prepare before you really start pouring it on. If Jin is the toughest member of your party, use Heat occasionally to keep the enemy's attention on Jin. This also gives Jin more opportunities to counter attack.

Once the fight really begins, switch to your more damaging and costly techniques. Gale Blade, Gale Strike, and Assaulting Blade are all good choices. Having a Skin Down on the enemy makes these even more effective. Be ready to use a special attack as soon as you have enough boost. Jin moves the gauge very well and there is no point in wasting it. Only during exceptionally powerful enemies should you hold your special attacks until they reach a certain level of health.

Watch Jin's break limit as the fight progresses. If Jin is broken, a large portion of your damage ceases and the battle becomes much more dangerous for the rest of your party. Have a break heal ready and keep his break gauge well under half.

SKILLS

CORE SKILLS, TECHNIQUES, AND SPECIAL ATTACKS

LEVELING SKILLS

LEVEL	NAME
1	SPARK WALTZ
8	SKELETAL SLASH
15	BREAK HEAL S
18	HEAT
23	DRAGON DANCE
29	RAGING SEA I
34	GALE BLADE I

TECHNIQUES

NAME	TARGETS	RANGE	TYPE	EFFECT	EP COST
SKELETAL SLASH	SINGLE ENEMY	SHORT	PHYSICAL	SMALL ATTACK + EFFECTIVE ON TYPE-B ENEMY	6
RAGING SEA I	ALL ENEMIES	LONG	PHYSICAL	SMALL ATTACK	10
GALE BLADE I	SINGLE ENEMY	SHORT	PHYSICAL	MEDIUM ATTACK	10

ETHERS

NAME	TARGETS	TYPE	EFFECT	EP COST
BREAK HEAL S	SINGLE ALLY	HEAL	RECOVER SMALL AMOUNT OF BREAK DAMAGE	4
HEAT	ALL ENEMIES	N/A	SET THE TARGET FOR ALL ENEMIES TO SELF	8

SPECIAL ATTACKS

NAME	TARGETS	TYPE	EFFECT	BOOST COST
SPARK WALTZ	SINGLE ENEMY	PHYSICAL	LARGE ATTACK	2
DRAGON DANCE	SINGLE ENEMY	LIGHTNING	LARGE ATTACK	3
LIGHTNING WALTZ	SINGLE ENEMY	LIGHTNING	MASSIVE ATTACK	4

BASIC SKILLS

It's important to note that while extra skills can be taken at any time (provided you have acquired the necessary item), lower level skill blocks in the primary lines must be completed before later skill blocks can be taken.

TECHNIQUES

NAME	TARGETS	RANGE	TYPE	EFFECT	EP COST
ARMOR PIERCE	SINGLE ENEMY	SHORT	PHYSICAL	SMALL ATTACK + EFFECTIVE ON TYPE-M ENEMY	6

SKILLS

NAME	SP COST	NAME	SP COST
ARMOR PIERCE	25	EP+10	25
HP+100	25	STR+2	25

INTRODUCTION

ARCHIVES

CHARACTERS

TACTICAL FILES

EQUIPMENT

THREAT ASSESSMENT

REGIONAL ANALYSIS

SUPPLEMENTAL DATA

ATTACKER

The Attacker line is all about damage. The prolific strength bonuses are balanced a bit by the addition of multiple enemy techniques.

ATTACKER SKILLS

A-2	SP COST	A-3	SP COST	A-4	SP COST	A-5	SP COST	A-6	SP COST	A-7	SP COST	MASTER	SP COST
HP+100	35	TWIN DRAGON I	50	HP+100	70	TWIN DRAGON II	100	RAGING SEA II	200	GALE BLADE II	300	HEAVEN'S TRACKER	---
STR+2	35	STR+2	50	STR+2	70	VIT+2	100	STR+2	200	RAGING SEA III	300		
STR+2	35	STR+2	50	VIT+2	70	DEX+2	100	STR+2	200	EP+20	300		
AGI+2	35	AGI+2	50	DEX+2	70	AGI+2	100	AGI+2	200	STR+2	300		

TECHNIQUES

NAME	TARGETS	RANGE	TYPE	EFFECT	EP COST
TWIN DRAGON I	TWO ENEMIES	SHORT	PHYSICAL	SMALL ATTACK	6
TWIN DRAGON II	TWO ENEMIES	SHORT	PHYSICAL	SMALL ATTACK	12
RAGING SEA II	ALL ENEMIES	LONG	PHYSICAL	MEDIUM ATTACK	14
GALE BLADE II	SINGLE ENEMY	SHORT	PHYSICAL	HEAVY ATTACK	12
RAGING SEA III	ALL ENEMIES	LONG	PHYSICAL	MEDIUM ATTACK	18

ETHERS

NAME	TARGETS	TYPE	EFFECT	EP COST
HEAVEN'S TRACKER	SELF	BUFF	ALWAYS EXECUTE CRITICAL ATTACKS	99

COUNTER

Everyone can do damage on their turn. This line gives Jin the evasion and counter abilities to do damage on the enemy's turn, as well as giving him some more powerful single target techniques.

COUNTER SKILLS

B-2	SP COST	B-3	SP COST	B-4	SP COST	B-5	SP COST	B-6	SP COST	B-7	SP COST	MASTER	SP COST
HP+100	35	SHORT COUNTER	50	ASSAULTING BLADE	70	TYPE-M CRITICAL	100	FOLLOW-THROUGH	200	GALE STRIKE	300	GHOST DIVER	---
STR+2	35	TYPE-B CRITICAL	50	STR+2	70	HP+100	100	STR+2	200	DARK KNIGHT	300		
EVA+2	35	EP+10	50	EVA+2	70	STR+2	100	EVA+2	200	EP+20	300		
EVA+2	35	STR+2	50	EVA+2	70	EVA+2	100	LUCK+2	200	STR+2	300		

TECHNIQUES

NAME	TARGETS	RANGE	TYPE	EFFECT	EP COST
ASSAULTING BLADE	SINGLE ENEMY	SHORT	PHYSICAL	MEDIUM ATTACK + HIGHER CRITICAL RATE	8
FOLLOW-THROUGH	SELF	N/A	BUFF	INCREASE OWN ATTACK POWER AND ETHER ATTACK POWER	8
GALE STRIKE	SINGLE ENEMY	SHORT	PHYSICAL	HEAVY ATTACK + HIGHER CRITICAL RATE	12
DARK NIGHT	ALL ENEMIES	LONG	PHYSICAL	MEDIUM ATTACK + BALANCE DOWN	20

ETHERS

NAME	TARGETS	TYPE	EFFECT	EP COST
GHOST DIVER	SELF	BUFF	ALWAYS EXECUTE COUNTER	99

EXTRA SKILLS

These are unlocked as you collect the skill keys throughout the game. There are three keys that open the three levels of extra skills. Unlike the skill lines, skills in later blocks can be purchased at any time and you do not need to complete an earlier block first.

SKILL KEYS

SKILL KEY	SKILLS UNLOCKED	LOCATION
EX SKILL KEY I	EX-A, EX-B, EX-C, EX-D	MILTIAN FOREST: BEHIND THE WATERFALL
EX SKILL KEY II	EX-E, EX-F, EX-G, EX-H	THE MERKABAH: FIRST AREA
EX SKILL KEY III	EX-I, EX-J, EX-K, EX-L	ABEL'S ARK: JUST INSIDE

EXTRA SKILLS

EX-A	SP COST	EX-B	SP COST	EX-C	SP COST	EX-D	SP COST
MEDICA S	50	ANALYZE	30	STR+2	40	INFERNO I	70
MEDICA S ALL	70	POISON	40	↓STR+2	40	BLIZZARD I	70
BALANCE DOWN	40	RARE STEAL	40	EATK+2	40	LIGHTNING I	70
QUICK	40	SLOW	40	EATK+2	40	SATELLITE I	70

EX-E	SP COST	EX-F	SP COST	EX-G	SP COST	EX-H	SP COST
MEDICA M	100	DISENGAGE	100	FIST DOWN	150	INFERNO II	150
MEDICA M ALL	150	REFRESH	100	SOUL DOWN	150	BLIZZARD II	150
BREAK HEAL M	80	RECOVER HP	100	SKIN DOWN	150	LIGHTNING II	150
REVERT M	100	RECOVER EP	100	MIND DOWN	150	SATELLITE II	150

EX-I	SP COST	EX-J	SP COST	EX-K	SP COST	EX-L	SP COST
MEDICA L	300	EP VAMP	400	OFFENSIVE	400	INFERNO III	400
MEDICA L ALL	400	MISTY	400	DEFENSIVE	400	BLIZZARD III	400
BREAK HEAL L	200	BEST ALLY	800	BALANCE	400	LIGHTNING III	400
REVERT L	300	TYPE-G CRITICAL	400	RECOVER BREAK	300	SATELLITE III	400

⚡ ETHERS ⚡

NAME	TARGETS	TYPE	EFFECT	EP COST
MEDICA S	SINGLE ALLY	HEAL	RECOVER SMALL AMOUNT OF HP	4
MEDICA S ALL	ALL ALLIES	HEAL	RECOVER SMALL AMOUNT OF HP	12
BALANCE DOWN	ALL ENEMIES	DEBUFF	DECREASE ACCURACY AND EVASION	22
QUICK	ALL ALLIES	BUFF	INCREASE SPEED	18
ANALYZE	SINGLE ENEMY	N/A	ANALYZE AN ENEMY'S DATA	1
POISON	SINGLE ENEMY	POISON	DAMAGE EACH TURN TO A SINGLE ENEMY	4
RARE STEAL	SINGLE ENEMY	N/A	MEDIUM CHANCE OF STEALING AN ITEM	8
SLOW	ALL ENEMIES	DEBUFF	DECREASE SPEED	18
INFERNO I	ALL ENEMIES	FIRE	SMALL ATTACK	12
BLIZZARD I	ALL ENEMIES	ICE	SMALL ATTACK	12
LIGHTNING I	ALL ENEMIES	LIGHTNING	SMALL ATTACK	12
SATELLITE I	ALL ENEMIES	BEAM	SMALL ATTACK	12
MEDICA M	SINGLE ALLY	HEAL	RECOVER MEDIUM AMOUNT OF HP	10
MEDICA M ALL	ALL ALLIES	HEAL	RECOVER MEDIUM AMOUNT OF HP	22
BREAK HEAL M	SINGLE ALLY	HEAL	RECOVER MEDIUM AMOUNT OF BREAK DAMAGE	6
REVERT M	SINGLE ALLY	REVIVE	REVIVE AND RECOVER MEDIUM AMOUNT OF HP	20
DISENGAGE	ALL ENEMIES	DEBUFF	REMOVE ALL BUFFS	10
REFRESH	ALL ALLIES	HEAL	RECOVER STATUS EFFECTS	10
RECOVER HP	SINGLE ALLY	HEAL	RECOVER SMALL AMOUNT OF HP WITH EACH TURN	12
RECOVER EP	SINGLE ALLY	HEAL	RECOVER SMALL AMOUNT OF EP WITH EACH TURN	18
FIST DOWN	ALL ENEMIES	DEBUFF	DECREASE PHYSICAL ATTACK POWER	22
SOUL DOWN	ALL ENEMIES	DEBUFF	DECREASE ETHER ATTACK POWER	22
SKIN DOWN	ALL ENEMIES	DEBUFF	DECREASE PHYSICAL DEFENSE	22
MIND DOWN	ALL ENEMIES	DEBUFF	DECREASE ETHER DEFENSE	22
INFERNO II	ALL ENEMIES	FIRE	MEDIUM ATTACK	24
BLIZZARD II	ALL ENEMIES	ICE	MEDIUM ATTACK	24
LIGHTNING II	ALL ENEMIES	LIGHTNING	MEDIUM ATTACK	24
SATELLITE II	ALL ENEMIES	BEAM	MEDIUM ATTACK	24
MEDICA L	SINGLE ALLY	HEAL	RECOVER LARGE AMOUNT OF HP	18
MEDICA L ALL	ALL ALLIES	HEAL	RECOVER LARGE AMOUNT OF HP FOR ALL ALLIES	32
BREAK HEAL L	SINGLE ALLY	HEAL	RECOVER LARGE AMOUNT OF BREAK DAMAGE	10
REVERT L	SINGLE ALLY	REVIVE	REVIVE AND RECOVER LARGE AMOUNT OF HP	32
EP VAMP	SINGLE ENEMY	DRAIN	SMALL EP DAMAGE + RECOVER SMALL AMOUNT OF EP	1
MISTY	SINGLE ENEMY	DEBUFF	SEAL ETHER SPELLS	26
BEST ALLY	SINGLE ALLY	REVIVE	AUTO REVIVE AFTER DEATH WITH FULL HP	60
OFFENSIVE	ALL ALLIES	BUFF	INCREASE ATTACK POWER AND ETHER ATTACK POWER	22
DEFENSIVE	ALL ALLIES	BUFF	INCREASE DEFENSE AND ETHER DEFENSE	22
BALANCE	ALL ALLIES	BUFF	INCREASE ACCURACY AND EVASION	22
RECOVER BREAK	SINGLE ALLY	HEAL	RECOVER SMALL AMOUNT OF BL WITH EACH TURN	10
INFERNO III	ALL ENEMIES	FIRE	HEAVY ATTACK	36
BLIZZARD III	ALL ENEMIES	ICE	HEAVY ATTACK	36
LIGHTNING III	ALL ENEMIES	LIGHTNING	HEAVY ATTACK	36
SATELLITE III	ALL ENEMIES	BEAM	HEAVY ATTACK	36

INTRODUCTION

ARCHIVES

CHARACTERS

TACTICAL FILES

EQUIPMENT

THREAT ASSESSMENT

REGIONAL ANALYSIS

SUPPLEMENTAL DATA

JR.

BIOGRAPHICAL INFORMATION

HEIGHT: 140CM (4'7")
WEIGHT: 38KG (184 LBS)
HAIR: RED
EYES: BLUE

Legally, Gaignun Kukai Jr. is the son of Gaignun Kukai, the present chairman of the Kukai Foundation. In reality, Jr. is Gaignun's older brother and a U.R.T.V. named Rubedo.

Rubedo, Nigredo (Gaignun), Albedo, and Citrine were the final four U.R.T.V. units and were put through additional mutation experiments to strengthen their powers. Rubedo and Albedo were born as conjoined twins and were separated before their training began. Citrine was absent during most of the training, but the other three became strong friends and were used to help in the treatment of a human girl named Sakura Mizrahi. During the treatment, Rubedo came to care greatly for Sakura, but her illness claimed her life before anything could become of the strong friendship.

During the Miltian Conflict, the U.R.T.V. units were deployed to counter and destroy U-DO. Rubedo was the only one to have a perfect anti-U-DO wavelength and acted as the leader. When the U.R.T.V. units had fought to U-DO and linked, Rubedo had a vision of the entire planet being destroyed by their attack against U-DO. Unwilling to kill so many innocents, Rubedo broke the link with the others without realizing the danger it would put them in. Without being linked to Rubedo, the other U.R.T.V. units were vulnerable to U-DO and driven mad or killed. Only Rubedo and Nigredo (who was carried out by Rubedo) were reported to have survived the incident.

After the Miltian Conflict, Helmer, Nigredo, and Rubedo took the money from the Federation's secret operations and used it to start the Kukai Foundation. Nigredo and Rubedo changed their names and took identities as the heirs to the Foundation. As Jr. can stop his aging, he remained in a childlike state and became Gaignun's son. Under Gaignun's guidance, the financial wellbeing of the Foundation continued to grow while Jr. dealt more with the real mission; to keep U-TIC from ever becoming a power again.

It was during a mission regarding this duty that he met MOMO. MOMO is a Realian designed to be physically identical to Sakura Mizrahi. During the travels that followed, the two have become good friends.

Over the years, Jr. has learned some temperance from Gaignun, but never shies away from difficult decisions. He cares for his friends and the innocents of the universe. Anyone who endangers either will find twin pistols firing in their direction. With Mary and Shelley to handle the smaller decisions (and the major ones in his absence), he commands the Durandal and hunts U-TIC wherever they run to.

STRENGTHS

Jr. is very well balanced among damage type characters. If an enemy is strong to one damage type, he can switch to another. This flexibility means that only enemies strong to *all* damage types are even moderately safe from Jr.

Many of his physical attacks are slightly different those of other characters. Rather than hitting and enemy with a fist or sword, he shoots them. This keeps Jr. well out of counter or revenge range without hindering his damage.

With access to many buff, debuff, and recovery ethers, Jr. can quickly switch from dealing damage to supporting others and he has the ether attack power and energy to handle it.

WEAKNESSES

Jr. isn't very mean. He's better at killing enemies than breaking them. He has only one technique that does break damage and it doesn't do much. The only other way for Jr. to move the enemy break gauge is through sheer damage or by using his level two special attack.

Jr. also isn't very big. While genetically altered, he doesn't have the staying power of the cyborgs, androids, or full-grown men of the party. He gets relatively few bonuses to his vitality or ether defense, so he takes a good bit of damage every time an enemy attacks him and he doesn't gain any evasion to escape attacks.

TRAINING

Early on, Jr. won't be as threatening as the other damage dealers in your party. Since he has several damage types, it takes him a while before they become as potent as some of the other attacks available to other characters.

Beyond the basic skills, grab strength, and ether attack bonuses along with attack ethers of all elemental types. Locked and Ready is almost essential because it is his only break technique. Jr. should also learn Rare Steal and enough recover ethers to be a suitable backup if things go poorly. Avoid the buff and debuff ethers with him until later to concentrate on his damage. The enemies at this stage in the game generally don't last long enough to make the buffs or debuffs worth the damage he could have done in a short amount of time.

As you progress, continue scooping up the abilities, ethers, and techniques that increase his damage potential. Spare skill points should be used to learn buff ethers. Don't grab the debuff ethers until later, but get enough of the recovery ethers to keep Jr. as a solid backup healer. If you haven't needed Jr. as a backup, consider ignoring the recovery ethers until later. Watch for the Recover EP ether. Grab this ability as soon as you can.

In terms of later-game choices, Best Ally, the criticals, and the damage ethers should be prime choices. This gives Jr. the ability to act as backup healer by reviving the healer if they fall. The critical abilities push his damage even further and make him quite a formidable opponent, unless the enemy is truly unfair.

EQUIPMENT

As with chaos, Jr. has a little more customization than many of the other characters. That's because chaos and Jr. can wear each other's clothing. This gives both of them access to armor that has strength or ether attack bonuses. Grab armor with higher ether attack as it affects four of his damage types while the strength armor only affects one.

Keeping Jr. in equipment that limits or negates the effects of Misty and Rasp is very important. Without the use of ether or techniques, Jr. is a sitting duck and of little use to a party.

Since he'll be using ether points every round of every fight, watch for equipment that increases his ether points as well as his hit points. Since he has enough healing to be a backup, he only needs to be able to survive a single volley from enemies. Adding elemental damage to his attacks doesn't do much because he doesn't use his basic attacks as often and can simply use his ether attacks to exploit enemy vulnerabilities.

Equipping an item that displays enemy data will change Jr. from a moderate damage dealer to a killer. Knowing exactly which ether to use and having it at his disposal is a lethal combination.

INTRODUCTION

ARCHIVES

CHARACTERS

TACTICAL FILES

EQUIPMENT

THREAT ASSESSMENT

REGIONAL ANALYSIS

SUPPLEMENTAL DATA

COMBAT

While the actions taken differ between large groups of enemies or single tough enemies, the idea behind them remains the same; find the weakness and exploit it.

If Jr. starts the fight against a large group of enemies, check the resistances of each enemy in the group and decide on an attack that none are resistant to. It's more important that they not resist, null, or absorb that damage than it is for one to be weak to it. Use the area of effect ether (or technique if physical damage is needed) and blast away. This lowers their health and increases your boost gauge in preparation of the next party member's turn.

When another party member has damaged the enemies before Jr., check their health levels. If you have the boost for a special attack that can kill multiple enemies, do so. Blast them with an area of effect ether if they need a bit more tenderizing before they're ready. When confronted with a boss, start the fight by using Recover EP (if you have it) and stealing. Once that's done, start blasting away. Watch the boss' elemental weaknesses and strengths as many will change during the fight. Put Safety on the party healer if you're high enough that the ether point cost won't crimp your damage capability. Only heal when your healer can't keep up as much of your ether points will be needed for doing damage. Use Skin Down and Mind Down if no one else has learned them. If someone else has, let them use it and keep the damage pouring on.

Use Locked and Ready to assist others with breaking the enemy, but don't use it if you're the only one. It doesn't do break damage fast enough to be the only breaker. Only use your special attacks if you can finish the enemy with it. There are other party members who have special attacks more suited for single targets and you may be better off just boosting to get another round of blasting. As an enemy's health drops, take the time to throw Misty and/or Lock on them to hinder their more powerful attacks. Keep an eye on Jr.'s health. Keep him at full or near. He doesn't have substantial vitality or ether defense and any hits against him will hurt dearly. The last thing you want is to lose a damage dealer by being careless.

SKILLS

CORE SKILLS, TECHNIQUES, AND SPECIAL ATTACKS

LEVELING SKILLS

LEVEL	NAME	LEVEL	NAME
1	REQUIEM	27	INFERNO II
8	DEAD FIST	30	STORM WALTZ
12	FIRE BOLT I	32	FIRE BOLT III
14	FULL THROTTLE I	38	TWIN HANDS I
17	INFERNO I	40	MISTY
21	FIRE BOLT II	43	RED DRAGON
24	RODEO SPIKE I	46	LOCK

TECHNIQUES

NAME	TARGETS	RANGE	TYPE	EFFECT	EP COST
DEAD FIST	SINGLE ENEMY	LONG	PHYSICAL	SMALL ATTACK + FIST DOWN	8
FULL THROTTLE I	SINGLE ENEMY	SHORT	PHYSICAL	SMALL ATTACK	4
RODEO SPIKE I	ALL ENEMIES	LONG	PHYSICAL	SMALL ATTACK	10
TWIN HANDS I	SINGLE ENEMY	LONG	PHYSICAL	MEDIUM ATTACK	10

ETHERS

NAME	TARGETS	TYPE	EFFECT	EP COST
FIRE BOLT I	SINGLE ENEMY	FIRE	SMALL ATTACK	6
INFERNO I	ALL ENEMIES	FIRE	SMALL ATTACK	12
FIRE BOLT II	SINGLE ENEMY	FIRE	MEDIUM ATTACK	10
INFERNO II	ALL ENEMIES	FIRE	MEDIUM ATTACK	24
FIRE BOLT III	SINGLE ENEMY	FIRE	MEDIUM ATTACK	16
MISTY	SINGLE ENEMY	DEBUFF	SEAL ETHER SPELLS	26
LOCK	SINGLE ENEMY	DEBUFF	SEAL BOOST CAPABILITY	26

🔥 SPECIAL ATTACKS 🔥

NAME	TARGETS	TYPE	EFFECT	BOOST COST
REQUIEM	SINGLE ENEMY	PHYSICAL	LARGE ATTACK + ABSORB SOUL OF TYPE-B AND G IF FINISH STRIKE	2
STORM WALTZ	ALL ENEMIES	PHYSICAL	MEDIUM ATTACK + LARGE BREAK	2
RED DRAGON	ALL ENEMIES	FIRE	LARGE ETHER ATTACK (+SOUL FOR HIGHER POWER)	3

BASIC SKILLS

It's important to note that while extra skills can be taken at any time (provided you have acquired the necessary item), lower level skill blocks in the primary lines must be completed before later skill blocks can be taken.

🔌 TECHNIQUES 🔌

NAME	TARGETS	RANGE	TYPE	EFFECT	EP COST
DEAD SOUL	SINGLE ENEMY	LONG	PHYSICAL	SMALL ATTACK + SOUL DOWN	8

SKILLS

NAME	SP COST
DEAD SOUL	25
EP+10	25
STR+2	25
EATK+2	25

HYBRID SKILLS

A-2	SP COST	A-3	SP COST	A-4	SP COST	A-5	SP COST	A-6	SP COST	A-7	SP COST	MASTER	SP COST
ICE BOLT I	35	LOCKED AND READY	50	ICE BOLT II	70	RODEO SPIKE II	100	RODEO SPIKE III	200	TWIN HANDS II	300	OVERTAKER	---
THUNDER BOLT I	35	EATK+2	50	THUNDER BOLT II	70	ICE BOLT III	100	FULL THROTTLE II	200	FULL THROTTLE III	300		
BEAM BOLT I	35	DEX+2	50	BEAM BOLT II	70	THUNDER BOLT III	100	SHORT REVENGE	200	EP+20	300		
STR+2	35	AGI+2	50	EATK+2	70	BEAM BOLT III	100	STR+2	200	LUCK+2	300		

HYBRID

The Hybrid skill line perfects the adaptability of Jr.'s damage. Ether skills of each damage type and physical techniques combine to make Jr. a very versatile damage dealer.

🔌 TECHNIQUES 🔌

NAME	TARGETS	RANGE	TYPE	EFFECT	EP COST
LOCKED AND READY	SINGLE ENEMY	LONG	PHYSICAL	SMALL BREAK ATTACK	8
RODEO SPIKE II	ALL ENEMIES	LONG	PHYSICAL	MEDIUM ATTACK	14
RODEO SPIKE III	ALL ENEMIES	LONG	PHYSICAL	HEAVY ATTACK	18
FULL THROTTLE II	SINGLE ENEMY	SHORT	PHYSICAL	MEDIUM ATTACK	6
TWIN HANDS II	SINGLE ENEMY	LONG	PHYSICAL	HEAVY ATTACK	12
FULL THROTTLE III	SINGLE ENEMY	SHORT	PHYSICAL	HEAVY ATTACK	8

ETHERS

NAME	TARGETS	TYPE	EFFECT	EP COST
ICE BOLT I	SINGLE ENEMY	ICE	SMALL ATTACK	6
THUNDER BOLT I	SINGLE ENEMY	LIGHTNING	SMALL ATTACK	6
BEAM BOLT I	SINGLE ENEMY	BEAM	SMALL ATTACK	6
ICE BOLT II	SINGLE ENEMY	ICE	MEDIUM ATTACK	10
THUNDER BOLT II	SINGLE ENEMY	LIGHTNING	MEDIUM ATTACK	10
BEAM BOLT II	SINGLE ENEMY	BEAM	MEDIUM ATTACK	10
ICE BOLT III	SINGLE ENEMY	ICE	HEAVY ATTACK	16
THUNDER BOLT III	SINGLE ENEMY	LIGHTNING	HEAVY ATTACK	16
BEAM BOLT III	SINGLE ENEMY	BEAM	HEAVY ATTACK	16
OVERTAKER	SELF	BUFF	LARGE INCREASE IN BOOST RATE	99

SUPPORTER

Jr. has the ability to act as backup for healing, buffing and debuffing. This line gives him a wide spread of abilities that can be used to make others more powerful as well as a number of ether attack and ether point bonuses.

SUPPORTER SKILLS

B-2	SP COST	B-3	SP COST	B-4	SP COST	B-5	SP COST	B-6	SP COST	B-7	SP COST	MASTER	SP COST
MEDICA S	35	MEDICA M	50	FIST DOWN	70	MEDICA M ALL	100	MEDICA L	200	MEDICA L ALL	300	PHANTOM FLY	---
BREAK HEAL S	35	EP+10	50	SOUL DOWN	70	REFRESH	100	REVERT M	200	EP+20	300		
MEDICA S ALL	35	EATK+2	50	QUICK	70	DISENGAGE	100	BREAK HEAL M	200	EATK+2	300		
EDEF+2	35	AGI+2	50	EDEF+2	70	EATK+2	100	SLOW	200	LUCK+2	300		

ETHERS

NAME	TARGETS	TYPE	EFFECT	EP COST
MEDICA S	SINGLE ALLY	HEAL	RECOVER SMALL AMOUNT OF HP	4
BREAK HEAL S	SINGLE ALLY	HEAL	RECOVER SMALL AMOUNT OF BREAK DAMAGE	4
MEDICA S ALL	ALL ALLIES	HEAL	RECOVER SMALL AMOUNT OF HP	12
MEDICA M	SINGLE ALLY	HEAL	RECOVER MEDIUM AMOUNT OF HP	10
FIST DOWN	ALL ENEMIES	DEBUFF	DECREASE PHYSICAL ATTACK POWER	22
SOUL DOWN	ALL ENEMIES	DEBUFF	DECREASE ETHER ATTACK POWER	22
QUICK	ALL ALLIES	BUFF	INCREASE SPEED	18
MEDICA M ALL	ALL ALLIES	HEAL	RECOVER MEDIUM AMOUNT OF HP	22
REFRESH	ALL ALLIES	HEAL	RECOVER STATUS EFFECTS	10
DISENGAGE	ALL ENEMIES	DEBUFF	REMOVE ALL BUFFS	10
MEDICA L	SINGLE ALLY	HEAL	RECOVER LARGE AMOUNT OF HP	18
REVERT M	SINGLE ALLY	REVIVE	REVIVE AND RECOVER MEDIUM AMOUNT OF HP	20
BREAK HEAL M	SINGLE ALLY	HEAL	RECOVER MEDIUM AMOUNT OF BREAK DAMAGE	6
SLOW	ALL ENEMIES	DEBUFF	DECREASE SPEED	18
MEDICA L ALL	ALL ALLIES	HEAL	RECOVER LARGE AMOUNT OF HP FOR ALL ALLIES	32
PHANTOM FLY	SELF	BUFF	ALWAYS EXECUTE EVASION	99

INTRODUCTION

ARCHIVES

CHARACTERS

TACTICAL FILES

EQUIPMENT

THREAT ASSESSMENT

SUPPLEMENTAL OR REGIONAL

EXTRA SKILLS

These are unlocked as you collect the skill keys throughout the game. There are three keys that open the three levels of extra skills. Unlike the skill lines, skills in later blocks can be purchased at any time and you do not need to complete an earlier block first.

SKILL KEYS

SKILL KEY	SKILLS UNLOCKED	LOCATION
EX SKILL KEY I	EX-A, EX-B, EX-C, EX-D	MILTIAN FOREST: BEHIND THE WATERFALL
EX SKILL KEY II	EX-E, EX-F, EX-G, EX-H	THE MERKABAH: FIRST AREA
EX SKILL KEY III	EX-I, EX-J, EX-K, EX-L	ABEL'S ARK: JUST INSIDE

EXTRA SKILLS

EX-A	SP COST	EX-B	SP COST	EX-C	SP COST	EX-D	SP COST
ANALYZE	30	BALANCE	50	HP+100	50	BLIZZARD I	70
BALANCE DOWN	50	DEX+2	40	EP+10	50	LIGHTNING I	70
RARE STEAL	40	DEX+2	40	STR+2	40	SATELLITE I	70
POISON	40	EVA+2	40	EATK+2	40	EVA+2	40

EX-E	SP COST	EX-F	SP COST	EX-G	SP COST	EX-H	SP COST
OFFENSIVE	150	SAFETY	150	HP+200	100	BLIZZARD II	150
DEFENSIVE	150	RECOVER HP	100	EP+20	100	LIGHTNING II	150
SKIN DOWN	150	RECOVER EP	100	VIT+2	80	SATELLITE II	150
MIND DOWN	150	RECOVER BREAK	100	EDEF+2	80	LUCK+2	80

EX-I	SP COST	EX-J	SP COST	EX-K	SP COST	EX-L	SP COST
BREAK HEAL L	200	HP VAMP	400	TYPE-B CRITICAL	400	INFERNO III	400
REVERT L	300	EP VAMP	400	TYPE-M CRITICAL	400	BLIZZARD III	400
HEAT	200	CURSE	800	TYPE-G CRITICAL	400	LIGHTNING III	400
RARE HUNTER	300	BEST ALLY	800	SHORT COUNTER	400	SATELLITE III	400

⚡ ETHERS ⚡

NAME	TARGETS	TYPE	EFFECT	EP COST
ANALYZE	SINGLE ENEMY	N/A	ANALYZE AN ENEMY'S DATA	1
BALANCE DOWN	ALL ENEMIES	DEBUFF	DECREASE ACCURACY AND EVASION	22
RARE STEAL	SINGLE ENEMY	N/A	MEDIUM CHANCE OF STEALING AN ITEM	8
POISON	SINGLE ENEMY	POISON	DAMAGE EACH TURN TO A SINGLE ENEMY	4
BALANCE	ALL ALLIES	BUFF	INCREASE ACCURACY AND EVASION	22
BLIZZARD I	ALL ENEMIES	ICE	SMALL ATTACK	12
LIGHTNING I	ALL ENEMIES	LIGHTNING	SMALL ATTACK	12
SATELLITE I	ALL ENEMIES	BEAM	SMALL ATTACK	12
OFFENSIVE	ALL ALLIES	BUFF	INCREASE ATTACK POWER AND ETHER ATTACK POWER	22
DEFENSIVE	ALL ALLIES	BUFF	INCREASE DEFENSE AND ETHER DEFENSE	22
SKIN DOWN	ALL ENEMIES	DEBUFF	DECREASE PHYSICAL DEFENSE	22
MIND DOWN	ALL ENEMIES	DEBUFF	DECREASE ETHER DEFENSE	22
SAFETY	SINGLE ALLY	REVIVE	AUTO REVIVE AFTER DEATH WITH 50% OF HP (1 TIME)	40
RECOVER HP	SINGLE ALLY	HEAL	RECOVER SMALL AMOUNT OF HP WITH EACH TURN	12
RECOVER EP	SINGLE ALLY	HEAL	RECOVER SMALL AMOUNT OF EP WITH EACH TURN	18
RECOVER BREAK	SINGLE ALLY	HEAL	RECOVER SMALL AMOUNT OF BL WITH EACH TURN	10
BLIZZARD II	ALL ENEMIES	ICE	MEDIUM ATTACK	24
LIGHTNING II	ALL ENEMIES	LIGHTNING	MEDIUM ATTACK	24
SATELLITE II	ALL ENEMIES	BEAM	MEDIUM ATTACK	24
BREAK HEAL L	SINGLE ALLY	HEAL	RECOVER LARGE AMOUNT OF BREAK DAMAGE	10
REVERT L	SINGLE ALLY	REVIVE	REVIVE AND RECOVER LARGE AMOUNT OF HP	32
HEAT	ALL ENEMIES	N/A	SET THE TARGET FOR ALL ENEMIES TO SELF	8
RARE HUNTER	SINGLE ENEMY	N/A	HIGH CHANCE OF STEALING AN ITEM	14
HP VAMP	SINGLE ENEMY	DRAIN	SMALL HP DAMAGE + RECOVER SMALL AMOUNT OF HP	10
EP VAMP	SINGLE ENEMY	DRAIN	SMALL EP DAMAGE + RECOVER SMALL AMOUNT OF EP	1
CURSE	SINGLE ENEMY	DEBUFF	REFLECT INFLICTED DAMAGE	32
BEST ALLY	SINGLE ALLY	REVIVE	AUTO REVIVE AFTER DEATH WITH FULL HP (1 TIME)	60
INFERNO III	ALL ENEMIES	FIRE	HEAVY ATTACK	36
BLIZZARD III	ALL ENEMIES	ICE	HEAVY ATTACK	36
LIGHTNING III	ALL ENEMIES	LIGHTNING	HEAVY ATTACK	36
SATELLITE III	ALL ENEMIES	BEAM	HEAVY ATTACK	36

KOS-MOS

BIOGRAPHICAL INFORMATION

Developed by Kevin Winnicot, KOS-MOS was designed to be the premier anti-Gnosis weapon. During a rather tragic incident, where KOS-MOS was awakened prematurely, she killed Kevin and most of the development team. Shion Uzuki was one of the only survivors at the incident. With Kevin dead, Shion was promoted to Chief Engineer of the KOS-MOS Project General Operation System Research Center, Vector Industries First R&D Division.

KOS-MOS continued to be outfitted and tested, but the core remained the same as in the archetype. This lead to the division spending a great deal of time collecting data to determine what was in her black box.

When Planet Ariadne vanished, the Woglinde was sent by Vector to investigate. As a precaution against Gnosis attack, the KOS-MOS project was taken as well. Though not fully combat ready, KOS-MOS self-started to protect Shion when the Gnosis attacked. During the travels that followed, KOS-MOS' combat capabilities were fully realized.

Some noticed that at times KOS-MOS' eyes turned blue and she spoke very differently. On these occasions, her power level became much greater, but they never lasted long. The one person most experienced with KOS-MOS, Shion, has yet to see this transformation.

KOS-MOS' actions are dictated by logic and a list of directives. She follows these with precision and lethality (as was seen when she killed Lt. Virgil when he would have lowered her abilities). Some of her directives are still a mystery, even to Shion.

HEIGHT:	167CM (5'6")
WEIGHT:	92KG (203 LBS)
HAIR:	BLUE
EYES:	RED/BLUE

STRENGTHS

KOS-MOS is an android. With a body made of metal and nano-machines, she can take quite a pounding. With plentiful ether defense, vitality, and hit point bonuses, there are few that can stand up to damage the way she can. Neither physical nor ether attacks leave much of a dent in KOS-MOS.

She doesn't lack in fire power either. With break attacks, single and multiple target techniques, and so many strength bonuses to learn, KOS-MOS stands shoulder to shoulder with many of the damage dealers in your party. KOS-MOS also gains several techniques that are specifically designed for one type of enemy or another.

WEAKNESSES

KOS-MOS is a machine with a set purpose. Any skills outside that purpose are unavailable. While she has a good array of ethers, KOS-MOS is sorely lacking in any ethers that buff the party or debuff the enemy. Nearly all buffing and debuffing will have to be done by other party members.

With lower ether attack power and ether points, KOS-MOS isn't great at dealing damage with ether attacks. These are a poor backup for when enemies are resistant to her techniques, but you can't rely on them.

KOS-MOS has only a few techniques that are long range and not physical. With so much time spent in short range, enemy revenge attacks and counters are likely to occur. Equipment to prevent this is very helpful, but until you find or buy it, KOS-MOS is likely to get a bit beaten up during some engagements.

TRAINING

Learn her basic skills and start scooping up many of her passive abilities. Strength should be toward the top of your list at first. This increases her damage across the board. Grab the techniques as soon as they become available. K-Pike

and K-Axe are both break attacks that come in quite handy for tougher enemies. Air Burst is her first multiple target technique and should be taken as soon as possible.

Now that her damage base is set, continue grabbing skills from the two primary lines. There are only a few extra skills that make KOS-MOS more powerful without diluting her strengths. Rare Steal is nearly a must for everyone. Refresh and some Break Heals are good emergency measures. Toss in the Recover EP and HP ethers and KOS-MOS is set for the long haul.

As you continue to advance, grab the multi-target attack ethers and recovery ethers. On occasions where you fight enemies strong to her damage types, this will keep you from losing a round to change characters and having the ability to heal in a pinch keeps the tougher encounters from being as nerve racking. Remember to keep your primary focus on getting her techniques and passive bonuses.

EQUIPMENT

Equipment that increases KOS-MOS' damage is rare, since she can't use accessories that add an elemental type to her attacks. Use items that increase her counter and revenge rate in combination with bonus hit points. This gives her the staying power to capitalize on the extra attacks.

Items that prevent or decrease the potency of debuffs are especially important. Accuracy down, attack down, and defense down all substantially impair KOS-MOS. Nullifying enemy evade and revenge will pay for itself! Look for items that increase her ether points to finish rounding out her equipment.

COMBAT

KOS-MOS operates fairly differently depending on your target. She can deal with smaller enemies well, but her true power lies against tougher opponents.

In battles of several weaker opponents, have KOS-MOS target the toughest one and destroy it. An alternate option is to weaken or finish the group by using A-BURST or X-BUSTER if you have either ability. If you have neither, but have access to a "hit all" ether attack, use it instead. Another alternative is to use Heat to focus all enemy attention onto her and let the others kill the enemy.

G-BUSTER, M-BUSTER, and B-BUSTER are great at dealing damage against the appropriate enemy type without costing many ether points. These should become your mainstay of standard damage. Substitute CANNON when fighting enemies that have high revenge rates or are weak to fire. Battles against tougher machines and Gnosis warrant the use of Hilbert Effect. This is one of her only debuffs, but it is quite effective (even if it is a bit expensive).

INTRODUCTION

ARCHIVES

CHARACTERS

TACTICAL FILES

EQUIPMENT

THREAT ASSESSMENT

Tougher enemies offer much more for KOS-MOS to do. Start the fights by using Recover EP if you have it. K-AXE, K-PIKE, W-FANG, and VALKYRIE are all decent break attacks. Whether she is assisting or the only breaking character, KOS-MOS is up to the challenge. Bring the enemy near their break point, then relax into doing generic damage.

Be ready to boost KOS-MOS and finish breaking the enemy if your party sustains massive damage or the enemy is preparing a special attack. Once the enemy is broken, let loose your most damaging attacks. Leave recovery to other characters unless your healer is out of the action.

If the enemy still has a great deal of health when the break ends, start breaking again. Weakened enemies should be finished quickly, since they tend to become desperate and use more powerful attacks.

SKILLS
CORE SKILLS, TECHNIQUES, AND SPECIAL ATTACKS

LEVELING SKILLS

LEVEL	NAME
1	G-SHOT
10	HEAT
11	M-BUSTER
16	CANNON I
31	X-BUSTER
39	HILBERT EFFECT

TECHNIQUES

NAME	TARGETS	RANGE	TYPE	EFFECT	EP COST
M-BUSTER	SINGLE ENEMY	SHORT	PHYSICAL	SMALL ATTACK + EFFECTIVE ON TYPE-M ENEMY	6
CANNON I	SINGLE ENEMY	LONG	FIRE	MEDIUM ATTACK	4

ETHERS

NAME	TARGETS	TYPE	EFFECT	EP COST
HEAT	ALL ENEMIES	N/A	SET THE TARGET FOR ALL ENEMIES TO SELF	8
HILBERT EFFECT	ALL ENEMIES	DEBUFF	DECREASE ALL ABILITIES OF TYPE-M AND G ENEMIES	38

SPECIAL ATTACKS

NAME	TARGETS	TYPE	EFFECT	BOOST COST
G-SHOT	SINGLE ENEMY	PHYSICAL	LARGE ATTACK	2
X-BUSTER	ALL ENEMIES	BEAM	MEDIUM ETHER ATTACK	2
D-TENERITAS	SINGLE ENEMY	FIRE	MASSIVE ETHER ATTACK	4

BASIC SKILLS

SKILLS

NAME	SP COST
G-BUSTER	25
STR+2	25
EATK+2	25
VIT+2	25

TECHNIQUES

NAME	TARGETS	RANGE	TYPE	EFFECT	EP COST
G-BUSTER	SINGLE ENEMY	SHORT	PHYSICAL	SMALL ATTACK + EFFECTIVE ON TYPE-G ENEMY	6

It's important to note that while extra skills can be taken at any time (provided you have acquired the necessary item), lower level skill blocks in the primary lines must be completed before later skill blocks can be taken.

ATTACKER

Bringing her programming and physical form to bear, there are few enemies that can stand up to a KOS-MOS well versed in the Attacker skill line. Passive abilities and techniques swell this skill line and pave the way for frightening attacks.

ATTACKER SKILLS

A-2	SP COST	A-3	SP COST	A-4	SP COST	A-5	SP COST	A-6	SP COST	A-7	SP COST	MASTER	SP COST
B-BUSTER	35	K-AXE	50	A-BURST I	70	CANNON II	100	W-BLADE	200	NEMESIS	300	BLOOD DANCER	---
STR+2	35	HP+100	50	TYPE-M CRITICAL	70	SHORT REVENGE	100	A-BURST II	200	SHORT DOUBLE	300		
EATK+2	35	STR+2	50	STR+2	70	TYPE-B CRITICAL	100	TYPE-G CRITICAL	200	EP+20	300		
DEX+2	35	EATK+2	50	LUCK+2	70	STR+2	100	EP+10	200	STR+2	300		

TECHNIQUES

NAME	TARGETS		TYPE	EFFECT	EP COST
B-BUSTER	SINGLE ENEMY	SHORT	PHYSICAL	SMALL ATTACK + EFFECTIVE ON TYPE-B ENEMY	6
K-AXE	SINGLE ENEMY	SHORT	PHYSICAL	MEDIUM BREAK ATTACK + HIGHER CRITICAL RATE TO TYPE-G ENEMY	8
A-BURST I	ALL ENEMIES	LONG	FIRE	SMALL ATTACK	10
CANNON II	SINGLE ENEMY	LONG	FIRE	HEAVY ATTACK	6
W-BLADE	SINGLE ENEMY	SHORT	PHYSICAL	MEDIUM ATTACK + HIGHER CRITICAL RATE ON TYPE-G ENEMY	10
A-BURST II	ALL ENEMIES	LONG	FIRE	MEDIUM ATTACK	14
NEMESIS	SINGLE ENEMY	SHORT	PHYSICAL/FIRE	MASSIVE ATTACK + HIGHER CRITICAL RATE TO TYPE-G ENEMY	16

ETHERS

NAME	TARGETS	TYPE	EFFECT	EP COST
BLOOD DANCER	SELF	BUFF	INCREASE ATTACK POWER AND ETHER ATTACK POWER	99

BLOCKER

The vitality, hit point, and ether defense bonuses in the Blocker line make KOS-MOS a force to be reckoned with. She gains enough techniques to still do effective damage, but the primary focus of this line is survivability.

BLOCKER SKILLS

B-2	SP COST	B-3	SP COST	B-4	SP COST	B-5	SP COST	B-6	SP COST	B-7	SP COST	MASTER	SP COST
HP +100	35	K-PIKE	50	B-BIND	70	HP+200	100	W-FANG	200	VALKYRIE	300	PLATINUM SINGER	---
VIT+2	35	HP+100	50	HP+200	70	VIT+2	100	VIT+2	200	B-SPIKE	300		
EDEF+2	35	VIT+2	50	EP+10	70	EDEF+2	100	EDEF+2	200	HP+300	300		
EVA+2	35	EDEF+2	50	VIT+2	70	EVA+2	100	AGI+2	200	EP+20	300		

INTRODUCTION

ARCHIVES

CHARACTERS

TACTICAL FILES

EQUIPMENT

THREAT ASSESSMENT

SUPPLEMENTS

TECHNIQUES

NAME	TARGETS	RANGE	TYPE	EFFECT	EP COST
K-PIKE	SINGLE ENEMY	SHORT	PHYSICAL	MEDIUM BREAK ATTACK + HIGHER CRITICAL RATE TO TYPE-B ENEMY	8
B-BIND	SINGLE ENEMY	SHORT	PHYSICAL	MEDIUM ATTACK + SMALL CHANCE OF SEALING BOOST	8
W-FANG	SINGLE ENEMY	SHORT	PHYSICAL	HEAVY ATTACK + MEDIUM BREAK ATTACK	12
VALKYRIE	SINGLE ENEMY	SHORT	PHYSICAL/FIRE	MASSIVE ATTACK + MEDIUM BREAK ATTACK	16
B-SPIKE	SINGLE ENEMY	SHORT	PHYSICAL	MEDIUM ATTACK + SMALL CHANCE OF REFLECTING DAMAGE	8

ETHERS

NAME	TARGETS	TYPE	EFFECT	EP COST
PLATINUM SINGER	SELF	BUFF	INCREASE DEFENSE AND ETHER DEFENSE	99

EXTRA SKILLS

These are unlocked as you collect the skill keys throughout the game. There are three keys that open the three levels of extra skills. Unlike the skill lines, skills in later blocks can be purchased at any time and you do not need to complete an earlier block first.

SKILL KEYS

SKILL KEY	SKILLS UNLOCKED	LOCATION
EX SKILL KEY I	EX-A, EX-B, EX-C, EX-D	MILTIAN FOREST: BEHIND THE WATERFALL
EX SKILL KEY II	EX-E, EX-F, EX-G, EX-H	THE MERKABAH: FIRST AREA
EX SKILL KEY III	EX-I, EX-J, EX-K, EX-L	ABEL'S ARK: JUST INSIDE

EXTRA SKILLS

EX-A	SP COST	EX-B	SP COST	EX-C	SP COST	EX-D	SP COST
MEDICA S	50	ANALYZE	30	FIRE BOLT I	50	INFERNO I	70
MEDICA S ALL	70	POISON	40	ICE BOLT I	50	BLIZZARD I	70
BREAK HEAL S	40	RARE STEAL	40	THUNDER BOLT I	50	LIGHTNING I	70
QUICK	40	SLOW	40	BEAM BOLT I	50	SATELLITE I	70

EX-E	SP COST	EX-F	SP COST	EX-G	SP COST	EX-H	SP COST
MEDICA M	100	DISENGAGE	100	FIRE BOLT II	100	INFERNO II	150
MEDICA M ALL	150	REFRESH	100	ICE BOLT II	100	BLIZZARD II	150
BREAK HEAL M	80	RECOVER HP	100	THUNDER BOLT II	100	LIGHTNING II	150
REVERT M	100	RECOVER EP	100	BEAM BOLT II	100	SATELLITE II	150

EX-I	SP COST	EX-J	SP COST	EX-K	SP COST	EX-L	SP COST
MEDICA L	300	EP VAMP	400	FIRE BOLT III	300	INFERNO III	400
MEDICA L ALL	400	CURSE	800	ICE BOLT III	300	BLIZZARD III	400
BREAK HEAL L	200	BEST ALLY	800	THUNDER BOLT III	300	LIGHTNING III	400
REVERT L	300	SHORT COUNTER	400	BEAM BOLT III	300	SATELLITE III	400

INTRODUCTION

ARCHIVES

CHARACTERS

TACTICAL FILES

EQUIPMENT

THREAT ASSESSMENT

⚡ ETHERS ⚡

NAME	TARGETS	TYPE	EFFECT	EP COST
MEDICA S	SINGLE ALLY	HEAL	RECOVER SMALL AMOUNT OF HP	4
MEDICA S ALL	ALL ALLIES	HEAL	RECOVER SMALL AMOUNT OF HP	12
BREAK HEAL S	SINGLE ALLY	HEAL	RECOVER SMALL AMOUNT OF BREAK DAMAGE	22
QUICK	ALL ALLIES	BUFF	INCREASE SPEED	18
ANALYZE	SINGLE ENEMY	N/A	ANALYZE AN ENEMY'S DATA	1
POISON	SINGLE ENEMY	POISON	DAMAGE EACH TURN TO A SINGLE ENEMY	4
RARE STEAL	SINGLE ENEMY	N/A	MEDIUM CHANCE OF STEALING AN ITEM	8
SLOW	ALL ENEMIES	DEBUFF	DECREASE SPEED	18
FIRE BOLT I	SINGLE ENEMY	FIRE	SMALL ATTACK	6
ICE BOLT I	SINGLE ENEMY	ICE	SMALL ATTACK	6
THUNDER BOLT I	SINGLE ENEMY	LIGHTNING	SMALL ATTACK	6
BEAM BOLT I	SINGLE ENEMY	BEAM	SMALL ATTACK	6
INFERNO I	ALL ENEMIES	FIRE	SMALL ATTACK	12
BLIZZARD I	ALL ENEMIES	ICE	SMALL ATTACK	12
LIGHTNING I	ALL ENEMIES	LIGHTNING	SMALL ATTACK	12
SATELLITE I	ALL ENEMIES	BEAM	SMALL ATTACK	12
MEDICA M	SINGLE ALLY	HEAL	RECOVER MEDIUM AMOUNT OF HP	10
MEDICA M ALL	ALL ALLIES	HEAL	RECOVER MEDIUM AMOUNT OF HP	22
BREAK HEAL M	SINGLE ALLY	HEAL	RECOVER MEDIUM AMOUNT OF BREAK DAMAGE	6
REVERT M	SINGLE ALLY	REVIVE	REVIVE AND RECOVER MEDIUM AMOUNT OF HP	20
DISENGAGE	ALL ENEMIES	DEBUFF	REMOVE ALL BUFFS	10
REFRESH	ALL ALLIES	HEAL	RECOVER STATUS EFFECTS	10
RECOVER HP	SINGLE ALLY	HEAL	RECOVER SMALL AMOUNT OF HP WITH EACH TURN	12
RECOVER EP	SINGLE ALLY	HEAL	RECOVER SMALL AMOUNT OF EP WITH EACH TURN	18
FIRE BOLT II	SINGLE ENEMY	FIRE	MEDIUM ATTACK	10
ICE BOLT II	SINGLE ENEMY	ICE	MEDIUM ATTACK	10
THUNDER BOLT II	SINGLE ENEMY	LIGHTNING	MEDIUM ATTACK	10
BEAM BOLT II	SINGLE ENEMY	BEAM	MEDIUM ATTACK	10
INFERNO II	ALL ENEMIES	FIRE	MEDIUM ATTACK	24
BLIZZARD II	ALL ENEMIES	ICE	MEDIUM ATTACK	24
LIGHTNING II	ALL ENEMIES	LIGHTNING	MEDIUM ATTACK	24
SATELLITE II	ALL ENEMIES	BEAM	MEDIUM ATTACK	24
MEDICA L	SINGLE ALLY	HEAL	RECOVER LARGE AMOUNT OF HP	18
MEDICA L ALL	ALL ALLIES	HEAL	RECOVER LARGE AMOUNT OF HP FOR ALL ALLIES	32
BREAK HEAL L	SINGLE ALLY	HEAL	RECOVER LARGE AMOUNT OF BREAK DAMAGE	10
REVERT L	SINGLE ALLY	REVIVE	REVIVE AND RECOVER LARGE AMOUNT OF HP	32
EP VAMP	SINGLE ENEMY	DRAIN	SMALL EP DAMAGE + RECOVER SMALL AMOUNT OF EP	1
CURSE	SINGLE ENEMY	DEBUFF	REFLECT INFLICTED DAMAGE	32
BEST ALLY	SINGLE ALLY	REVIVE	AUTO REVIVE AFTER DEATH WITH FULL HP (1 TIME)	60
FIRE BOLT III	SINGLE ENEMY	FIRE	HEAVY ATTACK	16
ICE BOLT III	SINGLE ENEMY	ICE	HEAVY ATTACK	16
THUNDER BOLT III	SINGLE ENEMY	LIGHTNING	HEAVY ATTACK	16
BEAM BOLT III	SINGLE ENEMY	BEAM	HEAVY ATTACK	16
INFERNO III	ALL ENEMIES	FIRE	HEAVY ATTACK	36
BLIZZARD III	ALL ENEMIES	ICE	HEAVY ATTACK	36
LIGHTNING III	ALL ENEMIES	LIGHTNING	HEAVY ATTACK	36
SATELLITE III	ALL ENEMIES	BEAM	HEAVY ATTACK	36

MOMO

HEIGHT:	141CM (4'8")
WEIGHT:	36KG (179 LBS)
HAIR:	PINK
EYES:	GOLD

Joachim Mizrahi built MOMO in his daughter's image in an attempt to connect the senses of his autistic daughter to the real world. When Sakura died during treatment, Joachim changed his goal slightly and sought to reclaim her spirit from beyond and resurrect her into MOMO.

As Joachim worked with MOMO, he came to a realization. MOMO was not his daughter Sakura. MOMO had become an entirely new person. Joachim encrypted a copy of his Y-Data and stored it within MOMO. During the Miltian Conflict he was killed and MOMO was rescued by the Federation forces. She was sent to live with Juli Mizrahi (who was her legal guardian).

Programmed with the emotions of a 12 year old girl, MOMO considered Joachim and Juli to be her parents. This caused her great pain as she wanted attention from Juli Mizrahi, but was turned away from any real affection. Juli disliked that MOMO was designed in her daughter's image and avoided MOMO when possible.

The existence of the Y-Data buried in her mind became known to a number of organizations and kidnapping attempts began. One eventually succeeded and U-TIC took possession of MOMO on Pleroma Station. Ziggurat 8 (nicknamed Ziggy by MOMO) rescued her from the station with the aid of the Elsa and crew. It was during the travels on the Elsa that MOMO met Jr. She grew to consider both him and Ziggy as good friends.

Several attempts have been made to recover the Y-Data from her mind, but they have been largely unsuccessful. Albedo staged a surprise attack and was able to gather much of the Y-Data and opened the way through the Abyss to Old Miltian. This attack nearly cost MOMO her life and shocked Juli. It was during this event that Juli realized she cared for MOMO.

In the time since, Juli has acted much more as MOMO's mother. With Ziggy as a constant companion and bodyguard, MOMO is never far from friends.

INTRODUCTION

ARCHIVES

CHARACTERS

TACTICAL FILES

EQUIPMENT

THREAT ASSESSMENT

REGIONAL ANALYSIS

SUPPLEMENTAL DATA

STRENGTHS

Even though she has the form of a 12 year old girl, MOMO is far from useless. Her superior understanding of ether abilities is second to none. She has access to almost every ether in the game and has the ether points to use them with near impunity, and the ether attack to make them count.

She also gains a number of strength bonuses and physical techniques that make enemies melt from this little damage wonder. With a number of break techniques, MOMO can supplement the primary breaker until the time is right to unleash her fury.

The higher ether attack also makes her recovery ethers more powerful and the buff and debuff ethers round out her expansive repertoire.

Break Arrow is her first break attack and should be chosen just before Angel Arrow and Twin Head Shot. These give her access to multi-target physical damage. Keep taking the attack ethers as you progress.

Grab Skin Down or Mind Down depending on whether your party uses ether or physical damage more. Disengage and the Recovery ethers are fairly important to get. These won't be used very often, but they pay for themselves when they are used.

Keep choosing any vitality, ether defense, or hit point bonus that presents itself. Short Revenge gives MOMO the ability to strike back at anyone that attacks her in close range and is nice to have.

The critical types are worth the time and skill points to get them as well as Best Ally. With the remaining survivability passives taken, work toward finishing the Spell Attacker line and gaining access to Blood Dancer. This is designed for boss encounters.

WEAKNESSES

As a 4'8" young girl, MOMO isn't that sturdy. Even with all the vitality, ether defense, and hit points she can grab, she'll never stand up to concentrated damage very well. Without a party member to keep her out of the enemy's field of view, MOMO will spend all her ether points keeping herself alive instead of dealing damage. Without all the vitality, ether defense, and hit points, it's quite likely for more powerful enemies to knock MOMO out of the fight in a single attack.

MOMO has a large ether point supply, but sustained fights can take their toll. Should she ever run out of ether points, MOMO is nearly useless. The long places between save points will likely have MOMO gobbling your ether packs or getting them from the active party.

EQUIPMENT

With so few hit points, it's no wonder that MOMO should be equipped with the highest hit point bonus possible. If you know ahead of time what element an enemy will be using, use items that will increase MOMO's resistance to that type of damage. Minimizing or nullifying any debuffs (especially Misty and Rasp) are good options as well.

With all that in mind, have MOMO (or someone else in your party) equipped with an item that displays the enemy's strengths and weaknesses. This allows MOMO to use the most devastating attack possible and fully capitalize on her variable damage.

TRAINING

Once you have the basic skills, choose her area of effect ethers. This gives you a good base for damage. As MOMO gains many of her recovery ethers by levels, don't worry about not seeing them available. Look for ether defense, vitality, and hit point bonuses. These aren't important in the very early parts of the game, but become absolutely necessary later.

COMBAT

As with many characters, using MOMO varies greatly on what you are fighting. With such a large breadth of damage types, she always has what you need at any one time.

Check the elemental strengths and weaknesses of each target when fighting large groups. Strengths are to be avoided. If you can find an element that all are weak or neutral toward, perfect!

If not, settle for an element that none are strong to. Once you know what damage type, decide if you want them dead or just wounded (so another party member can use a special attack to finish them). Use your most powerful area of effect ether if you want them dead, but scale it back a rank if you only want them wounded (your most powerful spells may only wound the enemies depending on what you're fighting).

Another option is to open the fight with Erde Kaiser (if you've gotten it). MOMO has enough ether points that this won't substantially deplete it and will likely leave all enemies broken and your boost gauge full. If your enemies are already wounded when MOMO's turn begins, consider using a special attack to finish one or more. Guilty Rain is great for this because it can finish multiple targets and rake in the bonus skill points, experience, and money.

Stronger foes present more varied actions. Start the fight by helping to break the enemy. Toss Recover EP on MOMO to keep her ether points high. Use Disengage anytime the enemy buffs themselves and Refresh anytime they debuff your party. Keep everyone's health high and break damage low while the enemy's break gauge is filled. Put Safety or Best Ally on yourself or other party members that might be killed in a single enemy barrage.

Once the enemy is nearly broken, use Offensive on your party (or Blood Dancer if you have it). Check for an elemental weakness (by item or by Analyze) and begin exploiting it as soon as the enemy is broken. If the only weakness is physical, have MOMO buff and support one of your physical damage dealers. Weakness to any of the ether elements means fun for MOMO.

Use the highest rank of your single target damage ether that corresponds with the enemy's weakness. If the enemy is below half health, burn your boosts to give MOMO extra turns while the enemy is broken. This maximizes her damage while keeping the party safe from retribution. If the enemy survives the onslaught, be prepared to fall into a healing role and keep your party alive at all costs.

SKILLS

CORE SKILLS, TECHNIQUES, AND SPECIAL ATTACKS

LEVELING SKILLS

LEVEL	NAME	LEVEL	NAME
1	MEDICA S	27	MEDICA L
1	FREEZE SHOCK	30	REVERT L
2	ANALYZE	32	REFRESH
9	MEDICA S ALL	34	SAFETY
15	REVERT M	37	MEDICA L ALL
17	MEDICA M	41	HILBERT EFFECT
22	MEDICA M ALL	45	MEDICA REST
24	GUILTY RAIN	48	GOLD CROWN

ETHERS

NAME	TARGETS	TYPE	EFFECT	EP COST
MEDICA S	SINGLE ALLY	HEAL	RECOVER SMALL AMOUNT OF HP	4
ANALYZE	SINGLE ENEMY	N/A	ANALYZE AN ENEMY'S DATA	1
MEDICA S ALL	ALL ALLIES	HEAL	RECOVER SMALL AMOUNT OF HP	12
REVERT M	SINGLE ALLY	REVIVE	REVIVE AND RECOVER MEDIUM AMOUNT OF HP	20
MEDICA M	SINGLE ALLY	HEAL	RECOVER MEDIUM AMOUNT OF HP	10
MEDICA M ALL	ALL ALLIES	HEAL	RECOVER MEDIUM AMOUNT OF HP	22
MEDICA L	SINGLE ALLY	HEAL	RECOVER LARGE AMOUNT OF HP	18
REVERT L	SINGLE ALLY	REVIVE	REVIVE AND RECOVER LARGE AMOUNT OF HP	32
REFRESH	ALL ALLIES	HEAL	RECOVER STATUS EFFECTS	10
SAFETY	SINGLE ALLY	REVIVE	AUTO REVIVE AFTER DEATH WITH 50% OF HP	40
MEDICA L ALL	ALL ALLIES	HEAL	RECOVER LARGE AMOUNT OF HP FOR ALL ALLIES	32
HILBERT EFFECT	ALL ENEMIES	DEBUFF	DECREASE ALL ABILITIES OF TYPE-M AND G ENEMIES	38
MEDICA REST	ALL ALLIES	HEAL	RECOVER SUBSTANTIAL AMOUNT OF HP	42

SPECIAL ATTACKS

NAME	TARGETS	TYPE	EFFECT	BOOST COST
FREEZE SHOCK	SINGLE ENEMY	ICE	LARGE ETHER ATTACK	2
GUILTY RAIN	ALL ENEMIES	LIGHTNING	MEDIUM ETHER ATTACK	2
GOLD CROWN	ALL ALLIES	BUFF	OFFENSIVE, DEFENSIVE, AND BALANCE UP	2

BASIC SKILLS

It's important to note that while extra skills can be taken at any time (provided you have acquired the necessary item), lower level skill blocks in the primary lines must be completed before later skill blocks can be taken.

SKILLS	
NAME	SP COST
FIRE BOLT I	25
ICE BOLT I	25
THUNDER BOLT I	25
BEAM BOLT I	25

ETHERS				
NAME	TARGETS	TYPE	EFFECT	EP COST
FIRE BOLT I	SINGLE ENEMY	FIRE	SMALL ATTACK	6
ICE BOLT I	SINGLE ENEMY	ICE	SMALL ATTACK	6
THUNDER BOLT I	SINGLE ENEMY	LIGHTNING	SMALL ATTACK	6
BEAM BOLT I	SINGLE ENEMY	BEAM	SMALL ATTACK	6

SPELL ATTACKER

MOMO's mastery of ether attacks only gets more potent through this line. She learns every elemental single and multiple target ether as well as boosting her ether points to frightening levels.

SPELL ATTACKER SKILLS													
A-2	SP COST	A-3	SP COST	A-4	SP COST	A-5	SP COST	A-6	SP COST	A-7	SP COST	MASTER	SP COST
INFERNO I	35	FIRE BOLT II	50	INFERNO II	70	FIRE BOLT III	100	INFERNO III	200	MISTY	300	BLOOD DANCER	---
BLIZZARD I	35	ICE BOLT II	50	BLIZZARD II	70	ICE BOLT III	100	BLIZZARD III	200	LOCK	300		
LIGHTNING I	35	THUNDER BOLT II	50	LIGHTNING II	70	THUNDER BOLT III	100	LIGHTNING III	200	EP+30	300		
SATELLITE I	35	BEAM BOLT II	50	SATELLITE II	70	BEAM BOLT III	100	SATELLITE III	200	EP+30			

ETHERS				
NAME	TARGETS	TYPE	EFFECT	EP COST
INFERNO I	ALL ENEMIES	FIRE	SMALL ATTACK	12
BLIZZARD I	ALL ENEMIES	ICE	SMALL ATTACK	12
LIGHTNING I	ALL ENEMIES	LIGHTNING	SMALL ATTACK	12
SATELLITE I	ALL ENEMIES	BEAM	SMALL ATTACK	12
FIRE BOLT II	SINGLE ENEMY	FIRE	MEDIUM ATTACK	10
ICE BOLT II	SINGLE ENEMY	ICE	MEDIUM ATTACK	10
THUNDER BOLT II	SINGLE ENEMY	LIGHTNING	MEDIUM ATTACK	10
BEAM BOLT II	SINGLE ENEMY	BEAM	MEDIUM ATTACK	10
INFERNO II	ALL ENEMIES	FIRE	MEDIUM ATTACK	24
BLIZZARD II	ALL ENEMIES	ICE	MEDIUM ATTACK	24
LIGHTNING II	ALL ENEMIES	LIGHTNING	MEDIUM ATTACK	24
SATELLITE II	ALL ENEMIES	BEAM	MEDIUM ATTACK	24

NAME	TARGETS	TYPE	EFFECT	EP COST
FIRE BOLT III	SINGLE ENEMY	FIRE	HEAVY ATTACK	16
ICE BOLT III	SINGLE ENEMY	ICE	HEAVY ATTACK	16
THUNDER BOLT III	SINGLE ENEMY	LIGHTNING	HEAVY ATTACK	16
BEAM BOLT III	SINGLE ENEMY	BEAM	HEAVY ATTACK	16
INFERNO III	ALL ENEMIES	FIRE	HEAVY ATTACK	36
BLIZZARD III	ALL ENEMIES	ICE	HEAVY ATTACK	36
LIGHTNING III	ALL ENEMIES	LIGHTNING	HEAVY ATTACK	36
SATELLITE III	ALL ENEMIES	BEAM	HEAVY ATTACK	36
MISTY	SINGLE ENEMY	DEBUFF	SEAL ETHER SPELLS	26
LOCK	SINGLE ENEMY	DEBUFF	SEAL BOOST CAPABILITY	26
BLOOD DANCER	SELF	BUFF	INCREASE ATTACK POWER AND ETHER ATTACK POWER	99

ATTACKER

MOMO's physical damage isn't as high as her ether damage, but it's not terrible. Combine the break techniques and strength and hit point bonuses in this line and MOMO can be a nearly five foot wrecking machine.

ATTACKER SKILLS

B-2	SP COST	B-3	SP COST	B-4	SP COST	B-5	SP COST	B-6	SP COST	B-7	SP COST	MASTER	SP COST
BREAK ARROW I	35	DOUBLE HEAD SHOT	50	OFFENSIVE	70	BREAK ARROW II	100	DOUBLE SHOT I	200	DOUBLE SHOT II	300	ABYSS WALKER	---
HP+100	35	ANGEL ARROW	50	DEFENSIVE	70	RARE STEAL	100	HEAT	200	SWORD FISH	300		
STR+2	35	STR+2	50	BALANCE	70	SHORT REVENGE	100	HP+300	200	SHORT COUNTER	300		
STR+2	35	STR+2	50	QUICK	70	STR+2	100	EP+30	200	SHORT DOUBLE	300		

TECHNIQUES

NAME	TARGETS	RANGE	TYPE	EFFECT	EP COST
BREAK ARROW I	SINGLE ENEMY	LONG	PHYSICAL	SMALL BREAK ATTACK	8
DOUBLE HEAD SHOT	TWO ENEMIES	SHORT	PHYSICAL	SMALL ATTACK	6
ANGEL ARROW	ALL ENEMIES	LONG	PHYSICAL	SMALL ATTACK	10
BREAK ARROW II	SINGLE ENEMY	LONG	PHYSICAL	MEDIUM BREAK ATTACK	10
DOUBLE SHOT I	SINGLE ENEMY	LONG	PHYSICAL	MEDIUM ATTACK	10
DOUBLE SHOT II	SINGLE ENEMY	LONG	PHYSICAL	HEAVY ATTACK	12
SWORD FISH	SINGLE ENEMY	SHORT	PHYSICAL	HEAVY ATTACK + HEAVY BREAK ATTACK	18

ETHERS

NAME	TARGETS	TYPE	EFFECT	EP COST
OFFENSIVE	ALL ALLIES	BUFF	INCREASE ATTACK POWER AND ETHER ATTACK POWER	22
DEFENSIVE	ALL ALLIES	BUFF	INCREASE DEFENSE AND ETHER DEFENSE	22
BALANCE	ALL ALLIES	BUFF	INCREASE ACCURACY AND EVASION	22
QUICK	ALL ALLIES	BUFF	INCREASE SPEED	18
RARE STEAL	SINGLE ENEMY	N/A	MEDIUM CHANCE OF STEALING AN ITEM	8
HEAT	ALL ENEMIES	N/A	SET THE TARGET FOR ALL ENEMIES TO SELF	8
ABYSS WALKER	SELF	BUFF	NULLIFY PHYSICAL ATTACK DAMAGE	99

EXTRA SKILLS

These are unlocked as you collect the skill keys throughout the game. There are three keys that open the three levels of extra skills. Unlike the skill lines, skills in later blocks can be purchased at any time and you do not need to complete an earlier block first.

SKILL KEYS

SKILL KEY	SKILLS UNLOCKED	LOCATION
EX SKILL KEY I	EX-A, EX-B, EX-C, EX-D	MILTIAN FOREST: BEHIND THE WATERFALL
EX SKILL KEY II	EX-E, EX-F, EX-G, EX-H	THE MERKABAH: FIRST AREA
EX SKILL KEY III	EX-I, EX-J, EX-K, EX-L	ABEL'S ARK: JUST INSIDE

EXTRA SKILLS

EX-A	SP COST	EX-B	SP COST	EX-C	SP COST	EX-D	SP COST
BREAK HEAL S	40	BREAK HEAL M	70	STR+2	40	HP+100	50
POISON	40	BALANCE DOWN	50	VIT+2	40	EP+10	50
SLOW	40	EDEF+2	40	EATK+2	40	STR+2	40
EATK+2	40	EDEF+2	40	EDEF+2	40	STR+2	40

EX-E	SP COST	EX-F	SP COST	EX-G	SP COST	EX-H	SP COST
FIST DOWN	150	DISENGAGE	100	VIT+2	80	HP+100	100
SOUL DOWN	150	RECOVER BREAK	100	VIT+2	80	EP+10	100
SKIN DOWN	150	RECOVER HP	100	DEX+2	80	STR+2	80
MIND DOWN	150	RECOVER EP	100	DEX+2	80	STR+2	80

EX-I	SP COST	EX-J	SP COST	EX-K	SP COST	EX-L	SP COST
BREAK HEAL L	200	HP VAMP	400	TYPE-B CRITICAL	400	HP+200	300
RARE HUNTER	300	EP VAMP	400	TYPE-M CRITICAL	400	EP+10	300
EDEF+2	250	CURSE	800	TYPE-G CRITICAL	400	STR+2	250
EDEF+2	250	BEST ALLY	800	DEX+2	250	STR+2	250

ETHERS

NAME	TARGETS	TYPE	EFFECT	EP COST
BREAK HEAL S	SINGLE ALLY	HEAL	RECOVER SMALL AMOUNT OF BREAK DAMAGE	4
POISON	SINGLE ENEMY	POISON	DAMAGE EACH TURN TO A SINGLE ENEMY	4
SLOW	ALL ENEMIES	DEBUFF	DECREASE SPEED	18
BREAK HEAL M	SINGLE ALLY	HEAL	RECOVER MEDIUM AMOUNT OF BREAK DAMAGE	6
BALANCE DOWN	ALL ENEMIES	DEBUFF	DECREASE ACCURACY AND EVASION	22
FIST DOWN	ALL ENEMIES	DEBUFF	DECREASE PHYSICAL ATTACK POWER	22
SOUL DOWN	ALL ENEMIES	DEBUFF	DECREASE ETHER ATTACK POWER	22
SKIN DOWN	ALL ENEMIES	DEBUFF	DECREASE PHYSICAL DEFENSE	22
MIND DOWN	ALL ENEMIES	DEBUFF	DECREASE ETHER DEFENSE	22
DISENGAGE	ALL ENEMIES	DEBUFF	REMOVE ALL BUFFS	10
RECOVER BREAK	SINGLE ALLY	HEAL	RECOVER SMALL AMOUNT OF BL WITH EACH TURN	10
RECOVER HP	SINGLE ALLY	HEAL	RECOVER SMALL AMOUNT OF HP WITH EACH TURN	12
RECOVER EP	SINGLE ALLY	HEAL	RECOVER SMALL AMOUNT OF EP WITH EACH TURN	18
BREAK HEAL L	SINGLE ALLY	HEAL	RECOVER LARGE AMOUNT OF BREAK DAMAGE	10
RARE HUNTER	SINGLE ENEMY	N/A	HIGH CHANCE OF STEALING AN ITEM	14
HP VAMP	SINGLE ENEMY	DRAIN	SMALL HP DAMAGE + RECOVER SMALL AMOUNT OF HP	10
EP VAMP	SINGLE ENEMY	DRAIN	SMALL EP DAMAGE + RECOVER SMALL AMOUNT OF EP	1
CURSE	SINGLE ENEMY	DEBUFF	REFLECT INFLICTED DAMAGE	32
BEST ALLY	SINGLE ALLY	REVIVE	AUTO REVIVE AFTER DEATH WITH FULL HP (1 TIME)	60

SHION

BIOGRAPHICAL INFORMATION

HEIGHT: 163CM (5'4")
WEIGHT: 48KG (106 LBS)
HAIR: BROWN
EYES: GREEN

As a young girl, Shion's life was turned upside down. She lived with both of her parents on Miltian before the conflict. Her mother was immobile and drifted in and out of comas, so she was cared for in a hospital. Shion's father spent a great deal of time working, so Shion was cared for by a Realian named Febronia a good part of the time.

During the Third Descent operation at the end of the Miltian Conflict, Shion's hometown came under direct attack by Federation forces. During the battle, the young Shion made her way to the hospital to find her parents. She found far more than any child should as both her parents were killed by renegade Realians right before her eyes. Shion would have perished as well, but her brother Jin rescued her.

Jin took Shion in until she could support herself. As she was exceptionally bright, this wasn't long. She landed a job at Vector Industries' First R&D Division at the age of 18. Her youth, appearance, and cheerful personality earned her many friends in the division while her sharp intellect advanced her quickly through the ranks.

She was promoted to Junior Chief Engineer of the KOS-MOS Project under Kevin Winnicot. The two were a terrific match and quickly fell in love. The project progressed quickly until Kevin was killed by KOS-MOS when she was awakened prematurely. Shion was present as her and Kevin's creation killed her lover.

Though traumatized and now afraid of thunder (both her parents and Kevin were killed during storms), she continued with the KOS-MOS project. She buried her past as deeply as she could and put on her cheerful personality once again. Some of those close to her, like Allen Ridgeley, could see through this, but they continued to offer support.

Just after Planet Ariadne vanished, Shion was aboard the Woglinde when it was attacked by a large group of Gnosis. She was grabbed by one, but KOS-MOS self started and was able to save Shion. The consequent destruction of the Woglinde left Shion and Allen inside an escape pod with Andrew Cherenkov clinging to the outside. The Elsa found them and Shion's trip into history began.

She has since left Vector after suspecting that the U.M.N. (supposedly constructed by Vector Industries) was closely tied to the Gnosis terrorism. She's had many doubts about the events of the Miltiann Conflict and has teamed up with Scientia to uncover the truth.

STRENGTHS

Shion has been supporting people most of her life. She's very comfortable and good at it. She obtains party buffs earlier than most other characters and she's very adept at healing people's break damage. This keeps the party away from danger and operating at maximum capacity.

She also has several techniques that cause break damage. She isn't the best at it, but she it is always good to use her in this capacity. Against human targets, there is only one character better at breaking than Shion.

The many ether attack bonuses give Shion the power to use both attack and recovery ethers. She gets access to all elemental types and can heal along with the best.

WEAKNESSES

Shion isn't the best at taking damage. She's far from the worst, but even with all the vitality, ether defense, and hit point bonuses, she takes quite a beating if the enemy focuses on her. She's pretty balanced between ether defense and vitality, but neither is high enough to have her at the head of your assault.

Without ether points, Shion's attacks become very weak. When not using ether or break attacks, Shion is better used for healing or buffing because her standard damage output is quite minimal.

TRAINING

Getting the basic skills gives you a pretty good idea what Shion does well. Be sure to gain Break Blow and Break Heal M quickly. This gives her a break technique and getting Break Heal M as early as possible is a godsend. She'll be your best break healer for quite some time.

Hit point and ether point bonuses should be near the top of your list. These increase Shion's staying power and will never become obsolete. Collect the buff ethers and Refresh as you gain levels. Shion really cements her ability to back up the party with these. Many of your tougher opponents will be humans, so grab Fallen Eagle II when it becomes available.

Short Double and the critical types can greatly increase Shion's damage potential and are obvious choices. Don't get the ice and thunder ether attacks just yet. Scoop up the strength bonuses followed by the ether attack power bonuses. This increases Shion's physical damage and more importantly...her breaking power!

Reach for Rare Hunter and Safety. These are very powerful ethers. Safety allows Shion to revive people before they die while Rare Hunter is an upgrade for Rare Steal. Choosing Double Shot I and II, and Break Blow III finish off her techniques nicely.

The Recover ethers, Misty, and Lock are good weapons to have. Crippling the enemy's ability to do anything worthwhile has become something that Shion is very good at. Once you have these, go back and pick up the remaining attack ethers to fully round out her damage capability.

EQUIPMENT

Shion sits in a difficult position in the party. As part healer, part breaker, the equipment she needs to operate at maximum power is hard to find. Equipment that increases her survivability through either decreasing damage dealt to her or increasing her hit points is important. This shores up her worst weakness.

Filling the remaining slots with equipment that increases her damage completes the set. Look for items that add an elemental type to her damage. This also counts when she uses her break attacks. Finding items that add damage types and increase her hitpoints are pure gold!

COMBAT

With her buffs, debuffs, and break techniques, Shion is better suited for tougher enemies. However, she has enough area of effect ether attacks and multiple target techniques to get the job done.

Against larger groups of weaker enemies, start the fight with either an area of effect attack to weaken the enemies and gain boost, or use Offensive on your party. The added power increases your party's damage greatly.

Pick the toughest enemy and start using Break Blow while watching the health and break damage of the party. Use healing and break healing ethers as needed to keep trivial enemies from ever bringing any member of your party down. As you gain levels and Shion learns more debuff ethers (such as Skin Down and Mind Down), these should be used just after Offensive to truly put the hurt on the enemies.

Begin fights against tougher opponents much the same. Buff the party with Offensive and Defensive to tip the scales in your favor. Put Recover EP (if you have it) on Shion to increase her staying power and start breaking the enemy. Use Disengage any time your opponent uses a buff.

As your foe closes in on half health (or starts spouting nonsense about destroying you), start stacking debuffs. Skin Down and Mind Down are great starts and Misty and Lock are terribly mean. Finish breaking the enemy and lay on your most damaging attacks. Avoid using your break attacks until the enemy is back on their feet.

If your party is wounded, use the time to revive or heal them. Shion's damage isn't terribly high and those couple of turns while the enemy is broken are better spent getting your group back to full health, little or no break damage, and renew buffs and debuffs.

Human enemies are especially vulnerable to breaking. Use Fallen Eagle II rather than Break Blow as it deals more break damage to humans. Keep the enemy as weak as possible by breaking and debuffing them and watch your party tear them apart.

SKILLS

CORE SKILLS, TECHNIQUES, AND SPECIAL ATTACKS

LEVELING SKILLS

LEVEL	NAME	LEVEL	NAME
1	ANALYZE	21	MEDICA M
1	BREAK BASH	23	DISENGAGE
3	MEDICA S	26	LOCK SHOT
6	LUNAR BLADE I	29	MEDICA M ALL
12	RARE STEAL	32	MEDICA L
14	MEDICA S ALL	36	REVERT L
16	FALLEN EAGLE I	41	MS2
19	REVERT M	43	MEDICA L ALL

⚡ ETHERS ⚡

NAME	TARGETS	TYPE	EFFECT	EP COST
ANALYZE	SINGLE ENEMY	N/A	ANALYZE AN ENEMY'S DATA	1
MEDICA S	SINGLE ALLY	HEAL	RECOVER SMALL AMOUNT OF HP	4
RARE STEAL	SINGLE ENEMY	N/A	MEDIUM CHANCE OF STEALING AN ITEM	8
MEDICA S ALL	ALL ALLIES	HEAL	RECOVER SMALL AMOUNT OF HP	12
REVERT M	SINGLE ALLY	REVIVE	REVIVE AND RECOVER MEDIUM AMOUNT OF HP	20
MEDICA M	SINGLE ALLY	HEAL	RECOVER MEDIUM AMOUNT OF HP	10
DISENGAGE	ALL ENEMIES	DEBUFF	REMOVE ALL BUFFS	10
MEDICA M ALL	ALL ALLIES	HEAL	RECOVER MEDIUM AMOUNT OF HP	22
MEDICA L	SINGLE ALLY	HEAL	RECOVER LARGE AMOUNT OF HP	18
REVERT L	SINGLE ALLY	REVIVE	REVIVE AND RECOVER LARGE AMOUNT OF HP	32
MEDICA L ALL	ALL ALLIES	HEAL	RECOVER LARGE AMOUNT OF HP FOR ALL ALLIES	32

⚔ TECHNIQUES ⚔

NAME	TARGETS	RANGE	TYPE	EFFECT	EP COST
LUNAR BLADE I	SINGLE ENEMY	SHORT	PHYSICAL	MEDIUM ATTACK	4
FALLEN EAGLE I	SINGLE HUMAN ENEMY	SHORT	PHYSICAL	SMALL BREAK ATTACK	8

🔥 SPECIAL ATTACKS 🔥

NAME	TARGETS	TYPE	EFFECT	BOOST COST
BREAK BASH	SINGLE ENEMY	PHYSICAL	HEAVY BREAK ATTACK + HIGHER CRITICAL RATE TO TYPE-B ENEMIES	2
LOCK SHOT	ALL ENEMIES	BEAM/DEBUFF	MEDIUM ETHER ATTACK + SEAL BOOST	2
MS2	SINGLE ENEMY	FIRE	LARGE ATTACK	3

BASIC SKILLS

It's important to note that while extra skills can be taken at any time (provided you have acquired the necessary item), lower level skill blocks in the primary lines must be completed before later skill blocks can be taken.

SKILLS

NAME	SP COST
QUICK	25
BREAK HEAL S	25
FIRE BOLT I	25
BEAM BOLT I	25

ETHERS

NAME	TARGETS	TYPE	EFFECT	EP COST
QUICK	ALL ALLIES	BUFF	INCREASE SPEED	18
BREAK HEAL S	SINGLE ALLY	HEAL	RECOVER SMALL AMOUNT OF BREAK DAMAGE	4
FIRE BOLT I	SINGLE ENEMY	FIRE	SMALL ATTACK	6
BEAM BOLT I	SINGLE ENEMY	BEAM	SMALL ATTACK	6

SUPPORT

With only a few attack ethers, Support is much more about helping others. The powerful buffs and debuffs ensure that even if Shion deals no damage in a turn, the time is far from wasted.

SUPPORT SKILLS

A-2	SP COST	A-3	SP COST	A-4	SP COST	A-5	SP COST	A-6	SP COST	A-7	SP COST	MASTER	SP COST
OFFENSIVE	35	REFRESH	50	FIRE BOLT II	70	SKIN DOWN	100	FIRE BOLT III	200	BREAK HEAL L	300	STAND KEEPER	---
DEFENSIVE	35	EATK+2	50	BEAM BOLT II	70	MIND DOWN	100	BEAM BOLT III	200	INFERNO II	300		
BALANCE	35	EATK+2	50	INFERNO I	70	BALANCE DOWN	100	SAFETY	200	SATELLITE II	300		
BREAK HEAL M	35	EP+20	50	SATELLITE I	70	SLOW	100	EP+20	200	RARE HUNTER			

ETHERS

NAME	TARGETS	TYPE	EFFECT	EP COST
OFFENSIVE	ALL ALLIES	BUFF	INCREASE ATTACK POWER AND ETHER ATTACK POWER	22
DEFENSIVE	ALL ALLIES	BUFF	INCREASE DEFENSE AND ETHER DEFENSE	22
BALANCE	ALL ALLIES	BUFF	INCREASE ACCURACY AND EVASION	22
BREAK HEAL M	SINGLE ALLY	HEAL	RECOVER MEDIUM AMOUNT OF BREAK DAMAGE	6
REFRESH	ALL ALLIES	HEAL	RECOVER STATUS EFFECTS	10
FIRE BOLT II	SINGLE ENEMY	FIRE	MEDIUM ATTACK	10
BEAM BOLT II	SINGLE ENEMY	BEAM	MEDIUM ATTACK	10
INFERNO I	ALL ENEMIES	FIRE	SMALL ATTACK	12
SATELLITE I	ALL ENEMIES	BEAM	SMALL ATTACK	12
SKIN DOWN	ALL ENEMIES	DEBUFF	DECREASE PHYSICAL DEFENSE	22
MIND DOWN	ALL ENEMIES	DEBUFF	DECREASE ETHER DEFENSE	22

NAME	TARGETS	TYPE	EFFECT	EP COST
BALANCE DOWN	ALL ENEMIES	DEBUFF	DECREASE ACCURACY AND EVASION	22
SLOW	ALL ENEMIES	DEBUFF	DECREASE SPEED	18
FIRE BOLT III	SINGLE ENEMY	FIRE	HEAVY ATTACK	16
BEAM BOLT III	SINGLE ENEMY	BEAM	HEAVY ATTACK	16
SAFETY	SINGLE ALLY	REVIVE	AUTO REVIVE AFTER DEATH WITH 50% OF HP	40
BREAK HEAL L	SINGLE ALLY	HEAL	RECOVER LARGE AMOUNT OF BREAK DAMAGE	10
INFERNO II	ALL ENEMIES	FIRE	MEDIUM ATTACK	24
SATELLITE II	ALL ENEMIES	BEAM	MEDIUM ATTACK	24
RARE HUNTER	SINGLE ENEMY	N/A	HIGH CHANCE OF STEALING AN ITEM	14
STAND KEEPER	SELF	BUFF	NULLIFY BREAK DAMAGE	99

ATTACKER

Attacker capitalizes on the martial arts training Shion received from her grandfather. With the criticals, counter, revenge, and double, the techniques she learns are even more powerful.

ATTACKER SKILLS

B-2	SP COST	B-3	SP COST	B-4	SP COST	B-5	SP COST	B-6	SP COST	B-7	SP COST	MASTER	SP COST
BREAK BLOW I	35	SLOW EDGE	50	FALLEN EAGLE II	70	LUNAR BLADE II	100	DOUBLE SHOT I	200	DOUBLE SHOT II	300	PHANTOM FLY	---
HP+100	35	SHORT COUNTER	50	HP+100	70	HEAT	100	FALLEN EAGLE III	200	BREAK BLOW II	300		
EP+20	35	STR+2	50	SHORT DOUBLE	70	TYPE-B CRITICAL	100	HP+100	200	SHORT REVENGE	300		
STR+2	35	VIT+2	50	LUCK+2	70	TYPE-M CRITICAL	100	EP+20	200	LUCK+2	300		

TECHNIQUES

NAME	TARGETS	RANGE	TYPE	EFFECT	EP COST
BREAK BLOW I	SINGLE ENEMY	SHORT	PHYSICAL	SMALL BREAK ATTACK	8
SLOW EDGE	SINGLE ENEMY	SHORT	PHYSICAL	SMALL ATTACK + SLOW	8
FALLEN EAGLE II	SINGLE HUMAN ENEMY	SHORT	PHYSICAL	MEDIUM BREAK ATTACK	10
LUNAR BLADE II	SINGLE ENEMY	SHORT	PHYSICAL	HEAVY ATTACK	6
DOUBLE SHOT I	SINGLE ENEMY	LONG	PHYSICAL	MEDIUM ATTACK	10
FALLEN EAGLE III	SINGLE HUMAN ENEMY	SHORT	PHYSICAL	HEAVY BREAK ATTACK	12
DOUBLE SHOT II	SINGLE ENEMY	LONG	PHYSICAL	HEAVY ATTACK	12
BREAK BLOW II	SINGLE ENEMY	SHORT	PHYSICAL	MEDIUM BREAK ATTACK	10

ETHERS

NAME	TARGETS	TYPE	EFFECT	EP COST
HEAT	ALL ENEMIES	N/A	SET THE TARGET FOR ALL ENEMIES TO SELF	8
PHANTOM FLY	SELF	BUFF	ALWAYS EXECUTE EVASION	99

EXTRA SKILLS

These are unlocked as you collect the skill keys throughout the game. There are three keys that open the three levels of extra skills. Unlike the skill lines, skills in later blocks can be purchased at any time and you do not need to complete an earlier block first.

SKILL KEYS

SKILL KEY	SKILLS UNLOCKED	LOCATION
EX SKILL KEY I	EX-A, EX-B, EX-C, EX-D	MILTIAN FOREST: BEHIND THE WATERFALL
EX SKILL KEY II	EX-E, EX-F, EX-G, EX-H	THE MERKABAH: FIRST AREA
EX SKILL KEY III	EX-I, EX-J, EX-K, EX-L	ABEL'S ARK: JUST INSIDE

INTRODUCTION

ARCHIVES

CHARACTERS

TACTICAL FILES

EQUIPMENT

THREAT ASSESSMENT

REGIONAL ANALYSIS

SUPPLEMENTAL DATA

EXTRA SKILLS

EX-A	SP COST	EX-B	SP COST	EX-C	SP COST	EX-D	SP COST
ICE BOLT I	50	BLIZZARD I	50	STR+2	40	STR+2	40
THUNDER BOLT I	50	LIGHTNING I	50	VIT+2	40	VIT+2	40
HP+100	50	POISON	50	EATK+2	40	EATK+2	40
EP+10	50	EATK+2	40	EDEF+2	40	EDEF+2	40

EX-E	SP COST	EX-F	SP COST	EX-G	SP COST	EX-H	SP COST
ICE BOLT II	100	BLIZZARD II	150	STR+2	80	HP+100	100
THUNDER BOLT II	100	LIGHTNING II	150	VIT+2	80	EP+10	100
FIST DOWN	150	RECOVER HP	100	EATK+2	80	DEX+2	80
SOUL DOWN	150	RECOVER EP	100	EDEF+2	80	DEX+2	80

EX-I	SP COST	EX-J	SP COST	EX-K	SP COST	EX-L	SP COST
ICE BOLT III	300	HP VAMP	400	TYPE-G CRITICAL	400	INFERNO III	400
THUNDER BOLT III	300	EP VAMP	400	HP+200	300	BLIZZARD III	400
MISTY	400	MEDICA REST	999	EP+10	300	LIGHTNING III	400
LOCK	400	BEST ALLY	800	LUCK+2	250	SATELLITE III	400

ETHERS

NAME	TARGETS	TYPE	EFFECT	EP COST
ICE BOLT I	SINGLE ENEMY	ICE	SMALL ATTACK	6
THUNDER BOLT I	SINGLE ENEMY	LIGHTNING	SMALL ATTACK	6
BLIZZARD I	ALL ENEMIES	ICE	SMALL ATTACK	12
LIGHTNING I	ALL ENEMIES	LIGHTNING	SMALL ATTACK	12
POISON	SINGLE ENEMY	POISON	DAMAGE EACH TURN TO A SINGLE ENEMY	4
ICE BOLT II	SINGLE ENEMY	ICE	MEDIUM ATTACK	10
THUNDER BOLT II	SINGLE ENEMY	LIGHTNING	MEDIUM ATTACK	10
FIST DOWN	ALL ENEMIES	DEBUFF	DECREASE PHYSICAL ATTACK POWER	22
SOUL DOWN	ALL ENEMIES	DEBUFF	DECREASE ETHER ATTACK POWER	22
BLIZZARD II	ALL ENEMIES	ICE	MEDIUM ATTACK	24
LIGHTNING II	ALL ENEMIES	LIGHTNING	MEDIUM ATTACK	24
RECOVER HP	SINGLE ALLY	HEAL	RECOVER SMALL AMOUNT OF HP WITH EACH TURN	12
RECOVER EP	SINGLE ALLY	HEAL	RECOVER SMALL AMOUNT OF EP WITH EACH TURN	18

NAME	TARGETS	TYPE	EFFECT	EP COST
ICE BOLT III	SINGLE ENEMY	ICE	HEAVY ATTACK	16
THUNDER BOLT III	SINGLE ENEMY	LIGHTNING	HEAVY ATTACK	16
MISTY	SINGLE ENEMY	DEBUFF	SEAL ETHER SPELLS	26
LOCK	SINGLE ENEMY	DEBUFF	SEAL BOOST CAPABILITY	26
HP VAMP	SINGLE ENEMY	DRAIN	SMALL HP DAMAGE + RECOVER SMALL AMOUNT OF HP	10
EP VAMP	SINGLE ENEMY	DRAIN	SMALL EP DAMAGE + RECOVER SMALL AMOUNT OF EP	1
MEDICA REST	ALL ALLIES	HEAL	RECOVER SUBSTANTIAL AMOUNT OF HP	42
BEST ALLY	SINGLE ALLY	REVIVE	AUTO REVIVE AFTER DEATH WITH FULL HP	60
INFERNO III	ALL ENEMIES	FIRE	HEAVY ATTACK	36
BLIZZARD III	ALL ENEMIES	ICE	HEAVY ATTACK	36
LIGHTNING III	ALL ENEMIES	LIGHTNING	HEAVY ATTACK	36
SATELLITE III	ALL ENEMIES	BEAM	HEAVY ATTACK	36

ZIGGY

BIOGRAPHICAL INFORMATION

HEIGHT: 191CM (6'3")
WEIGHT: 162KG (357 LBS)
HAIR: BLONDE
EYES: BLUE

Captain Jan Sauer was a member of the Federation Police Counter Terrorism Division. Jan's happy life ended when his subordinate (Erich Weber) betrayed him and became the cyber-terrorist Voyager. This wasn't the end of Voyager's betrayal as he plotted and eventually succeeded in murdering both Jan's wife and stepson. When confronted by Erich, Captain Sauer killed himself.

Due to the Life Recycling Act, Jan's body was donated to Ziggurat Industries. Revived as a battle cyborg, he was given the name Ziggurat 8 to denote his construction number. Rather than grasping this second chance at life, Ziggurat 8 opted to replace his organic tissue with machine upgrades at every opportunity.

Since cyborgs have no rights (not even the rights of Realians), Ziggurat 8 was at the mercy of his employers and could not simply stop living. He opted for the most dangerous missions and started on a personal journey...to eliminate everything human about himself.

This journey was interrupted when Subcommittee Member Juli Mizrahi (to whom he was assigned) ordered him to rescue a 100-series Observational Realian from Pleroma Station. The Realian was MOMO. During the rescue, MOMO began calling him "Ziggy." The two escaped Pleroma Station, but were pursued. They were rescued by the Elsa and joined with the other passengers for a trip of a lifetime.

Ziggy has been at MOMO's side ever since. Juli Mizrahi has assigned him as MOMO's personal bodyguard and the two are actually becoming friends. Ziggy seems to have taken a liking to his new name and is no longer as eager to destroy his humanity.

Dark shadows still lurk within his past, but his friends need him in the present. He's as dependable as the metal much of his body is constructed of. He won't back down from a fight and approaches many of the difficulties with a very practical mind that balances some of the more imaginative members of the party.

STRENGTHS

Ziggy is a battle cyborg! When it comes to taking damage, there isn't a single other character that can match him. His hit points and vitality are immense. Any battle you're worried about enemy attacks killing all members instantly, put Ziggy in.

He's been around the block a few times and knows how to break people. Ziggy is terrifyingly good at breaking humans and only terrific at breaking anything else. He even possesses multiple target break techniques. Being able to break later bosses multiple times is worth his weight in gold.

WEAKNESSES

When it comes to ether attacks, Ziggy isn't the one for the job. He can learn all the area of effect ether attacks, but these are very costly in terms of ether points and his ether attack isn't high enough to make them really count. He gets some buffs and debuffs, but ether abilities are definitely not his realm of expertise.

Aside from his breaking ability, his physical damage isn't very high. He gets a number of strength bonuses, but they don't make up the difference well. Against enemies that are very resistant to breaking, Ziggy doesn't have as much to do since none of his other damage types are very effective.

TRAINING

After obtaining the basic skills, start scooping up any techniques that present themselves. Ziggy's normal attacks aren't very powerful, so he has to rely on his powerful techniques. Devil Break is a wonderful ability because it breaks and lowers the enemy's accuracy.

Grab vitality and hit point bonuses as they become available. One of Ziggy's jobs will likely be surviving. Avoid the ether attacks and ether attack power bonuses until you have spare points. These aren't as important to Ziggy and in most cases you can just change a more ether-based character in.

Keep learning any passive bonuses that increase Ziggy's survivability while you work toward Revert M and the Recover ethers. If Ziggy is going to be the last one standing, it would be nice if he could revive other members. The Recover ethers and Refresh give Ziggy a good number of ethers that don't rely on his lower ether attack power to be effective.

As more techniques show up in his two primary lines, learn them. These are the bread and butter of Ziggy and should not be ignored. Watch for ether point bonuses as well. Breaking people takes a lot of work and as the enemies become tougher, Ziggy will need the added power.

Road Rage I is an absolute must. This is Ziggy's first multiple target break technique and will make random fights great fun. With his break potential well on the way, consider grabbing the third rank of attack ethers. This way you don't use skill points on the lower tiers, but you still have them available for the more difficult fights (the fights up until now haven't really warranted them).

Polish off Ziggy's training with Best Ally and Revert L. These, along with any recovery ethers you've picked up, allow Ziggy to act as an emergency healer on top of breaking the enemies. Misty and Lock can be quite powerful against some enemies and if no one else in your party has learned them, have Ziggy do so.

EQUIPMENT

Ziggy's base hit points are immense, but even that won't stop the more dangerous enemies. Watch for items that increase his hit points and break limit. There are foes that have hit all break abilities and Ziggy is the best candidate to survive them.

Rasp is the bane of Ziggy. Without access to his techniques he must rely on his less powerful ethers until the effect can be removed. Equipping items that prevent Rasp (or Misty so he can use Refresh) will keep this break train moving.

Finishing his equipment off with more bonuses to hit points or ether points and you have a character that will survive pretty much everything that can be thrown at him.

COMBAT

Before you get Road Rage, fights against multiple weaker foes seem a little uncertain for Ziggy. He doesn't have much in the way of "hit all" abilities and doesn't do enough damage to kill most enemies outright. In these cases, use Heat to pull all enemy attacks to you. Ziggy can take the damage and it frees up the other members to focus on nothing but doing damage. As you gain levels, Ziggy gets Hind. With a multiple target special attack, the chance of multiple finishing strikes each battle increases greatly.

If the group of enemies has a substantially tougher member, take the time to break it rather than using Heat. Heavy Tackle is effective if you're fighting non-humans. Stick with Choke for humans because the amount of break damage it deals is insane.

Against single strong opponents, Ziggy really starts to shine. Use Recover EP early on along with Recover Break. This gives Ziggy a lot more staying power without taking a great deal of time. Once those are active, start breaking. Use Choke against human targets and Heavy Tackle or Sword Fish against inhuman foes.

Once an enemy is broken, switch to Painkiller, Sword Edge, or Sword Rush to help throw on the damage. If anyone in the party is terribly wounded, consider using Ziggy's turn to help them (usually with an item) and free other members up to do damage. Taking the time to heal break damage on party members before they are fully broken often pays for itself. With Ziggy's Break Heals, he's very good at it.

Watch for blanket debuffs hitting your party and buffs stacking on the enemy. Refresh and Disengage are spectacular. It's a careful balance deciding when to deal break damage and when to use an ether. If you're unsure, use a break technique as breaking an enemy gives you more time to think.

Though Ziggy has very high hit points, he isn't indestructible. Keep his health high, since the purpose of his hit points is to keep the enemy from killing everyone in a single attack. If other party members should fall, use your highest Revert or a revive item (Seven Moons are great for this) to bring them back with as much health as possible.

As Recover EP falls, use it again to keep your ether points flowing. Be ready to finish a break any time the opponent begins charging a special attack or if your party needs time to recover.

SKILLS

CORE SKILLS, TECHNIQUES, AND SPECIAL ATTACKS

LEVELING SKILLS			
LEVEL	**NAME**	**LEVEL**	**NAME**
1	PENETRATE	26	HIND
8	HEAT	30	BACK TACKLE
10	BREAK HEAL S	33	BREAK HEAL L
16	CHOKE	40	INTRUDER
18	BREAK HEAL M	48	SWORD RUSH
23	BACK FISH		

⚡ ETHERS ⚡				
NAME	**TARGETS**	**TYPE**	**EFFECT**	**EP COST**
MEDICA S	SINGLE ALLY	HEAL	RECOVER SMALL AMOUNT OF HP	4
ANALYZE	SINGLE ENEMY	N/A	ANALYZE AN ENEMY'S DATA	1
MEDICA S ALL	ALL ALLIES	HEAL	RECOVER SMALL AMOUNT OF HP	12
REVERT M	SINGLE ALLY	REVIVE	REVIVE AND RECOVER MEDIUM AMOUNT OF HP	20
MEDICA M	SINGLE ALLY	HEAL	RECOVER MEDIUM AMOUNT OF HP	10
MEDICA M ALL	ALL ALLIES	HEAL	RECOVER MEDIUM AMOUNT OF HP	22
MEDICA L	SINGLE ALLY	HEAL	RECOVER LARGE AMOUNT OF HP	18
REVERT L	SINGLE ALLY	REVIVE	REVIVE AND RECOVER LARGE AMOUNT OF HP	32
REFRESH	ALL ALLIES	HEAL	RECOVER STATUS EFFECTS	10
SAFETY	SINGLE ALLY	REVIVE	AUTO REVIVE AFTER DEATH WITH 50% OF HP (1 TIME)	40
MEDICA L ALL	ALL ALLIES	HEAL	RECOVER LARGE AMOUNT OF HP FOR ALL ALLIES	32
HILBERT EFFECT	ALL ENEMIES	DEBUFF	DECREASE ALL ABILITIES OF TYPE-M AND G ENEMIES	38
MEDICA REST	ALL ALLIES	HEAL	RECOVER SUBSTANTIAL AMOUNT OF HP	42

INTRODUCTION

ARCHIVES

CHARACTERS

TACTICAL FILES

EQUIPMENT

THREAT ASSESSMENT

REGIONAL ANALYSIS

SUPPLEMENTAL DATA

TECHNIQUES

NAME	TARGETS	RANGE	TYPE	EFFECT	EP COST
CHOKE	SINGLE HUMAN ENEMY	SHORT	PHYSICAL	HEAVY BREAK ATTACK	12
BACK FISH	SINGLE ENEMY	SHORT	PHYSICAL	SMALL CHANCE OF EXECUTING SWORD FISH FROM BEHIND	6
BACK TACKLE	SINGLE ENEMY	SHORT	PHYSICAL	SMALL CHANCE OF EXECUTING HEAVY TACKLE FROM BEHIND	6
SWORD RUSH	SINGLE ENEMY	SHORT	PHYSICAL	HEAVY PHYSICAL ATTACK	12

ETHERS

NAME	TARGETS	TYPE	EFFECT	EP COST
HEAT	ALL ENEMIES	N/A	SET THE TARGET FOR ALL ENEMIES TO SELF	8
BREAK HEAL S	SINGLE ALLY	HEAL	RECOVER SMALL AMOUNT OF BREAK DAMAGE	4
BREAK HEAL M	SINGLE ALLY	HEAL	RECOVER MEDIUM AMOUNT OF BREAK DAMAGE	6
BREAK HEAL L	SINGLE ALLY	HEAL	RECOVER LARGE AMOUNT OF BREAK DAMAGE	10

SPECIAL ATTACKS

NAME	TARGETS	TYPE	EFFECT	BOOST COST
PENETRATE	SINGLE ENEMY	PHYSICAL	LARGE ATTACK	2
HIND	ALL ENEMIES	FIRE	MEDIUM ATTACK	2
INTRUDER	SINGLE ENEMY	FIRE	MASSIVE ATTACK + MEDIUM BREAK ATTACKS	4

BASIC SKILLS

It's important to note that while extra skills can be taken at any time (provided you have acquired the necessary item), lower level skill blocks in the primary lines must be completed before later skill blocks can be taken.

SKILLS

NAME	SP COST	NAME	SP COST
PAIN KILLER I	25	EP+10	25
HP+100	25	VIT+2	25

TECHNIQUES

NAME	TARGETS	RANGE	TYPE	EFFECT	EP COST
PAIN KILLER I	SINGLE ENEMY	SHORT	PHYSICAL	MEDIUM ATTACK	4

BLOCKER

The plentiful hit point, vitality, and other defensive bonuses in Blocker give Ziggy more survivability than most and barely what he needs at the same time. Enemies in the later game are going to try his durability.

BLOCKER SKILLS

A-2	SP COST	A-3	SP COST	A-4	SP COST	A-5	SP COST	A-6	SP COST	A-7	SP COST	MASTER	SP COST
HP+100	35	DEVIL BREAK	50	HP+200	70	PAIN KILLER II	100	SWORD EDGE	200	ROAD STORM	300	ROYAL GUARD	---
VIT+2	35	VIT+2	50	VIT+2	70	HP+200	100	DEFENSIVE	200	HP+300	300		
EDEF+2	35	EDEF+2	50	EDEF+2	70	EP+20	100	HP+300	200	EP+30	300		
EVA+2	35	EVA+2	50	EVA+2	70	VIT+2	100	VIT+2	200	VIT+2	300		

TECHNIQUES

NAME	TARGETS	RANGE	TYPE	EFFECT	EP COST
DEVIL BREAK	SINGLE ENEMY	SHORT	PHYSICAL	MEDIUM BREAK ATTACK + LOWER ACCURACY	8
PAIN KILLER II	SINGLE ENEMY	SHORT	PHYSICAL	HEAVY ATTACK	6
SWORD EDGE	SINGLE ENEMY	SHORT	PHYSICAL	MEDIUM ATTACK + HIGHER CRITICAL RATE	10
ROAD STORM	ALL ENEMIES	LONG	PHYSICAL	MEDIUM ATTACK + DECREASE IN PHYSICAL ATTACK POWER	20

ETHERS

NAME	TARGETS	TYPE	EFFECT	EP COST
DEFENSIVE	ALL ALLIES	BUFF	INCREASE DEFENSE AND ETHER DEFENSE	22
ROYAL GUARD	SELF	BUFF	ALWAYS EXECUTE GUARD	99

BREAKER

Ziggy can't be matched in his ability to break enemies. Higher break techniques as well as multiple target break techniques are complimented by plentiful strength bonuses in this line.

BREAKER SKILLS

B-2	SP COST	B-3	SP COST	B-4	SP COST	B-5	SP COST	B-6	SP COST	B-7	SP COST	MASTER	SP COST
HEAVY TACKLE I	35	HP+100	50	HEAVY TACKLE II	70	ROAD RAGE I	100	HEAVY TACKLE III	200	ROAD RAGE II	300	HEARTBREAKER	---
STR+2	35	EP+10	50	HP+100	70	TYPE-M CRITICAL	100	BACK CHOKE	200	STR+2	300		
DEX+2	35	STR+2	50	EP+10	70	STR+2	100	OFFENSIVE	200	EP+20	300		
DEX+2	35	LUCK+2	50	TYPE-B CRITICAL	70	AGI+2	100	STR+2	200	LUCK+2	300		

TECHNIQUES

NAME	TARGETS	RANGE	TYPE	EFFECT	EP COST
HEAVY TACKLE I	SINGLE ENEMY	SHORT	PHYSICAL	SMALL BREAK ATTACK	8
HEAVY TACKLE II	SINGLE ENEMY	SHORT	PHYSICAL	MEDIUM BREAK ATTACK	10
ROAD RAGE I	ALL ENEMIES	LONG	PHYSICAL	SMALL BREAK ATTACK	10
HEAVY TACKLE III	SINGLE ENEMIES	SHORT	PHYSICAL	HEAVY BREAK ATTACK	12
BACK CHOKE	SINGLE HUMAN ENEMY	SHORT	PHYSICAL	SMALL CHANCE OF EXECUTING CHOKE FROM BEHIND	8
ROAD RAGE II	ALL ENEMIES	LONG	PHYSICAL	MEDIUM BREAK ATTACK	12

ETHERS

NAME	TARGETS	TYPE	EFFECT	EP COST
OFFENSIVE	ALL ALLIES	BUFF	INCREASE ATTACK POWER AND ETHER ATTACK POWER	22
HEARTBREAKER	SELF	BUFF	LARGE INCREASE IN BREAK ATTACK POWER	99

EXTRA SKILLS

These are unlocked as you collect the skill keys throughout the game. There are three keys that open the three levels of extra skills. Unlike the skill lines, skills in later blocks can be purchased at any time and you do not need to complete an earlier block first.

SKILL KEYS

SKILL KEY	SKILLS UNLOCKED	LOCATION
EX SKILL KEY I	EX-A, EX-B, EX-C, EX-D	MILTIAN FOREST: BEHIND THE WATERFALL
EX SKILL KEY II	EX-E, EX-F, EX-G, EX-H	THE MERKABAH: FIRST AREA
EX SKILL KEY III	EX-I, EX-J, EX-K, EX-L	ABEL'S ARK: JUST INSIDE

INTRODUCTION

ARCHIVES

CHARACTERS

TACTICAL FILES

EQUIPMENT

THREAT ASSESSMENT

REGIONAL ANALYSIS

SUPPLEMENTAL DATA

EXTRA SKILLS

EX-A	SP COST	EX-B	SP COST	EX-C	SP COST	EX-D	SP COST
MEDICA S	50	ANALYZE	30	STR+2	40	INFERNO I	70
MEDICA S ALL	70	POISON	40	STR+2	40	BLIZZARD I	70
BALANCE DOWN	40	RARE STEAL	40	EATK+2	40	LIGHTNING I	70
QUICK	40	SLOW	40	EATK+2	40	SATELLITE I	70

EX-E	SP COST	EX-F	SP COST	EX-G	SP COST	EX-H	SP COST
MEDICA M	100	DISENGAGE	100	FIST DOWN	150	INFERNO II	150
MEDICA M ALL	150	REFRESH	100	SOUL DOWN	150	BLIZZARD II	150
RECOVER BREAK	100	RECOVER HP	100	SKIN DOWN	150	LIGHTNING II	150
REVERT M	100	RECOVER EP	100	MIND DOWN	150	SATELLITE II	150

EX-I	SP COST	EX-J	SP COST	EX-K	SP COST	EX-L	SP COST
MEDICA L	300	BALANCE	400	HP VAMP	400	INFERNO III	400
MEDICA L ALL	400	BEST ALLY	800	EP VAMP	400	BLIZZARD III	400
RARE HUNTER	300	SHORT COUNTER	400	MISTY	400	LIGHTNING III	400
REVERT L	300	TYPE-G CRITICAL	400	LOCK	400	SATELLITE III	400

ETHERS

NAME	TARGETS	TYPE	EFFECT	EP COST
MEDICA S	SINGLE ALLY	HEAL	RECOVER SMALL AMOUNT OF HP	4
MEDICA S ALL	ALL ALLIES	HEAL	RECOVER SMALL AMOUNT OF HP	12
BALANCE DOWN	ALL ENEMIES	DEBUFF	DECREASE ACCURACY AND EVASION	22
QUICK	ALL ALLIES	BUFF	INCREASE SPEED	18
ANALYZE	SINGLE ENEMY	N/A	ANALYZE AN ENEMY'S DATA	1
POISON	SINGLE ENEMY	POISON	DAMAGE EACH TURN TO A SINGLE ENEMY	4
RARE STEAL	SINGLE ENEMY	N/A	MEDIUM CHANCE OF STEALING AN ITEM	8
SLOW	ALL ENEMIES	DEBUFF	DECREASE SPEED	18
INFERNO I	ALL ENEMIES	FIRE	SMALL ATTACK	12
BLIZZARD I	ALL ENEMIES	ICE	SMALL ATTACK	12
LIGHTNING I	ALL ENEMIES	LIGHTNING	SMALL ATTACK	12
SATELLITE I	ALL ENEMIES	BEAM	SMALL ATTACK	12
MEDICA M	SINGLE ALLY	HEAL	RECOVER MEDIUM AMOUNT OF HP	10
MEDICA M ALL	ALL ALLIES	HEAL	RECOVER MEDIUM AMOUNT OF HP	22
RECOVER BREAK	SINGLE ALLY	HEAL	RECOVER SMALL AMOUNT OF BL WITH EACH TURN	10
REVERT M	SINGLE ALLY	REVIVE	REVIVE AND RECOVER MEDIUM AMOUNT OF HP	20
DISENGAGE	ALL ENEMIES	DEBUFF	REMOVE ALL BUFFS	10
REFRESH	ALL ALLIES	HEAL	RECOVER STATUS EFFECTS	10
RECOVER HP	SINGLE ALLY	HEAL	RECOVER SMALL AMOUNT OF HP WITH EACH TURN	12
RECOVER EP	SINGLE ALLY	HEAL	RECOVER SMALL AMOUNT OF EP WITH EACH TURN	18
FIST DOWN	ALL ENEMIES	DEBUFF	DECREASE PHYSICAL ATTACK POWER	22
SOUL DOWN	ALL ENEMIES	DEBUFF	DECREASE ETHER ATTACK POWER	22
SKIN DOWN	ALL ENEMIES	DEBUFF	DECREASE PHYSICAL DEFENSE	22
MIND DOWN	ALL ENEMIES	DEBUFF	DECREASE ETHER DEFENSE	22
INFERNO II	ALL ENEMIES	FIRE	MEDIUM ATTACK	24
BLIZZARD II	ALL ENEMIES	ICE	MEDIUM ATTACK	24
LIGHTNING II	ALL ENEMIES	LIGHTNING	MEDIUM ATTACK	24
SATELLITE II	ALL ENEMIES	BEAM	MEDIUM ATTACK	24
MEDICA L	SINGLE ALLY	HEAL	RECOVER LARGE AMOUNT OF HP	18
MEDICA L ALL	ALL ALLIES	HEAL	RECOVER LARGE AMOUNT OF HP FOR ALL ALLIES	32
RARE HUNTER	SINGLE ENEMY	N/A	HIGH CHANCE OF STEALING AN ITEM	14
REVERT L	SINGLE ALLY	REVIVE	REVIVE AND RECOVER LARGE AMOUNT OF HP	32
BALANCE	ALL ALLIES	BUFF	INCREASE ACCURACY AND EVASION	22
BEST ALLY	SINGLE ALLY	REVIVE	AUTO REVIVE AFTER DEATH WITH FULL HP	60
HP VAMP	SINGLE ENEMY	DRAIN	SMALL HP DAMAGE + RECOVER SMALL AMOUNT OF HP	10
EP VAMP	SINGLE ENEMY	DRAIN	SMALL EP DAMAGE + RECOVER SMALL AMOUNT OF EP	1
MISTY	SINGLE ENEMY	DEBUFF	SEAL ETHER SPELLS	26
LOCK	SINGLE ENEMY	DEBUFF	SEAL BOOST CAPABILITY	26
INFERNO III	ALL ENEMIES	FIRE	HEAVY ATTACK	36
BLIZZARD III	ALL ENEMIES	ICE	HEAVY ATTACK	36
LIGHTNING III	ALL ENEMIES	LIGHTNING	HEAVY ATTACK	36
SATELLITE III	ALL ENEMIES	BEAM	HEAVY ATTACK	36

E.S. ASHER

PRIMARY: JR.
SUPPORT: CHAOS

WEAKNESSES

The weapons of the Asher aren't as damaging. A number of the weapons have lower EN cost and do less damage to make up for it. This forces the Asher to attack multiple times to do the same amount of damage. With more attacks, comes more times for the enemy to interrupt your attack chain.

EQUIPMENT

While keeping the most up-to-date frame, generator, and cpu is pretty obvious, the disks to load up and weapons to choose aren't always so.

Since the Asher doesn't do as much damage on its own, use weapons with high Team. This gives others extra attacks while giving you the Anima for any damage they deal. Your damage still counts and the more damage party members get to add a couple times a round!

Early on, D-Sensor and D-Guard are fairly useful. D-Sensor really never loses its place as it gives you a lot of information for a very low slot cost. D-Guard is tolerable until your selection increases.

Look for D-Charge and C-Clean. These two disks will keep your E.S. in good shape while any disks that increase your maximum hit points are excellent choices.

If you plan on using the Pile Bunker weapons often, equip D-Kill C and D-Kill R to keep enemies from capitalizing on your short attacks. The Double Gatling Guns are highly recommended whenever possible.

STRENGTHS

With missiles as backup, the Asher has a good blend of fire and physical damage. This allows it to attack with either damage type depending on any elemental weaknesses or strengths of the enemy. This can be pushed further with the use of various Anima attacks that have more attack types.

The Asher is also one of the sturdiest of the E.S. units. Its frames tend to be able to sustain more damage. Many of the Asher's weapons are long range. This keeps it well away from enemy revenges and counters. With some of the highest Team weapons available, the Asher rarely attacks alone.

COMBAT

Against large groups of weaker opponents, Charge any time the Asher reaches half hit points or less and keep firing otherwise. Use your most damaging attack as these enemies will rarely evade you. When only one enemy is left, be sure to give yourself a round of Charges to bring all E.S.'s back to full health.

Battles against tougher opponents require a bit more finesse. Having a D-Sensor equipped tells you what damage types the enemy is strong or weak to.

Use attacks the enemy is weak to later in the attack chain. This gives them the maximum damage bonus before weakness is taken into account.

Avoid using short range attacks against enemies that have high evasion, counter, or revenge. Instead stick with long range weapons. If you have the spare EN, start the chain with Missles. These have high accuracy and hit multiple times. The end result is your real weapons get an accuracy and damage boost from being later in the chain.

Using your Anima can be very powerful. The outright damage is very nice, but there is another way to do as much or more damage. Using weapons with such high Team, the Asher leads ambushes quite frequently. The damage from these can be more than a single Anima attack!

ANIMA AWAKENINGS

ANIMA ATTACKS				
ANIMA LEVEL	NAME	DAMAGE TYPE	TARGETS	EFFECT
1	SHOT BUSTER	BEAM	SINGLE ENEMY	MEDIUM ETHER ATTACK
2	FLARE BUSTER	FIRE	ALL ENEMIES	LARGE ETHER ATTACK
3	CERBERUS	LIGHTNING	SINGLE ENEMY	MASSIVE ATTACK

E.S. DINAH
PILOT INFORMATION

PRIMARY: SHION, KOS-MOS
SUPPORT: MIYUKI, SHION, ALLEN

STRENGTHS

The Dinah is one of your damage dealers. The sword in the primary hand never really becomes obsolete and the other weapons never slack in damage. Having weapons that add Mind Down and Soul Down effects on top of the damage is just icing on the cake.

Having both long and short range weapons, the Dinah can do damage from the safety of long range or increase the damage by getting up close and personal. The Dinah also tends to attack more often then the other units as its speed is considerably higher.

INTRODUCTION

ARCHIVES

CHARACTERS

TACTICAL FILES

EQUIPMENT

THREAT ASSESSMENT

REGIONAL ANALYSIS

SUPPLEMENTAL

WEAKNESSES

One look at the weapon list will tell you the Dinah's largest weakness. The Dinah is restricted to beam weapons. Every single weapon the Dinah will ever have will be a beam weapon. Against enemies that are resistant (or even immune) to beam damage, the Dinah has substantial trouble dealing damage in the attack chain.

EQUIPMENT

With such a powerful close range weapon, it's safe to assume that you'll be using it a lot. As the Dinah often jumps in on Co-ops and Ambushes, the Dinah uses it even more. Equip a weapon in the other hand that gives has a debuff effect to make the enemy's life even worse.

The primary drawback of a short range weapon is the opening for enemies to counter or revenge. Equipping disks that prevent this (such as the D-Kill R or D-Kill C) are worth the cpu space. Filling out the cpu with disks that give revenge and increased revenge make the Dinah very dangerous to attack.

The D-Charge is nearly a must as it enables the Dinah to repair a great deal of damage quickly.

COMBAT

For larger fights of smaller enemies, mindlessly attack with the Dinah. It's likely the Dinah will kill an enemy every single round. If there are no bosses nearby, use your level 2 Anima attack (if you have it) to kill all enemies quickly and gain the finishing strike bonus.

Tougher enemies are a bit different, but not as much as you might think. Use your Lasers at the beginning of the attack chain to give an accuracy bonus to your real attacks. Early in the fight, use any weapons that have a debuff effect. Re-use these as necessary to keep the debuff active.

After that, it comes to hacking and slashing. Use the Dinah's sword as often as possible. The blade does substantial damage and has a modest Team. This gives others the ability to gain extra attacks, but the Dinah's primary purpose is straight damage. Charge whenever the Dinah gets damaged. In late-game fights any damage can be fatal so watch your E.S.

As the Dinah has lower Team weapons, use your special attack any time you use your Anima. The turn afterward (when you still have the EN cost bonus) will still be an attack-fest.

ANIMA AWAKENINGS

ANIMA ATTACKS				
ANIMA LEVEL	NAME	DAMAGE TYPE	TARGETS	EFFECT
1	R-FANG	BEAM	SINGLE ENEMY	MEDIUM ETHER ATTACK
2	X-BUSTER	BEAM	ALL ENEMIES	LARGE ETHER ATTACK
3	X-CANNON	BEAM	SINGLE ENEMY	MASSIVE ETHER ATTACK

INTRODUCTION

ARCHIVES

CHARACTERS

TACTICAL FILES

EQUIPMENT

THREAT ASSESSMENT

REGIONAL ANALYSIS

SUPPLEMENTAL DATA

E.S. REUBEN
PILOT INFORMATION

PRIMARY: JIN
SUPPORT: CANAAN

STRENGTHS

The Reuben is all about damage. Nearly all of its weapons are high EN cost and low number of hits. This makes for hits that are quite damaging. Having the Reuben to capitalize on Co-op and Ambush attacks is frighteningly powerful. Anything that gives the Reuben more attacks is worth the time and money.

With a choice of either fire or physical weapons, the Reuben has some flexibility in which damage type it can equip for a fight. Enemies that are strong to one are unlikely to be strong to both.

The Reuben's more powerful weapons almost invariably have low accuracy. This leads to tougher enemies evading and countering often.

WEAKNESSES

All of the Reuben's weapons are short range. This leaves it at the mercy of any enemy it can't kill in a single attack. Even as one of your sturdier E.S. units, getting hit with counters and revenges can really add up.

EQUIPMENT

Since the Reuben is going to be the target of many counters and revenges, there are two ways to fix this. Use disks that boost the maximum hit points of the Reuben is one option. The other is to use disks that prevent the enemy from countering and revenging. D-Kill R, D-Kill C, and D-Nullify Evade are priceless for the Reuben.

The Reuben's attacks tend to cost a lot of EN and are very damaging. Disks that boost your EN can give the Reuben another attack, but don't use them if this isn't the case. Instead, look for ways to give the Reuben more attacks. D-Revenge(+) and D-Counter(+) can be very effective when combined with a sword that is many stories tall.

COMBAT

Fights against weaker enemies are pretty mindless with the Reuben. Simply cleave the enemy into smaller pieces each round. The Reuben will likely kill an enemy every large attack. Use missles to finish off your EN for the small chance that an ally can jump in and finish off your second enemy.

Against tougher foes, the attack chain is a bit different. The enemy often has a higher evade and will make the Reuben's life difficult if you're not careful. Start the attack chain with as many missles as you can fire without limiting the number of sword attacks you get. The missles have high accuracy and will build an accuracy bonus for the low accuracy of your sword.

The Reuben can take damage very quickly if the enemy starts using counter or revenge, so watch its hit points closely. Don't worry about losing a round of damage so you can Charge. It's worth it to avoid losing the damage for the rest of the fight if the Reuben goes down.

If you have the EN to spare (without lowering the number of big attacks you can make), consider putting one of your missle attacks at the end of the chain. Missles have a higher Team rating and can give others an extra attack.

Using your special attack after awakening your Anima is highly recommended. The special attacks do more damage than the Reuben can ordinarily do and the Reuben doesn't have the Team to count on Ambush attacks.

ANIMA AWAKENINGS

ANIMA ATTACKS				
ANIMA LEVEL	NAME	DAMAGE TYPE	TARGETS	EFFECT
1	IRON BLADE	PHYSICAL	SINGLE ENEMY	MEDIUM ATTACK
2	GARUDA'S WRATH	LIGHTNING	ALL ENEMIES	LARGE ATTACK
3	LOTUS BLADES	BEAM	SINGLE ENEMY	MASSIVE ATTACK

E.S. ZEBULUN
PILOT INFORMATION

PRIMARY: MOMO
SUPPORT: ZIGGY

STRENGTHS

The Zebulun is your only E.S. with lightning attacks. At first that may not sound like much, but the Zebulun isn't restricted to lightning attacks. This means it can attack with your other E.S. units until you come across an enemy that is only weak to lightning. While the other units can only do normal damage, the Zebulun is busy punching holes in the enemy.

A number of the Zebulun's weapons have debuff effects added to them. Again, this may not seem like much until you look and realize how rare Balance Down is! Combine this with the high Team of a number of the weapons and the Zebulun helps the other units quite a bit.

WEAKNESSES

Like anything surrounding MOMO, the Zebulun suffers from low hit points. If any of the E.S. units are going to get killed in a single shot, it's likely to be the Zebulun. It starts with substandard hit points and never catches up.

The other downside is the lack of actual damage the Zebulun deals. It relies on others to do damage. If your primary damage dealers fall, the Zebulun is generally unable to finish a tougher opponent.

EQUIPMENT

With the Zebulun's inferior hit points, avoid short range weapons. It can't survive too many counters and revenges, so eliminate the issue entirely and look for long range weapons. Don't get rid of the shield weapon as you don't want to be cornered into beam damage only. Grab a beam weapon in your left hand to compliment the lightning weapon in your right hand.

The Zebulun's damage isn't as much an issue as other E.S. units. No matter which weapon you choose, the Zebulun isn't going to be the most damaging E.S. Instead, choose weapons that compliment your other party members. Weapons that cause Soul Down work well when paired with the Dinah's beam damage while Balance Down works well to help the Reuben and Dinah land their more powerful attacks more often.

The EN cost of a number of the Zebulun's attacks is fairly low. Grab disks that increase your maximum EN early on. These become obsolete later, but make a difference until then. Disks that protect against revenge and counter will keep the enemy from disciplining the Zebulun during Co-op and Ambush attacks (The Zebulun will always use the shield weapon if you have it equipped).

COMBAT

The Zebulun is a bit different than the other E.S. units. Even against large groups of weaker foes, it will have trouble killing enemies outright. This leads to the strategies for all encounters being roughly the same.

Start the fight by putting a debuff on the enemy, but always end your attack chain with a high Team weapon. You goal is to take as many high Team attacks as possible once you get the debuff on. Restore the debuff as needed throughout the fight, but concentrate on getting Co-op attacks.

The Zebulun doesn't do much damage and has a harder time filling its Anima gauge. As damage caused during a Co-op or Ambush counts toward the originators gauge, having others to do the damage nets the Zebulun a decent rise in Anima.

With the lighter frame of the Zebulun, keeping it undamaged is very important. Charge after any round where the Zebulun took damage and don't be afraid to use items if the Charge won't fully repair the Zebulun.

Unless the enemy is weak to the damage type of your Anima attack, don't use it. If they are weak, your Anima will do tremendous damage, but if they aren't, you're better off getting an Ambush attack (which the Zebulun can do very regularly).

ANIMA AWAKENINGS

ANIMA ATTACKS				
ANIMA LEVEL	NAME	DAMAGE TYPE	TARGETS	EFFECT
1	AIRD STAR	BEAM	SINGLE ENEMY	MEDIUM ETHER ATTACK
2	AIRD RAIN	BEAM	ALL ENEMIES	LARGE ETHER ATTACK
3	METEOR BURST	FIRE	ALL ENEMIES	MASSIVE ETHER ATTACK

INTRODUCTION
ARCHIVES
CHARACTERS
TACTICAL FILES
EQUIPMENT
THREAT ASSESSMENT
REGIONAL ANALYSIS
SUPPLEMENTAL DATA

TACTICAL FILES

Xenosaga III is the type of game that people will say is both easy and difficult. Preparation and understanding the game's battle mechanics make such a huge difference in the performance of your party that it's really a night-and-day issue. This chapter tries to explain as many of the issues as possible, and bring both beginners and more advanced players onto a field with some common ground.

UNDERSTANDING STATISTICS & COMMON GAMEPLAY ELEMENTS

Xenosaga III has a developed system for combat and general gameplay. There are hidden items to collect (some of them from peripheral missions that span wide distances), and knowing what to do and where to look is essential. This section of the guide attempts to simplify many of the game's concepts.

CHARACTER PARAMETERS (ATTRIBUTES)

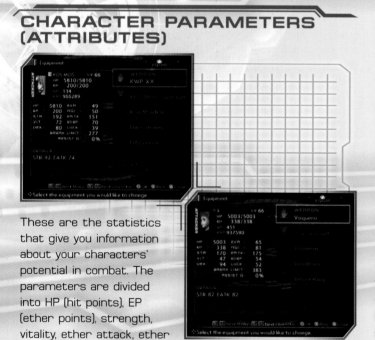

These are the statistics that give you information about your characters' potential in combat. The parameters are divided into HP (hit points), EP (ether points), strength, vitality, ether attack, ether defense, dexterity, evasion, agility, luck, and break limit.

Hit points measure the amount of damage a character can sustain before collapsing. Once your character reaches zero hit points, they are knocked out and won't be able to contribute in the battle until they are brought back to consciousness (with various abilities or items). If all three of your active characters are knocked out at the same time, the game ends. For increased odds of survival, work to raise hit points, vitality, and ether defense.

Ether points control how many ether abilities and tech attacks your characters can use before becoming exhausted. Once their EP total drops near zero, no more abilities can be used without relying on an Ether Pack or stopping at a Save Point to rest. Having a higher total allows a character to use more abilities in random encounters without the fear of being left overdrawn before reaching another Save Point.

Strength is the measure of a person's physical attack prowess. With a higher value, your characters can deal far more damage by using their normal attacks and any abilities that deal physical damage. While characters like Jin, KOS-MOS, and Jr. gain a great deal from strength, ether-based characters only improve marginally from gaining bonuses to strength.

Vitality defends characters against physical attacks; thus, they take less damage from physical attacks by having a higher vitality. This makes your hit points last longer, and saves people from dropping as easily in both burst-damage situations and from long-term attacks.

Ether attack is the measure of a character's damage potential with ether abilities. This also improves the recovery effects of various ether abilities, meaning that characters with a high ether attack make good healers as well as attackers. MOMO, Shion, and chaos are some of the better ether attack characters.

Ether defense protects a character against ether damage. Much like vitality, this extends the potential of your hit points.

Dexterity is your measure of accuracy for all types of attacks. Any physical attack has the potential to miss, dealing no damage at all when this happens. Characters with a high dexterity minimize this chance.

On the flipside, evasion allows your characters to avoid attacks.

Agility is not as powerful as it once was, earlier in the series. Though characters won't receive extra attacks from being extremely fast, they still are able to consistently act earlier in the round by having a higher agility. This parameter determines the order of combat within each round. Having a higher agility is wonderful in random encounters, where getting those early hits makes all the difference in the amount of damage taken.

Luck normally affects the chance of scoring a critical hit, but it also influences evasion for your characters. Some skills, such as Rare Steal, also benefit from having higher luck. This parameter is increased heavily by certain equipment choices; the damage increase from maintaining a high luck is well beyond similar increases in strength and dexterity!

Each person has a break limit, and that sum heavily influences the armor and accessory options you choose for your characters. Unlike hit points, this quantity starts each fight at zero and rises until hitting its maximum value. At that time, the character in question loses two rounds of combat and sustains far more critical hits from enemies. Thus, you want characters to have as high a break limit as possible without sacrificing their potential to deal damage to enemies. Note that recovery abilities exist to reduce characters' current break damage, but these abilities restore no hit points (so it's a tradeoff in what you want to accomplish).

USING SAVE POINTS

There are golden plates throughout the game world. These are Save Points, used to record your progress through the game. In *Xenosaga III*, these also have a function to restore all hit points and ether points to your characters, even if they are in your reserve party.

When clearing an area, always be mindful of Save Points and their potential to restore characters. This is especially useful when using many ether abilities to clear enemies quickly!

Also, remember that Save Points are always placed near boss fights. If you have been exploring a dungeon area for some time and suddenly come across a Save Point, use it immediately! Don't go forward another few steps just to look around. You might walk into a boss fight and be stuck trying to survive with half your resources expended.

SEARCHING FOR ITEMS

There are several ways to get items in **Xenosaga III**: breaking containers, completing battles, the stores, and running various missions.

Containers often offer some of the lighter loot that you will find (recovery items and such), but there are a number of hidden gems in the rough as well. Break containers that you pass using ● to see if anything is inside of them. Beyond that, running along the edges of each location to see if there are hidden objects in the terrain that your group can destroy. It is rarely useful to walk down the center of a corridor in the Xenosaga world!

THE SPOILS OF WAR

Defeating enemies is a necessary act, but there are some fun rewards that come with victory as well. Each foe that is struck down in battle is worth experience, skill points, and money. These sums are increased by defeating targets with a finishing strike (special attacks are used to do this in both character mode and E.S. mode).

Characters in the reserve party, whether in E.S. battles or normal encounters, receive only 80% of the experience and skill points that are given to the main combatants. This is only calculated at the very end of battle, so whoever is swapped in at the end of the fight is counted (even if they only came in for the final round).

Another interesting issue in battles is that you can flee (from non-boss fights), and retreat for a moment. This restores the enemy group to its full count, but you still receive the rewards for beating the enemies that went down before you fled. This method can be used for fast skill-point accrual in areas that have especially lucrative groups of enemies. To gain the most from this, reduce a fun enemy group to one member; flee, and stand still to wait for combat immunity to wear off. This puts you directly back into the engagement; repeat for free levels and skill points.

USING SKILL POINTS

Fairly early in the game, the Skill Line option becomes available for your characters. This section of the menu is then used to purchase skills, using the skill points that you gain in battle. Some of these skills offer passive improvements to your characters (more hit points, better strength, and such). Others offer new techniques and ether abilities.

To unlock higher-tier skills, purchase all four of the items in a given block. This opens the next level of skills above that group. Each character can advance along two paths, and it is up to you whether to try and specialize in one before taking anything from the other. For the best overall parameters at a given level, it's wise to take both lines to some extent. However, some people focus quite heavily on a single line until they can get a specific ability or technique that defines their character in combat.

At the end of the two primary skill lines are master skills; these are gained without cost after your characters complete the purchase of every skill in that line. The resulting powers are ether abilities that cost 99 ether points and provide medium-duration buffs that are extremely potent.

Once your group finds EX Skill Keys, two optional lines begin to appear. These can be taken without any prerequisites, and they serve to fill out each character's list of parameter choices and abilities.

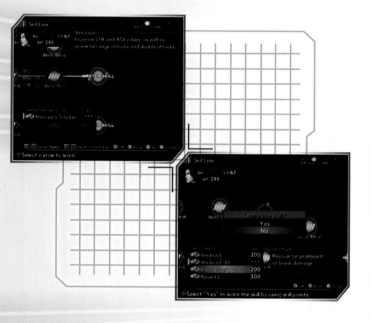

SETTING UP FIGHTS

Encounters with enemies are often foreseeable in this game. Unlike some RPGs, the monsters are walking around the maps of each dungeon. Thus, your party is able to avoid them at times, or set up the encounters to begin in a way that benefits your party.

Try to start fights by attacking enemies from behind. This grants a free combat round to your characters, allowing them to eliminate an enemy or two before any attacks can be made. All of this is quite nice, but beware enemies that are fast-moving. Your group can be attacked from behind as well, leading to just as troubling a dilemma for your characters. Face incoming opponents and stand still to avoid being flanked by tricky enemy groups.

For an even nastier start, place a trap in the corridor (by pressing [R2] and ● at the same time). Detonate these when monsters are close by using the ● by itself; this stuns the foes and gives you the ideal chance to engage them.

TRAP BONUSES	
EFFECT	DESCRIPTION
NO DANGER	ENEMIES INFLUENCED BY A TRAP CANNOT GET A BACK ATTACK AGAINST YOUR GROUP
INITIATIVE	YOUR GROUP GETS A FREE ROUND OF ACTIONS BEFORE THE ENEMIES CAN RESPOND
BOOST BONUS	YOUR BOOST GAUGE GETS A RANDOM BUMP WHEN STARTING THESE FIGHTS

ELEMENTAL PROPERTIES

There are five types of damage in **Xenosaga III**: Physical, Fire, Ice, Lightning, and Beam. These are represented by icons in the following table.

ELEMENTAL TYPES	
◆	PHYSICAL
🔥	FIRE
❄	ICE
⚡	LIGHTNING
✦	BEAM

Physical damage is delivered by normal attacks and techniques. These are best against most biological targets and Gnosis, and are usually less effective against mechanical foes.

INTRODUCTION

ARCHIVES

CHARACTERS

TACTICAL FILES

EQUIPMENT

ENEMY ASSESSMENT

REGIONAL ANALYSIS

SUPPLEMENTAL DATA

Fire, Ice, Lightning, and Beam damage are delivered by ether attacks and certain E.S. weapons. These damage types aren't as useful for blowing through enemies if they don't have any weaknesses. Instead, they are best used when enemies have a weakness versus their type (and many enemies do have weaknesses).

For many fights, it's easy to take out soft targets with generic Physical damage then switch to another element for hitting anything that is especially tough (e.g. a larger Gnosis or a mechanical enemy).

ELEMENTAL ATTRIBUTES		
DEFENSE		RESULT OF INCOMING DAMAGE
O	WEAK	50% DAMAGE BONUS
▲	STRONG	HALF DAMAGE TAKEN
–	ABSORB	RECOVERS HP EQUAL TO DAMAGE RECEIVED
X	NULLIFY	TAKES NO DAMAGE

Elemental attributes tell you which type of damage to use against a target. These are uncovered by using Analyze/ Analyze Balls, equipping a necklace with the Display Data property, or loading a D-Sensor onto an E.S. Once you are armed with the knowledge of an enemy's attributes in regard to each element, hit them where they are weak and avoid using anything that they are strong against.

ANALYSIS

The Analyze skill and Analyze Balls are used to get a full report on any enemy you meet. These are inexpensive, in terms of ether or financial cost, so it's worth using them if you like to find out a great deal about your opponents.

The chapter on Threat Assessment in this guide is used as a way of presenting such data in a single location. If you wish to look up monster statistics without wasting any of your character turns inside of combat, use that instead.

ENEMY TYPES

There are three classifications of enemies: biological, Gnosis, and mechanical. Certain techniques are especially good against a given type of enemy, so if something says that it is more effective against Type M enemies that means it is better against mechanical targets.

Biological targets are usually the easiest to Break. Ziggy, chaos, and Jr. are good at disrupting large groups of biological foes. In addition to this, biological targets are usually lower on hit points, so they are some of the fastest things to farm for quick skill point increases.

Mechanical targets are the worst to take down with brute force; they are made to withstand physical damage well, and they Break Limits are high. Use more ether abilities on such foes to push them out of the way. MOMO, chaos, and Shion are extremely good at exploiting elemental weaknesses of machines.

Gnosis are usually heavy with special attacks and abilities. Very few Gnosis are light targets, meaning that they take some investment to bring down. Break attacks and exploiting weaknesses all work well, but no single answer is clear until you grow used to the specific encounters in an area.

MINI-GAMES AND PERIPHERAL MISSIONS

Hakox is the primary mini-game for **Xenosaga III**, and it's a big one. Hidden within Hakox is a very important Segment Address (one of the fifteen you need), a Swimsuit for Ziggy, Jr's final weapon, and other goodies. Thus, if you want to see and collect everything, it's important to get good at Hakox.

Your party first finds a Hakox station on Fifth Jerusalem. After that, more stages are unlocked as your progress through the game and play this onboard the Elsa. Look on the left side of the Elsa's lounge. Not only is there a Hakox station there, but a nearby droid alerts the group each time a new world or new character are unlocked!

Peripheral missions are found most heavily on Fifth Jerusalem and Miltia. Some of these have no reward or only have modest rewards; others are extremely generous in what they provide.

Some of the largest missions in the game include getting all Segment Address information, restoring the entire database, and assembling the Federal Reports. Each of these missions is explained in the walkthrough and the Supplemental Data chapters. For the best equipment in **Xenosaga III**, pay careful attention to these!

INTRODUCTION

ARCHIVES

CHARACTERS

TACTICAL FILES

EQUIPMENT

ASSESSMENT

REGIONAL ANALYSIS

SUPPLEMENTAL DATA

BASICS OF GROUND COMBAT

Ground combat is engaged when your normal party encounters an enemy group or boss fight. This pits three of your characters against one or more foes. Read more about this to learn how to switch characters in battle (and why to do so), and how to overcome the many perils of fighting.

TECHNIQUES

Techniques offer enhanced physical attacks that deal more damage, hit more targets, have debuff properties against your enemies, and so forth. Some of these are learned by leveling up, and others are gained after being purchased in the skill lines.

Because they are physically based, the characters who are more physical in their capabilities gain even more by using techniques.

CHARACTER TECHNIQUE USAGE

CHARACTER	PRIMARY FOCUS	SECONDARY FOCUS
CHAOS	AREA-OF-EFFECT BREAKS	MODEST DAMAGE
JIN	SINGLE-TARGET DAMAGE	AREA-OF-EFFECT DAMAGE
JR.	AREA-OF-EFFECT DAMAGE	N/A
KOS-MOS	SINGLE-TARGET DAMAGE	SINGLE-TARGET BREAKS
MOMO	SINGLE-TARGET BREAKS	SINGLE-TARGET DAMAGE
SHION	SINGLE-TARGET DAMAGE	SINGLE-TARGET BREAKS
ZIGGY	AREA-OF-EFFECT BREAKS	SINGLE-TARGET BREAKS

Like ether abilities, techniques cost ether points, so they cannot be used ceaselessly unless you are near a Save Point. When dealing with wandering encounters, keep an area-of-effect technique person in the active party at all times; these characters are used to soften and destroy blocks of enemies for faster and safer fighting!

One important aspect of techniques is that they have a much higher percentage of Break abilities (there are almost no ether abilities with Break in the game). Thus, heavy Break strategies are often centered around technique usage.

ETHER ABILITIES

Ether abilities are used for several functions: recovery, status changes, and damage. Recovery ethers may be the most important of all, since just about every boss fight in the game is close to undoable without them. However, the potential for area-of-effect damage and both buffs and debuffs from ether abilities is also immense.

Recovery ethers are used to restore hit points and remove status ailments, including the art of returning knocked out characters to active combat status. Characters with a higher ether attack are best for healer, and these are also the people who learn healing/recovery spells the earliest. MOMO and Shion are both well known for their solid healing, and either is wonderful to put into the party during boss fights. During random encounters, however, recovery spells are often entirely unneeded; you can always restore the party's hit points between battles for those smaller skirmishes.

Status enhancements and ailments are usually subtle, because they are for the long-term rather than for fights that will last one or two rounds.

Thus, boss fights are the main time to see both categories come to the forefront. Use status enhancements to raise damage or survivability for your group; enact these at an early part of the battle if they are long lasting, or wait until the halfway point if the effects are only several-round affairs.

With status ailments, focus on lowering enemy resistance to damage. Anything that lowers an enemy's defenses is going to pay for itself heavily during the combat-intensive boss fights, and this is doubly useful if the opponent already has a weakness. For instance, an enemy with a fire weakness should be hit with Mind Down so ether attacks are more effective.

In terms of pure damage, ether attacks fall a bit behind a number of the physical attacks. However, enemies are more likely to be weak versus at least one of the ether damage types! Combined with the area-of-effect nature of ether abilities, these attacks are able to soften wandering encounter groups very quickly. In boss fights, a character with an extremely high ether attack can harp on an opponent's one weakness strike after strike. Toward the end of **Xenosaga III**, you start to see more foes with physical strengths, and that makes ether abilities essential.

SPECIAL ATTACKS AND BOOSTING

Outside of your E.S.s, characters are able to accrue Boost. This fills a gauge in the upper-right side of the screen, and you can use points from there to gain free attacks or unleash powerful special attacks. Both of these functions are essential for doing the most damage and surviving more difficult encounters.

Initially, groups are able to accrue up to three points of Boost. With certain items equipped, it is possible to reach much higher totals, but most of the items that raise Boost Limits for the party are not found until later in **Xenosaga III**.

Accruing Boost is done by dealing damage to enemies. The more damage you deal from an attack, the greater the amount of Boost given; this means that characters with area-of-effect attacks are able to give the group a massive infusion of Boost. Jin's techniques and MOMO's ether abilities are stellar for filling the Boost Gauge.

For a single Boost point, the party can gain a free attack for anyone in active combat. Boosting is shown at-length in the tutorials, but it still takes time to master its tactical purpose. If your group is in danger of a wipeout, for whatever reason, Boost one of your healers to give them a chance to get an area-of-effect recovery ability off before the enemy gets another round. On offense, use Boosts during an enemy's Break period to get additional attacks with increased critical rates.

When you do decide to use Boost, give your best person the free attack. If you need healing, let Shion or MOMO go again. If you want to do the most damage, let your person with the best attack for the battle have another shot (let Ziggy Break again, or Jin deal direct damage, or have MOMO use a second ether ability). Why waste a free attack by giving it to someone who can only do 75% of what your best character for the fight can accomplish?

Special attacks cost more than Boosting. There are three levels of special attacks, with each costing more and having a greater effect on a battle. See the table below for an idea of what most special attacks enable (although there are exceptions).

SPECIAL ATTACKS		
RANK	AREA OF EFFECT	BOOST COST
1	SINGLE TARGET	2
2	ALL ENEMIES	2
3	SINGLE TARGET	3-4

Use these not only to do a great deal of damage in a single strike, but rely on them for finishing your enemies. This grants a 50% bonus to experience, skill points, and gold. In boss battles, that adds up to an immense gain in rewards for the encounter with only a slight investment in time and caution.

USING ITEMS IN BATTLE

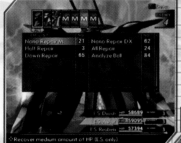

Although items must be replenished, unlike ether points (which are free at Save Points), there are major advantages to using items. First, these are useful in boss fights because they waste none of your ether points at a time when running out could be dangerous. Beyond that, some items accomplish things that few of your abilities can replicate. For example, the Seven Moons item is able to bring back a character with full health and ether points; even your best recovery ethers won't offer that!

Keep a clear eye on what items accomplish, and don't be afraid to use the more effective options during boss fights, even if that means using things that cost money to replenish. Money is easy to get in **Xenosaga III**, and anything that avoids a frustrating battle or the threat of a defeat is worthwhile.

GUARDING

Guarding reduces the damage a character takes by 50% until their next turn. Under normal circumstances, you won't have your characters do this very often. However, when a boss threatens to unleash a devastating attack, consider guarding until the danger has passed. This can be combined with the Shock Absorber accessory to further decrease the damage that is reduced by guarding.

WHEN TO RUN

Running isn't often needed, and some players might go through the entire game without giving this a try. Earlier in the chapter, a technique that allows a character to reset fights and quickly gain skill points and experience was listed; this is the most useful aspect of running in the game. Kill off all but one enemy in a group, run, and restart the fight; this is much faster than running between areas looking for lucrative battles, even in the EVS.

THE ART OF CHANGING CHARACTERS

Unlike in E.S. battles, the ability to change characters is always at hand when you are using your normal characters. This is a powerful feature that comes in handy all the time, especially for boss fights. Use ether attacks heavily with your main party and keep them in the battle as long as possible, but don't be shy about pulling in other characters when things get rough.

Not only does this act like a free heal (because you are bringing in a character that is likely to be full on hit points and ether points), but this also gives you a person with an empty Break Gauge! No single item or ability in the game can so quickly erase all the trouble that a boss has inflicted, so the loss of a single round to switch in the other character is actually trivial.

With high hit points and Break abilities, Ziggy is a wonderful closer for boss fights. His lower damage slows things early in the encounter, when the foes are easy to control anyway, and his ability to survive in the later stages of the fight is rivaled by few.

This brings up the idea of a party that intentionally starts off with its lighter characters, then moves into the heavier tanks toward the late stages of a fight. Imagine beginning a boss battle with Jin, MOMO, and Jr. They get to deal their damage quickly and have a good time doing so. When the crew starts to get bruised, KOS-MOS, Ziggy, and Shion enter the fray. Now, you have a solid healer with two damage dealers that don't drop easily. What a way to close the door on your opponent!

TARGET CONTROL

Each enemy has an A.I. routine dedicated to determining the target that they "want" to attack. For most enemies, this is revealed by Analyzing them. View the following table to see what the results indicate and what to do about the situations that develop.

ENEMY TARGETING PATTERNS		
TYPE	RESULT	COUNTER
RANDOM	CAN ATTACK ANYONE	HAVE YOUR TOUGHEST CHARACTER USE HEAT OR RELAX AND HEAL
BREAK KILLER	ATTACKS EASIEST CHARACTER TO BREAK	SWITCH OUT CHARACTERS WITH LOW BREAK LIMITS FROM THE GROUP AFTER THEY GET HIT
HEALER KILLER	CHARACTERS WITH MORE RECOVERY ABILITIES ARE HIT	HEALER HEAL THYSELF
HP KILLER	GOES AFTER LOW HP CHARACTERS	SWITCH IN HIGHER HP CHARACTERS WHEN INITIAL ONES GET LOW

Heat is an ether ability that is often associated with target control. This is because Heat forces most enemies to attack the person who used it. This reduces the number of area-of-effect attacks delivered against the group, and it certainly causes other characters in the party to take less damage.

You won't often need Heat to win battles; it forces both your group and the enemies to fight a slower engagement. For safety and survival, combine a good Heat character with a sound healer for a victory that is almost assured (e.g. Ziggy + Shion), but don't count on it being fast. To keep being effective with Heat, you must use it often.

THE BREAKING GAME

Both sides are trying to Break each other, even in wandering encounters. Break Status does so many things in this game that it is a valuable tool for almost any type of player.

EFFECTS OF BREAK STATUS

- TARGET IS UNABLE TO ACT FOR TWO TURNS

- NO BOOSTS CAN BE USED ON THE TARGET DURING THIS TIME

- EVADE/GUARD IS IMPOSSIBLE

- COUNTERATTACKS/REVENGE ALSO UNUSABLE

- CRITICAL HITS LANDS FAR MORE OFTEN AGAINST THE TARGET

- AT THE END OF THE BEAK PERIOD, THE TARGET'S BREAK GAUGE RETURNS TO ZERO

As you can see, this is a dangerous state. To reduce the dangers of this for your group, equip gear with higher Break Limits and use Break Heals to reduce characters' Break Gauge when they are under heavy attack. Because Break Heals don't restore any hit points, these should be maintained during rounds when the group isn't in dire straits; in other words, hit points are still the first priority for healing.

To return this favor, use Break techniques and Erde Kaiser ether abilities to put your enemies on the ropes. Once broken, almost all foes are easily dispatched. It usually takes a few Break cycles to pull down a major boss, but they too suffer once properly broken.

Because Break only lasts for two rounds, then fully resets the target's Gauge, don't waste time on Break abilities when a foe is already in that state. Instead, use your best attacks for dealing direct damage!

The best time to attempt a Break is when a boss is preparing for a special attack. It is often quite disruptive to Break them during these rounds, and your group might be able to prevent the foe from using their major attack even after getting out of their Break period. Thus, it's good to bring bosses up to a point near their Break limit and wait; hold off on further Break attacks until your enemy either has some advantage over you or is about to unleash something scary.

STATUS ENHANCEMENTS AND AILMENTS

Not all the names for the status enhancements and ailments in **Xenosaga III** are clearly linked with what they do. Read these tables to understand what the various abilities are used to enact. Note that it's always good to have a character or two with Refresh; this makes it so that there is always someone to cast Refresh and remove negative effects from your party. If you are still concerned about these, use defensive bracelets to negate many enemy ailments (e.g. equip the Grand Design on your first character with Refresh).

STATUS ENHANCEMENTS	
NAME	**EFFECT**
SAFETY	CAST AHEAD OF TIME TO RESTORE 50% OF A PERSON'S HPS IF THEY ARE KNOCKED OUT
BEST ALLY	CAST AHEAD OF TIME TO RESTORE ALL OF A PERSON'S HPS IF THEY ARE KNOCKED OUT
RECOVER HP	RECOVERS SOME HPS EVERY TURN
RECOVER EP	RECOVERS SOME EPS EVERY TURN
RECOVER BREAK	LOWERS BREAK GAUGE EVERY TURN
QUICK	RAISES AGILITY
OFFENSIVE	RAISES STRENGTH AND ETHER ATTACK
DEFENSIVE	RAISES VITALITY AND ETHER DEFENSE
BALANCE UP	RAISES ACCURACY AND EVASION
BOOST UP	IMPROVES RATE OF BOOST ACCRUAL
BREAK UP	RAISES BREAK DAMAGE
ABSOLUTE CRITICAL	ALL HITS ACT AS CRITICAL HITS
NULL PHYSICAL	IMMUNITY TO PHYSICAL DAMAGE
NULL BREAK	REDUCES BREAK DAMAGE TO ZERO
ABSOLUTE EVASION	ALL ATTACKS ARE EVADED
ABSOLUTE GUARD	ALL ATTACKS ARE GUARDED AGAINST
ABSOLUTE REVENGE	REVENGE TRIGGERS AFTER ANY ATTACK
ABSOLUTE COUNTER	COUNTER TRIGGERS AFTER ANY ATTACK
OMEGA FIST	IMPROVES STRENGTH AFTER A SUCCESSFUL GUARD; LASTS UNTIL END OF FIGHT
OMEGA SOUL	IMPROVES ETHER ATTACK AFTER A SUCCESSFUL GUARD; LASTS UNTIL END OF FIGHT
OMEGA SKIN	IMPROVES VITALITY AFTER A SUCCESSFUL GUARD; LASTS UNTIL END OF FIGHT
OMEGA MIND	IMPROVES ETHER DEFENSE AFTER A SUCCESSFUL GUARD; LASTS UNTIL END OF FIGHT

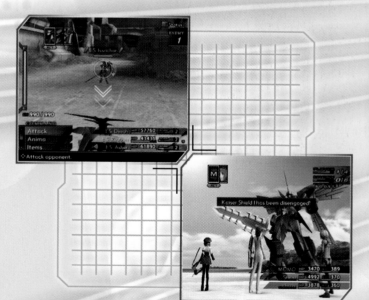

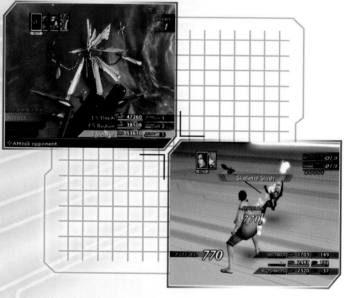

STATUS AILMENTS

NAME	EFFECT
BREAK	LOSE ALL ATTACK AND DEFENSE FOR TWO TURNS
HEAT	FORCES ENEMY TO ATTACK ONE PERSON, USUALLY WITH A WEAKER ATTACK TYPE
POISON	SUBTRACTS 20% OF A TARGET'S HPS PER TURN; WILL NOT KILL THE TARGET
FIST DOWN	LOWERS PHYSICAL ATTACK POWER
SOUL DOWN	LOWERS ETHER ATTACK POWER
SKIN DOWN	LOWERS PHYSICAL DEFENSE
MIND DOWN	LOWERS ETHER DEFENSE
BALANCE DOWN	LOWERS ACCURACY AND EVASION
SLOW	CAUSES TARGET TO GO LATER IN EACH ROUND
SEAL TECH	PREVENTS TECHNIQUES FROM BEING USED
SEAL ETHER	PREVENTS ETHER ABILITIES FROM BEING USED
SEAL BOOST	PREVENTS BOOST FROM BEING USED
CRYSTALLIZE	GIVES CHARACTER THREE TURNS UNTIL THEY ARE REMOVED FROM BATTLE PERMANENTLY (USE ANTI-CRYSTAL IN BATTLE OR 20 G VACCINES FOR PERMANENT IMMUNITY)
HILBERT	REDUCES THE PARAMETERS OF MACHINES AND GNOSIS
F MINE	GIVES E.S. FOUR TURNS UNTIL 80% OF TOTAL HP IS RECEIVED AS DAMAGE (USE ANIMA AWAKENING, DOWN REPAIR, OR CHARGE + D-CLEAN TO REMOVE)
CURSE	ALL DAMAGE DEALT IS ALSO DELIVERED TO THE TARGET; CANNOT KILL THE AFFECTED TARGET

E.S. BATTLES MADE EASY

E.S. battles have a flow that is only somewhat similar to ground fights. These skirmishes can have more enemies, and they often have a more epic feel as well. With a bit of practice, E.S. combat becomes an awesome way to farm extra experience and skill points. Beyond that, some of **Xenosaga III**'s best encounters are found here, so you should know how it's all done.

E.S. PARAMETERS

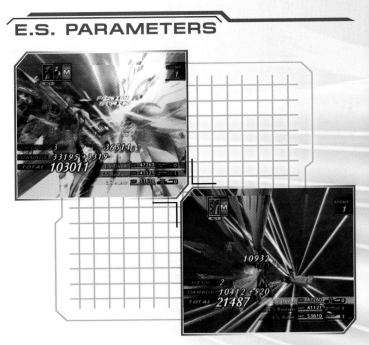

Most of the E.S. parameters are analogous to their character counterparts, but they can be calculated a bit strangely. Beyond that, there are a few new tricks to them, so all are listed here.

E.S. ATTRIBUTES

NAME	PURPOSE
HIT POINTS	FUNCTION JUST LIKE NORMAL CHARACTER HIT POINTS, THOUGH FALLING TO ZERO TAKES THE E.S. OUT OF THE COMBAT FULLY (THEY CANNOT BE REVIVED)
ENERGY	FILLS TO FULL AT THE BEGINNING OF EACH TURN; THESE ARE USED TO UNLEASH A CRAFT'S NORMAL WEAPONS
POWER	THE COMBINATION OF THE PILOT AND CO-PILOT'S STR VALUES; DETERMINES THE PHYSICAL DAMAGE THE CRAFT CAN DEAL IN COMBAT
ARMOR	SUM OF THE PILOT AND CO-PILOT'S VIT VALUES; DECREASES PHYSICAL DAMAGE TAKEN BY THE CRAFT
ETHER ATTACK	THE SUM OF THE PILOT AND CO-PILOT'S EATK VALUES; DETERMINES THE ETHER DAMAGE DONE BY THE CRAFT
ETHER DEFENSE	SUM OF THE PILOT AND CO-PILOT'S EDEF; REDUCES ETHER DAMAGE RECEIVED
DEXTERITY	IS CALCULATED ONLY BY THE MAIN PILOT'S DEX VALUE; INCREASES THE CHANCE OF STRIKING ENEMIES
EVASION	ALSO CALCULATED OFF OF THE MAIN PILOT, BASED FROM THEIR EVA VALUE; IMPROVES THE CHANCE FOR THE CRAFT TO EVADE INCOMING ATTACKS
AGILITY	TAKEN FROM THE PILOT'S AGI; ALLOWS THE CRAFT TO ACT SOONER THAN OTHERS
LUCK	RAISES THE CHANCE TO LAND A CRITICAL HIT OR TO EVADE ATTACKS

INTRODUCTION

ARCHIVES

CHARACTERS

TACTICAL FILES

EQUIPMENT

ENEMY ASSESSMENT

REGIONAL ANALYSIS

SUPPLEMENTAL DATA

ENERGY EXPLAINED

With energy filling every turn, your goal is usually to spend as much of it as possible. This means that you want a weapon grouping that delivers the greatest damage without leaving a spare 80-100 energy around.

First off, see if the enemies you are fighting are weak versus anything on each craft. E.S. attacks are already so devastating that one attack from a weapon that an enemy is weak versus spells victory.

Always keep a D-Sensor on one of your E.S.s so that it is clear what elements are most useful in a given encounter.

Next, see how many of your most-effective weapon attacks can be made in each round. Is it then possible to get a secondary attack? If not, see if sacrificing one primary attack can get you two secondary attacks. Sometimes this is worthwhile. Other times it is worthless! That is E.S. combat for you.

The way to tell is to think about what is needed the most. If raw damage is your goal, use heavy weapons and try to hit the enemy's weaknesses if you can. Accuracy, however, comes at a price. To hit consistently against some of the faster bosses, you are better off starting a chain of attacks with your light-damage, but high-accuracy, lasers/missiles. These are not only good for hitting the enemy and raising the accuracy of the chain; they also strike multiple times, raising the factor for the damage bonus later in the chain.

When choosing equipment, note the cost of a given selection (in terms of energy use). If you have an engine that puts out 800 energy per turn and a sword that uses 410 energy per swing, you have a problem! To fix it, look for a disk to raise your energy by just enough to be able to get that second swing off each turn. Suddenly, things are looking even worse for your enemies, yes?

Be wary of using disks to raise your energy beyond a certain point in the late game. The limit on energy for a given E.S. is 999. Engines at that point are able to provide 900 or 990 energy on their own, so disks that improve energy output are almost worthless. If you can't use the extra energy, don't bother with the disk (there are always more options for damage or survivability).

CHAINS

Chains offer improved accuracy and damage for consecutive hits against a target. This happens even if you gain a cooperative attack or ambush against an enemy, meaning that even multiple E.S.s benefit from chain accuracy/damage. To get the most out of this, use attacks that hit as many times as possible early in your sequence. This raises the damage total of the entire chain, and that is especially useful when your final attacks are likely to be the highest energy cost/damage ones of the bunch.

For each hit in a chain, a 5% damage bonus is added. This applies up to 20 times (leading to double damage for every single attack afterward). Combined with the accuracy boost of the chain, this is amazingly useful.

To give chains the best chance of stacking, use any extra energy that would be left after your primary weapons fire for high-accuracy/multiple-hit attacks from your secondary weapons. Lasers and missiles are ideal for this tactic. If one person tries to attack with Sword, Sword, Missile during an Anima Awakening, it will be far less effective than if they tried Missile, Sword, Sword. The initial missile burst puts the chain up to a decent damage plus right off the bat, and it raises accuracy enough to help the more difficult sword hits find their mark.

INTRODUCTION

ARCADES

CHARACTERS

TACTICAL FILES

EQUIPMENT

ENEMY ASSESSMENT

REGIONAL ANALYSIS

SUPPLEMENTAL DATA

If you miss or are otherwise stopped from completing your full sequence of weapon attacks, there is no chance for a Cooperative Attack or Ambush to occur. Thus, it's useful to rely on the standard chain techniques for high accuracy if you are hoping to start a solid combo.

Under normal circumstances, only a Cooperative Attack is available. This means that only a single E.S. can add to the end of your chain. During Anima Awakening, this is replaced by the potential for Ambushes; Team Combos that involve all of the E.S.s in the fighting group. By the end of those combos, the enemy is going to be experiencing a sandstorm's worth of deep hurting!

For the highest number of these long chains and combos, avoid using two-handed weapons on the Dinah and the Zebulun. While the damage per attack seems better with two-handed weapons, there is a major cost in terms of lost accuracy and team combos.

ANIMA

TEAM COMBOS (COOPERATIVE ATTACKS AND AMBUSHES)

Now that you know how to do the most with a chain of attacks from one E.S., it's time to learn how to get other E.S.s in on the fun. You might have noticed already that E.S. weapons have a Team rating. This lets you know how much of a relative chance they provide for other members of the group to score a free attack in addition to your current character's chain. Most weapons with a high Team rating are not quite as damaging on their own, but they do much more when combined with another character's Cooperative Attack or Ambush.

Anima is somewhat like Boost for E.S.s. Accrued through damage-dealing, it is used for special attacks. However, the similarities end there, because E.S.s are able to use Anima individually. Though they cannot Boost to give each other free turns, E.S.s are able to get ambushes while using Anima, and those are even better in some ways.

WHAT ANIMA DOES

- ANIMA AWAKENING GIVES YOU TWO OR MORE ROUNDS WITH DECREASED ENERGY COST FOR WEAPONS

- EACH LEVEL OF ANIMA AWAKENING CORRESPONDS TO A SPECIAL ATTACK

- DURING ANIMA AWAKENING, E.S.S CAN MAKE TRIPLE-ATTACK AMBUSHES FOR MAJOR BONUS DAMAGE

- ANIMA IS ACCRUED BY E.S. INDIVIDUALLY; IT IS ALSO SPENT INDIVIDUALLY

- ANIMA IS GAINED BY DELIVERING DAMAGE TO TARGETS, JUST LIKE BOOST

WHAT ANIMA ISN'T

- ANIMA DOES NOT GIVE YOUR E.S.S THE POTENTIAL FOR FREE TURNS

- THERE ARE NO ITEMS TO IMPROVE HOW MUCH ANIMA YOUR E.S.S CAN STORE; THAT IS PLOT-BASED

- YOUR E.S.S CANNOT GAIN ANIMA WHILE IN ANIMA AWAKENING MODE

Crafty use of Anima is so useful that it's something everyone must try for themselves. To get on the road to greatness, practice using Anima during simple encounters. You won't need to save Anima only for boss fights; indeed, doing so prevents your party from using finishing moves and getting bonus experience.

Practice using your favorite special attacks, and remember that frequent use raises their level. This adds bonus damage to that particular special attack, so it's extremely useful for single-target specials.

In some fights, having huge bursts from a special attack is all that you need. In others, the potential for ambushes far surpasses the special attacks in overall importance. When that happens, use level one Anima Awakenings instead of the more expensive tiers. It takes far less time to get the Anima back from a level one Awakening, and you still have the same potential for ambushes while under its effect.

For the most experience in random encounters, use level two Anima Awakenings from Anima that has been accrued in earlier battles. Have one person use an Anima at the beginning of the encounter when all of the enemies are still up and fighting. Immediately use your level two special attack and watch everything get splattered! Those finishing moves add up to major money, skill points, and so forth.

In boss battles, you don't want to fully deplete your Anima Gauges just to quickly bypass the easy part of the fight. Instead, use level one Anima Awakenings throughout the fight to increase the damage output of your group without taking everyone's Gauge down to nothing. Next, save everyone's Anima during the middle portion of the fight and use a burst of level three Anima Awakenings for a brilliant finish. It's a darn shame you don't get the third-level Anima Awakenings earlier in the game; they look so cool that it hurts not to have them!

CHARGE

Charge is even more
useful than using
guard on your normal
characters. This
places your E.S. into
a defensive stance
that lasts until their
next combat phase;
they take half damage during this time. Beyond
that, charge restores 15% of the E.S.s health
immediately. If you load a D-Charge, this percentage
improves by a huge quantity. Such E.S.s are able
to restore well over half of their health in a single
turn while guarding! This is able to protect your
craft from destruction even under the most brutal
of assaults.

If enemies are preparing a major special attack, have
all of your E.S.s charge. This brings their health closer
to full and does much to negate the effect of the
incoming move that it doesn't usually matter if the E.S. is
left without all of its HPs. In fact, unless your charge will
leave an E.S. with under half health, it's more powerful in
surviving an ugly round than if you healed it to full HPs.

INTRODUCTION

ARCHIVES

CHARACTERS

TACTICAL FILES

EQUIPMENT

THREAT ASSESSMENT

REGIONAL ANALYSIS

SUPPLEMENTAL DATA

EQUIPMENT DATABASE

Everything in the universe has a use, whether it's selling a rock or firing a gun. Listed within this section are the items of consequence encountered through your travels. These are separated into Items, Equipment, and E.S. Equipment so you can quickly find what you need.

ITEMS

While the term "items" covers a large portion of objects in the world, this section only focuses on items that are consumable, of value to merchants, or unlock an area or skill.

RECOVERY ITEMS

The most common and prolific items are recovery items. These recover a variety of statistics or dispel debuffs on one or more party members. These can be used in or out of battle.

RECOVERY ITEMS

ITEM NAME	COST	EFFECT
MED KIT S	100	RECOVER A SMALL AMOUNT OF HP
MED KIT M	500	RECOVER A MEDIUM AMOUT OF HP
MED KIT L	N/A	RECOVER ALL HP
MED KIT DX	N/A	RECOVER ALL HP FOR ALL ALLIES
REJUVENATOR M	N/A	RECOVER MEDIUM AMOUNT OF HP AND EP
REJUVENATOR L	N/A	RECOVER ALL HP AND EP
REJUVENATOR DX	N/A	RECOVER ALL HP AND EP FOR ALL ALLIES
ETHER PACK S	3000	RECOVER SMALL AMOUNT OF EP
ETHER PACK M	7000	RECOVER MEDIUM AMOUNT OF EP
ETHER PACK L	N/A	RECOVER ALL EP
ANTIDOTE	20	CURE A POISONED ALLY
CLEANSER	1000	CURE AN ALLY'S STATUS EFFECT EXCEPT FOR CRYSTALLIZATION
SEVEN MOONS	300	REVIVE AND RECOVER ALL HP AND EP
ANTI-CRYSTAL	1000	CURE A CRYSTALLIZED ALLY
REMOVER	50	CURE AN ALLY'S DECREASED ABILITY
REVIVE M	600	REVIVE AND RECOVER MEDIUM AMOUNT OF HP
REVIVE L	N/A	REVIVE AND RECOVER ALL HP.
NULLIFIER	1000	DISENGAGE AN ENEMY'S STATUS SUPPORT
NANO REPAIR M	400	RECOVER MEDIUM AMOUNT OF HP (E.S. ONLY)
NANO REPAIR DX	1000	RECOVER ALL HP (E.S. ONLY)
HALF REPAIR	1500	RECOVER MEDIUM AMOUNT OF HP FOR ALL ALLIES (E.S. ONLY)
ALL REPAIR	3800	RECOVER ALL HP FOR ALL ALLIES (E.S. ONLY)
DOWN REPAIR	50	CURE AN ALLY'S DECREASED ABILITY AND F MINE (E.S. ONLY)
LEMON ICE CREAM	80	RECOVER SMALL AMOUNT OF HP
BERRY ICE CREAM	480	RECOVER MEDIUM AMOUNT OF HP
MELON ICE CREAM	1000	RECOVER ALL HP

BATTLE ITEMS

ITEM NAME	COST	EFFECT
ANALYZE BALL	4	ANALYZE AN ENEMY. MUST BE USED DURING BATTLE
TRAP	200	IMMOBILIZE THE ENEMY IN THE AREA FOR A MOMENT. MUST BE USED BEFORE BATTLES

IMPROVEMENT ITEMS

These items are used only once (and only outside of combat). They permanently increase a statistic, add to a person's skill points, or grant another ability to your characters. The G Vaccine is the only item in this list that can be purchased from a store.

IMPROVEMENT ITEMS

ITEM NAME	EFFECT
SKILL UPGRADE A	INCREASE SKILL POINTS BY 10
SKILL UPGRADE B	INCREASE SKILL POINTS BY 50
SKILL UPGRADE C	INCREASE SKILL POINTS BY 100
SKILL UPGRADE D	INCREASE SKILL POINTS BY 500
HP UPGRADE	INCREASE MAXIMUM HP VALUE BY 25.
EP UPGRADE	INCREASE MAXIMUM EP VALUE BY 5.
STR UPGRADE	INCREASE STR VALUE BY 2.
VIT UPGRADE	INCREASE VIT VALUE BY 2.
EATK UPGRADE	INCREASE EATK VALUE BY 2.
EDEF UPGRADE	INCREASE EDEF VALUE BY 2.
EVA UPGRADE	INCREASE EVA VALUE BY 2.
DEX UPGRADE	INCREASE DEX VALUE BY 2.
AGI UPGRADE	INCREASE AGI VALUE BY 2.
LUCK UPGRADE	INCREASE LUCK VALUE BY 2.
G VACCINE	INCREASE CRYSTALLIZATION RESISTANCE BY 5%

EXTRA SKILLS!

The EX Skill Keys are extremely important and must be found during your travels. Because of this, they are listed in the Special Items section.

BARTER ITEMS

Some items have no apparent use. Don't throw them away! One man's trash is another man's treasure. Just because you don't have a use for something doesn't mean no one else does. Some of the merchants are willing to pay greatly for your "junk."

BARTER ITEMS

ITEM NAME	SELL PRICE
SCRAP IRON	15
SALT PILLAR	80
I.D. PLATE	100
JUNKED CIRCUIT	200
WHITE FRAGMENT	400
RANK BADGE	500
CARNELIAN EGG	1000
CRYSTAL OF SPITE	1000
ETHER CORE	1500
SEPHIROTIC CANE	5000

SPECIAL ITEMS

The primary difference between these items and the previously listed is they are found in very specific locations in the universe. The Decoders are listed in your special items and the EX Skill Keys are used from your inventory and unlock new skill groups.

EX SKILL KEYS

ITEM NAME	SKILL BLOCKS OPENED	AREA FOUND
EX SKILL KEY I	EX-A, EX-B, EX-C, EX-D	MILTIANN FOREST: BEHIND THE WATERFALL
EX SKILL KEY II	EX-E, EX-F, EX-G, EX-H	THE MERKABAH: FIRST AREA
EX SKILL KEY III	EX-I, EX-J, EX-K, EX-L	ABEL'S ARK: JUST INSIDE

DECODERS

SEGMENT ADDRESS #	DECODER LOCATION	OBTAIN BY
1	FLOATING LANDMASS, PUZZLE LEVEL ONE	TREASURE BOX
2	HAKOX MINI-GAME	DEFEAT BEGINNER LEVEL
3	PEDEA ISLAND	DEFEAT ERDE KAISER SIGMA
4	CAT TESTING GROUNDS, LOUNGE AREA	TREASURE BOX
5	HOSPITAL, 4TH FLOOR	TREASURE BOX
6	CAT TESTING GROUNDS, WEAPON'S DEVELOPMENT AREA	DEFEAT OMEGA ID
7	HOSPITAL, 2ND FLOOR	DELIVER ALL FEDERAL REPORTS TO LORIA
8	PEDEA ISLAND	TREASURE BOX
9	CAT TESTING GROUNDS, END BOSS	DEFEAT BOSS
10	MERKABAH, TOP OF SHAFT	TREASURE BOX
11	DABYRIE MINE, BOSS	DEFEAT BOSS
12	MERKABAH, HONEYCOMB	TREASURE BOX
13	LABYRINTHOS, AREA 13	TREASURE BOX
14	ABEL'S ARK, BLUE SPHERE	TREASURE BOX
15	DABRYE MINE, ENTRANCE	TALK TO MAI ABOUT HER FATHER

EQUIPMENT

Anything that can be put on a character and used multiple times is found in this section. These items only need to be equipped once (until you find an upgrade) and are used in every single battle. Equipment is broken into each of the slots on your character. Weapons and Armor are further split by character, as not everyone wears the same size.

WEAPONS

These are the items that greatly determine your ability to do damage of one form or another. All of them increase both STR and EATK; some of them have other bonuses as well.

CHAOS

NAME	COST	STR	VIT	DEX	EVA	AGI	EATK	EDEF	LUCK	BREAK LIMIT
PARAIBA HAND	N/A	13					15			
FORCE HAND	190	15					17			
PSYCHO DRIVER	590	21					23			
MEDES DRIVER	1700	26					28			
TIMAEUS	3200	32					34			
KRITIAS	5200	38	10				40			
CHAOS LORD	7800	47			10		49		10	
GOD BREATH	N/A	81					84			

JIN

NAME	COST	STR	VIT	DEX	EVA	AGI	EATK	EDEF	LUCK	BREAK LIMIT
BO YAN	N/A	15					9			
HINOKA SANJU	200	19					11			
QI YAN	300	19			3		11			
VB-RAIN	670	25					17			
YASOMA SANJU	N/A	28					20		7	30
VB-FALL	2000	30					22			
HINOKA KAGURA	N/A	36			10		28		10	
VB-FLAME	3500	36					28			
SHEN YAN	5600	42					34			
YASOMA KARUGA	N/A	49			14		35			
VB-CRIMSON	8500	51					36			
VB-DAWN	N/A	88					60			

JR.

NAME	COST	STR	VIT	DEX	EVA	AGI	EATK	EDEF	LUCK	BREAK LIMIT
BLOOD M9	N/A	14					13			
DESERT EAGLE	190	17					16			
LEGACY OF ZARA	590	23					22			
PHANTOM SILVER	1800	27					27			
BLOOD M40	3300	33					33			
BLACK RELIC	5400	39	10				39			
VI-SHOT	8200	48	15			5	47			
VAQUERO	N/A	82					82			

KOS-MOS

NAME	COST	STR	VIT	DEX	EVA	AGI	EATK	EDEF	LUCK	BREAK LIMIT
KWP-PI	N/A	16					8			
KWAP-PII	300	21	3				13			
KWP-XI	N/A	29	10				16	10		
KWP-XII	700	28					19			
KWP-XIII	2100	33					23			
KWP-XIV	3800	39					29			
KWP-XV	5800	48				6	38		5	
KWP-XX	300000	92					74			

MOMO

NAME	COST	STR	VIT	DEX	EVA	AGI	EATK	EDEF	LUCK	BREAK LIMIT
COMPOUND VI	N/A	9					15			
DELTA EDGE I	180	12					21			
COMPOUND VII	580	18					28			
DELTA EDGE II	1600	23					33			
ADONA SHOOTER	3200	29					39			
COMPOUND VIII	5200	34					45			
BARBIT SHOOTER	7900	36					53			
DELTA EDGE III	N/A	42					48		12	
MARKI SHOOTER	8600	36				10	53		10	
MOON BRIDGE	N/A	60					92			

SHION

NAME	COST	STR	VIT	DEX	EVA	AGI	EATK	EDEF	LUCK	BREAK LIMIT
WHITE SILVER	N/A	9					8			
AUTO MACER	200	12					13			
BLUE LADY	300	15					15			
RED CANCER	600	21					21			
TOLL BUNKER	1800	25					26			
VIPER BUNKER	3400	31					32			
GUARDIAN	N/A	36	6				35		4	
COMBAT LADY	5300	37					38			
NIGHT BUNKER	8000	46					47			
VI EMPEROR	N/A	46					45		10	
MIYUKI SPECIAL	N/A	79					81			

ZIGGY

NAME	COST	STR	VIT	DEX	EVA	AGI	EATK	EDEF	LUCK	BREAK LIMIT
BLAST KNUCKLE	N/A	15					9			
ZERO CRUSHER	210	18					11			
RANGER HUNT	610	24					17			
ROCK STAR	2000	29					22			
BREAK KNUCKLE	3200	35					28			
BLUE NAIL	5000	41				6	31			30
BARBELO KNUCKLE	8600	49	10				33			50
GNOSIS NAIL	N/A	85					54			

ALLEN

NAME	COST	STR	VIT	DEX	EVA	AGI	EATK	EDEF	LUCK	BREAK LIMIT
BENZER ACE	N/A	20					19			

CANAAN

NAME	COST	STR	VIT	DEX	EVA	AGI	EATK	EDEF	LUCK	BREAK LIMIT
NIGHT WALKER	N/A	11					8			

MIYUKI

NAME	COST	STR	VIT	DEX	EVA	AGI	EATK	EDEF	LUCK	BREAK LIMIT
MWS TYPE 76	N/A	9					9			

ARMOR

Like weapons, most armor can only be used by one member of your party. There are some exceptions to this, as some styles are very popular. In these cases, the armor is listed under both people.

CHAOS

NAME	COST	STR	VIT	DEX	EVA	AGI	EATK	EDEF	LUCK	BREAK LIMIT
COMBAT SUIT	N/A		3					3		
FIBER VEST	120		6					7		
SURVIVAL WEAR	N/A	4	6					6		
NEO PROTECTOR	380		9				4	11		
TECHTRON CLOTH	380	4	11					9		
HALF COAT	N/A		12		6			10	4	
BRIGAND	1050		13				8	15		
DOUBLE RIDERS	1050	8	15					13		
METAL SPRINT	N/A		16			6		18	6	
RIGID LEATHER	2200		18					20		
COAT HARDY	N/A		23		12			24		40
VECTOR CROSS	3500	6	23				6	25		
SHOCK ABSORBANT SHIRT	N/A		26					20		60
NANO CARE COAT	3500		26		8	5		27		
UNION LEATHER	5300		29					31	8	80
CHAOS'S SWIMSUIT	N/A					5			30	
FLAWLESS	N/A			3		20	3			

JIN

NAME	COST	STR	VIT	DEX	EVA	AGI	EATK	EDEF	LUCK	BREAK LIMIT
JADE PHOENIX	N/A		3					2		
GRANITE MANTLE	120		6					4		
HAZE ROBE	400		10					7		
DOUBLE VESTMENT	N/A	6	15		5			10		
MOONLIGHT ROBE	1200		15					10		
RAPTOR ROBE	2100		20					14		
WARLORD'S MANTLE	3500	12	24					15		
HEAVEN'S ROBE	3500		26		12			18		
SARASVATI'S ROBE	N/A	20	33					22		80
TRUE JADE	5300		33		15			22		80
JIN'S SWIMSUIT	N/A					5			30	

JR.

NAME	COST	STR	VIT	DEX	EVA	AGI	EATK	EDEF	LUCK	BREAK LIMIT
LEATHER JACKET	N/A		3					3		
FIBER VEST	120		6					7		
SURVIVAL WEAR	N/A	4	6					6		
NEO PROTECTOR	380		9				4	11		
TECHTRON CLOTH	380	4	11					9		
HALF COAT	N/A		12		6			10	4	
BRIGAND	1050		13				8	15		
DOUBLE RIDERS	1050	8	15					13		
METAL SPRINT	N/A		16			6		18	6	
RIGID LEATHER	2200		18					20		
COAT HARDY	N/A		23		12			24		40
VECTOR CROSS	3500	6	23				6	25		
SHOCK ABSORBANT SHIRT	N/A		26					20		60
NANO CARE COAT	3500		26		8	5		27		
LONG HORN	N/A		31			10		29		100
JR.'S SWIMSUIT	N/A					5			30	

KOS-MOS

NAME	COST	STR	VIT	DEX	EVA	AGI	EATK	EDEF	LUCK	BREAK LIMIT
KAP-AZA	N/A		4					4		
KAP-BEG	150		8					7		
KAP-CLE	450		12					11		
KAP-COS	1300		18					16		
KAP-GLA	2300		24					22		
KAP-NAR	N/A	10	30					28		40
KAP-SAL	3800		31					29		
KAP-SAN	5900	20	38					37		
KAP-VEN	5900		37				20	38		
KAP-VEL	N/A		46			10		45		100
KOS-MOS'S SWIMSUIT	N/A					5			30	

MOMO

NAME	COST	STR	VIT	DEX	EVA	AGI	EATK	EDEF	LUCK	BREAK LIMIT
KAJIC SHIRT	N/A		3					3		
DENIM JACKET	110		4					5		
METAL CORSET	120		5				3	6		
LACE TANK TOP	120		6		3			8		
BOLERO CAPE	370		7					10		
KAJIC CAPE	1000		9					14		30
BUTTERFLY SUIT	2000		11					18		50
GORGON COAT	3400		14				10	22		
KAJIC BLOUSE	5300		17				15	26		80
HONEY TEDDY	N/A		5		20			5	15	
MOMO'S SWIMSUIT	N/A					5			30	

SHION

NAME	COST	STR	VIT	DEX	EVA	AGI	EATK	EDEF	LUCK	BREAK LIMIT
PEARL WEAR	N/A		2					2		
DENIM JACKET	110		4					5		
METAL CORSET	120		5				3	6		
LACE TANK TOP	120		6		3			8		
GRAMPUS PANNIER	370		9					11		
PLATINUM BUSTIER	1000	7	12					14		
VELVET BOLERO	2000		15		8			17		
DRAGON BUSTIER	3400	10	18					20		
VELVET PANNIER	N/A		22					24	10	80
DIVE TEDDY	N/A		5		20			5	15	
SHION'S SWIMSUIT	N/A					5			30	

ZIGGY

NAME	COST	STR	VIT	DEX	EVA	AGI	EATK	EDEF	LUCK	BREAK LIMIT
SPEED I VEST	N/A		5					4		
SPEED II VEST	110		9					8		
SPEED III VEST	380		14					12		
GUSTAV ARMOR	1300	10	17					16		
GUSTAV VEST	1000		20		5			17		
ASSAULT VEST	N/A	15	27					23		60
PROTECT GEAR	2100		27					23		
ZIG-MUSCLE	3700	20	35					29		
ZIG-SKELETAL	3700		35					29		90
TOP SECRET SKELETAL	5300		43			12		35		120
ZIGGY'S SWIMSUIT	N/A					5			30	

ALLEN

NAME	COST	STR	VIT	DEX	EVA	AGI	EATK	EDEF	LUCK	BREAK LIMIT
NEO PROTECTOR	380		9				4	11		

CANAAN

NAME	COST	STR	VIT	DEX	EVA	AGI	EATK	EDEF	LUCK	BREAK LIMIT
COMBAT SUIT	N/A		3					3		

MIYUKI

NAME	COST	STR	VIT	DEX	EVA	AGI	EATK	EDEF	LUCK	BREAK LIMIT
PEARL WEAR	N/A		2					2		

NECKLACES

Necklaces provide passive combat improvements in a variety of ways. These can be very powerful for survivability or attack enhancements.

NAME	COST	EFFECT
SNAKE EYE	100	DISPLAY DATA
LEATHER CHOKER	150	BL +50
CYLINDER NECK	300	BL +100
RED CRYSTAL	300	SMALL RARE ITEM
OPEN HEART	450	SMALL ITEM+
BULLET NECK	600	HP +300
DOG TAG	600	BL +150
PANTHER EYE	1200	DISPLAY DATA, HP +300
CROSS CHOKER	1600	LARGE ITEM+
SUN CRY	1800	MEDIUM G+
EAGLE EYE	4500	DISPLAY DATA, HP +300, EP +50
ROSARIO OF LOVE	6000	EP +100
SWEET PAIN	N/A	MAX BOOST +1, RECOVERY ETHER+
UNION NECK	N/A	MAX BOOST +1
ROSARIO OF GRIEF	N/A	EP +50
DRAGON'S EYE	N/A	LARGE RARE ITEM+, DISPLAY DATA, EP +50
GOLD FALL	N/A	LARGE G+
GUSTAV NECK	N/A	MAX BOOST +2
GOD'S EXPERIENCE	N/A	LARGE EXP+
CRESCENT MOON	N/A	SMALL SP+
NIGHT MOON	N/A	LARGE SP+
EVANGELIST	N/A	MAX BOOST +3, LARGE EXP+, LARGE SP+
BRISINGAMEN	N/A	LARGE G+, LARGE RARE ITEM, EP +100
TALISMAN	N/A	HP +800
KAJIC NECK	N/A	RECOVERY ETHER+
TEARS RIVER	N/A	SMALL G+
BRAVE HEART	N/A	MAX BOOST +3
ANGEL'S EXPERIENCE	N/A	SMALL EXP+
IRON MAIDEN	N/A	MAX BOOST +2, SMALL EXP+, SMALL SP+
KIBISIS	N/A	MAX BOOST +3, HP +1500, EP +300
ANDVARI	N/A	SMALL G+, SMALL RARE ITEM
DRAUPNIR	N/A	MEDIUM G+, LARGE RARE ITEM

BRACELETS

Bracelets are usually defensive in nature; they provide resistances or immunities to status effects and damage types.

WATCHES AND BRACELETS

NAME	COST	EFFECT
COBRA BANGLE	100	1/2 POISON DAMAGE
SHOCK ABSORBER	100	1/2 GUARD DAMAGE
RARE BRACE	300	1/2 ACC+EVA DOWN, 1/2 POISON
KING JACK	700	1/2 LOCK, 1/2 CURSE
QUEEN JACK	700	1/2 RASP, 1/2 MISTY
VAN BRACE	700	1/2 ATTACK DOWN, 1/2 DEFENSE DOWN
BEAM WALL	1000	1/2 BEAM
FIRE WALL	1000	1/2 FIRE
ICE WALL	1000	1/2 ICE
THUNDER WALL	1000	1/2 LIGHTNING
UNKNOWN BRACELET	1400	NULL ACC+EVA DOWN
GOD CIRCLE	1700	NULL MISTY
IMPERIAL	1700	NULL LOCK
SOUL COLLECTOR	1700	NULL CURSE
DRAGON HEAD	3000	1/2 RASP, 1/2 MISTY, 1/2 LOCK
GROSS SOUL	3000	1/2 ATTACK DOWN, 1/2 DEFENSE DOWN, 1/2 ACC+EVA DOWN
TEMPEST BEADS	5600	NULL ATTACK DOWN, NULL DEFENSE DOWN
DOUBLE DEALER	7000	OMEGA MIND DURING GUARD
ROSENCRANTZ	7000	OMEGA SKIN DURING GUARD
RA'S BEADS	100000	NULL RASP, NULL MISTY, NULL LOCK
PLATINUM BANGLE	300000	2X DEFENSE VS. G
STEEL BANGLE	300000	2X DEFENSE VS. B
TITANIUM BANGLE	300000	2X DEFENSE VS. M
WISEMAN'S BEADS	450000	NULL STATUS EFFECTS
RESIST BEAM	600000	NULL BEAM
RESIST FIRE	600000	NULL FIRE
RESIST ICE	600000	NULL ICE
RESIST THUNDER	600000	NULL LIGHTNING
EMPEROR'S BRACELET	N/A	1/2 PHYSICAL, 1/2 GUARD DAMAGE
FIVE STONES	N/A	1/2 PHYSICAL
GENERAL'S BRACELET	N/A	1/2 FIRE, 1/2 ICE, 1/2 LIGHTNING
GRAND DESIGN	N/A	NULL STATUS EFFECTS
KAJIC WRIST	N/A	2X DEFENSE VS. M, 1/2 FIRE, 1/2 GUARD
NINE STONES	N/A	ABSORB PHYSICAL
BEAM ABSORBER	N/A	ABSORB BEAM
CORAL STONE	N/A	NULL RASP
GARUDA BANGLE	N/A	NULL POISON
GUSTAV WRIST	N/A	2X DEFENSE VS. B/M/G
HERO'S BRACELET	100000	1/2 FIRE, 1/2 ICE
HYDRA HEAL	N/A	ABSORB FIRE
SHIVA'S GUARD	N/A	ABSORB ICE
SIVA'S EYE	N/A	ABSORB LIGHTNING
UNION WRIST	N/A	2X DEFENSE VS. G, 1/2 ICE, 1/2 GUARD
VELVET BREATH	N/A	2X DEFENSE VS. B, 1/2 LIGHTNING, 1/2 GUARD
WARRIOR'S BRACELET	100000	1/2 LIGHTNING, 1/2 BEAM

RINGS

Through recent advances in metal technology, Vector Industries now produces rings that change size depending on the one holding them. These advanced rings automatically detect the size of the ring finger and change their size to accommodate. Note that KOS-MOS cannot use any ring that adds an elemental damage type to her attacks.

RINGS

NAME	COST	EFFECT
RED OASIS	150	BL +50
RED STAR	300	BL +100
COBALT RING	300	ADD ICE
CRIMSON RING	300	ADD FIRE
SILVER RING	300	ADD BEAM
YELLOW RING	300	ADD LIGHTNING
VELVET RING	600	BL +150
BEAM AVATAR	900	ADD BEAM, HP +300
FLAME AVATAR	900	ADD FIRE, HP +300
ICE AVATAR	900	ADD ICE, HP +300
LIGHTNING AVATAR	900	ADD LIGHTNING, HP +300
COUNTER RING	1800	INCREASE COUNTER
REVENGE RING	1800	INCREASE REVENGE
RUTHLESS RING	1800	INCREASE DOUBLE
GREEN STAR	2600	HP +800
ACALA'S PULSE	3000	INCREASE COUNTER, NULL E-COUNTER
HAMMURABI SPELL	3000	INCREASE REVENGE, NULL E-REVENGE
LOST KINGDOM	3000	INCREASE COUNTER, INCREASE REVENGE
PIERCE RING	12000	NULL E-GUARD
BIND RING	15000	NULL E-EVADE
BLUE STAR	N/A	EP +100
KAJIC RING	N/A	EP +300
LIFE DEMON	N/A	HP DRAIN, EP +100, BL +100
LIFE LEECH	N/A	HP DRAIN
BLUE OASIS	N/A	EP +50
GREEN OASIS	N/A	HP +300
GUSTAV RING	N/A	HP +1500
WITCH'S EYE	N/A	HP +300, EP +50, BL +50
SAGE'S RING	N/A	HP +800, EP +100, BL +100
ENHANCE RING	N/A	HP +1500, EP +300, BL +150
VENOM RING	N/A	ADDS POISON, EP +50
UNION RING	N/A	NULL E-GUARD AND E-EVADE
REAL WORLD	N/A	INCREASE COUNTER, REVENGE, DOUBLE
RING OF COERCION	N/A	NULL E-COUNTER AND E-REVENGE
RING OF EDEN	N/A	DECREASE CONSUMED EP BY 1/2
HEAVEN'S DOOR	N/A	DECREASE CONSUMED EP TO 1
THE UNIVERSE	N/A	DECREASE CONSUMED EP BY 1/2, NULL E-COUNTER, E-REVENGE
KNIGHT RING	N/A	OMEGA FIST DURING GUARD, HP +800
GYPSY RING	N/A	OMEGA SOUL DURING GUARD, HP +800
POWER HEAL	N/A	HP DRAIN, NULL E-GUARD AND E-EVADE
POWER LEECH	N/A	HP DRAIN, INCREASE COUNTER, DOUBLE

INTRODUCTION
ARCHIVES
CHARACTERS
TACTICAL FILES
EQUIPMENT
THREAT ASSESSMENT
REGIONAL ANALYSIS
SUPPLEMENTAL DATA

E.S. EQUIPMENT

The parts on your E.S.s determine how effective they are in combat. Weapons determine damage and damage type, frames provide armor, generators determine number of attacks per round, CPUs allow a maximum number of programs to be loaded, and disks control those programs.

WEAPONS

Like the operators, the E.S. have distinct weapon types. The weapons are listed by each E.S., then by which (or both) hands wield the weapon.

ASHER

Piloted by Jr. with chaos as backup, the Asher prefers physical or fire weapons.

RIGHT HAND

NAME	COST	WEAPON TYPE	DAMAGE TYPE	RAPID	POW	EATK	EN COST	HITS	ACC	ABILITIES
STING RAY	N/A	PILE BUNKER	PHYSICAL	10	42	42	230	2	LOW	NONE
STING RAY II	300	PILE BUNKER	PHYSICAL	10	47	43	230	2	LOW	NONE
STING RAY V	4400	PILE BUNKER	PHYSICAL	10	71	67	230	2	LOW	NONE

LEFT HAND

NAME	COST	WEAPON TYPE	DAMAGE TYPE	RAPID	POW	EATK	EN COST	HITS	ACC	ABILITIES
G88 ASSAULT	N/A	GATLING GUN	PHYSICAL	14	42	42	190	5	MEDIUM	NONE
G90 ASSAULT	300	GATLING GUN	PHYSICAL	14	47	43	190	5	MEDIUM	NONE
SG-M20	400	SHOTGUN	PHYSICAL	10	50	35	170	6	MEDIUM	NONE
SG-M30P	1600	SHOTGUN	PHYSICAL	10	55	54	170	6	MEDIUM	NONE
SG-M WOLF	2200	SHOTGUN	PHYSICAL	10	65	64	170	6	MEDIUM	NONE
TEMPEST	2200	BAZOOKA	FIRE	5	60	54	300	2	LOW	NONE
TEMPEST GP	2400	BAZOOKA	FIRE	5	67	64	300	2	LOW	NONE
DRACHE	4100	GRENADE RIFLE	FIRE	3	70	64	410	2	LOW	NONE
BZ AVENGER	4600	BAZOOKA	FIRE	5	73	67	300	2	LOW	NONE
DRACHE-RR	5300	GRENADE RIFLE	FIRE	3	75	67	410	2	LOW	NONE

TWO HANDS

NAME	COST	WEAPON TYPE	DAMAGE TYPE	RAPID	POW	EATK	EN COST	HITS	ACC	ABILITIES
V18 ASSAULT II	3900	DBL GATLING GUN	PHYSICAL	25	112	108	320	10	MEDIUM	NONE
V2 ASSAULT II	7500	DBL GATLING GUN	PHYSICAL	25	127	124	320	10	MEDIUM	NONE

*Rapid becomes Team in battle..

DINAH

KOS-MOS and Shion pilot this E.S. With such a difference in fighting styles, it's no wonder that the Dinah prefers to have both melee and ranged weapons.

RIGHT HAND

NAME	COST	WEAPON TYPE	DAMAGE TYPE	RAPID	POW	EATK	EN COST	HITS	ACC	ABILITIES
S SIFE	N/A	BLADE	BEAM	10	43	43	230	2	LOW	NONE
S SIFE FX	N/A	BLADE	BEAM	10	49	60	230	2	LOW	NONE

LEFT HAND

NAME	COST	WEAPON TYPE	DAMAGE TYPE	RAPID	POW	EATK	EN COST	HITS	ACC	ABILITIES
VOLANS	N/A	HANDGUN	BEAM	14	43	43	190	5	MEDIUM	NONE
VOLANS G	300	HANDGUN	BEAM	14	49	49	190	5	MEDIUM	NONE
G PHALANX	320	GATLING GUN	BEAM	16	49	50	200	7	MEDIUM	NONE
ARF-R5	350	RIFLE	BEAM	12	49	52	220	3	MEDIUM	SOUL DOWN
G PHALANX II	1800	GATLING GUN	BEAM	16	54	59	200	7	MEDIUM	NONE
ARF-R7	2000	RIFLE	BEAM	12	54	67	220	3	MEDIUM	SOUL DOWN
SR SHAULA A	2200	S RIFLE	BEAM	5	54	70	380	1	HIGH	MIND DOWN
SR SHAULA R2	2500	S RIFLE	BEAM	5	59	63	380	1	HIGH	MIND DOWN
DORADE RK-3	4200	GIANT BAZOOKA	BEAM	3	59	66	450	2	LOW	NONE
VOLANS SV	4500	HANDGUN	BEAM	14	74	78	190	5	MEDIUM	NONE
PHALANX XX	4600	GATLING GUN	BEAM	16	74	80	200	7	MEDIUM	NONE
ARF RASTABAN	4700	RIFLE	BEAM	12	74	82	220	3	MEDIUM	SOUL DOWN
DORADE RK-5	5000	GIANT BAZOOKA	BEAM	3	74	85	450	2	LOW	NONE

REUBEN

With a master swordsman at its helm, the Reuben's primary weapons are swords, and the bigger the better! Though the Reuben is always in harm's way, because it fights up close and personal, it is also the primary damage dealer of the group.

BOTH HANDS

NAME	COST	WEAPON TYPE	DAMAGE TYPE	RAPID	POW	EATK	EN COST	HITS	ACC	ABILITIES
TYPE II - GUST	N/A	LONG SWORDS	PHYSICAL	10	86	79	250	2	MEDIUM	NONE
TYPE II - GALE	600	LONG SWORDS	FIRE	10	93	87	250	2	MEDIUM	NONE
DAWNING MOON	1000	POLE SWORD	PHYSICAL	3	96	87	410	1	LOW	NONE
SHIRANUI	2200	PAIR OF SWORDS	PHYSICAL	12	100	93	180	2	HIGH	BALANCE DOWN
MISTY MOON	3400	POLE SWORD	FIRE	3	105	93	410	1	LOW	NONE
FOUR HEAVENS	4400	PAIR OF SWORDS	FIRE	12	109	97	180	2	HIGH	SKIN DOWN
NEW MOON	5000	POLE SWORD	PHYSICAL	3	112	97	410	1	LOW	NONE
FULL MOON	9000	POLE SWORD	FIRE	3	126	102	410	1	LOW	NONE

ZEBULUN

Ziggy provides backup for MOMO with the Zebulun. Its weapons are quite varied, but the preference for lightning based weapons holds steady.

RIGHT HAND

NAME	COST	WEAPON TYPE	DAMAGE TYPE	RAPID	POW	EATK	EN COST	HITS	ACC	ABILITIES
ST SWIFT	N/A	SHIELD WEAPON	LIGHTNING	10	42	42	220	2	LOW	NONE
ST SWIFT HG	300	SHIELD WEAPON	LIGHTNING	10	48	49	220	2	LOW	NONE
ST2-SWIFT	2400	SHIELD WEAPON	LIGHTNING	10	53	60	220	2	LOW	NONE

LEFT HAND

NAME	COST	WEAPON TYPE	DAMAGE TYPE	RAPID	POW	EATK	EN COST	HITS	ACC	ABILITIES
SCHWALBE	N/A	LASER GUN	BEAM	14	42	42	180	3	MEDIUM	MIND DOWN
LINDWURM	300	BEAM GUN	LIGHTNING	10	48	49	160	4	MEDIUM	MIND DOWN
EM FADEN	400	STUN GUN	LIGHTNING	18	48	52	180	1	MEDIUM	BALANCE DOWN
LINDWURM M2	1600	BEAM GUN	LIGHTNING	10	56	57	160	4	MEDIUM	MIND DOWN
SCHWALBE F	1800	LASER GUN	BEAM	14	56	59	180	3	MEDIUM	MIND DOWN
EM FADEN R	2100	STUN GUN	LIGHTNING	18	56	60	180	1	MEDIUM	BALANCE DOWN
SC LINDWURM	5000	BEAM GUN	LIGHTNING	10	70	70	160	4	MEDIUM	MIND DOWN
SCHWALBE SW	5400	LASER GUN	BEAM	14	70	75	180	3	MEDIUM	MIND DOWN

BOTH HANDS

NAME	COST	WEAPON TYPE	DAMAGE TYPE	RAPID	POW	EATK	EN COST	HITS	ACC	ABILITIES
AIRD-E	3000	AIRD LASER	BEAM	5	104	106	300	6	MEDIUM	NONE
AIRD-E+	4000	AIRD LASER	BEAM	5	108	111	300	6	MEDIUM	NONE
AIRD-C II	4200	AIRD CANNON	BEAM	3	108	115	450	3	MEDIUM	NONE
SENTIR A-L	8000	AIRD LASER	BEAM	5	123	124	300	6	MEDIUM	NONE
AIRD-C V	9000	AIRD CANNON	BEAM	3	123	126	450	3	MEDIUM	NONE

GENERATORS

What good is a weapon without power? Generators determine the amount of EN you have to attack with each turn. As new generators appear in the stores, scoop them up without hesitation. These provide an even bigger boost to damage output than weapon upgrades, so buy them first.

GENERATORS		
NAME	COST	MAX EN
G-ROX/25	N/A	250
G-LEGLE/42	N/A	420
G-ROX/43	480	430
G-ROX/56	1200	560
G-LEGLE/56	N/A	560
G-ROX/63	2000	630
G-IGNIS I	N/A	750
G-ROX/80	3000	800
G-LEGLE/85	N/A	850
G-ROX/90	5200	900
G-IGNIS III	N/A	990

CPUS

CPUs determine how many advanced programs you can have running at the same time. These programs are found on the Disks that are listed immediately after.

CPUS		
NAME	COST	MAX SLOTS
C-US1	N/A	1
C-US2	100	2
C-US3	150	3
C-US3G	N/A	3
C-US4	1000	4
C-US5	1500	5
C-US5G	N/A	5
C-US6	2000	6
C-US7	2500	7
C-US8	3000	8
C-US9	3500	9
C-US9G	N/A	9
C-US10	N/A	10

DISKS

The abilities granted by loading various disks into your CPU vary greatly. Choosing the disks to maximize your performance against a single enemy or using them to round out any weak spots you have are both valid choices.

DISKS			
NAME	COST	SLOTS USED	EFFECT
D-SENSOR	50	1	DISPLAY DATA
D-GUARD	200	2	1/2 GUARD DAMAGE
D-KILL C	300	2	NULL E-COUNTER
D-KILL R	300	2	NULL E-REVENGE
D-TREASURE I	500	2	SMALL RARE ITEM
D-FRAME I	750	2	HP + 2000
D-HALF A	800	5	1/2 ATTACK DOWN
D-HALF D	800	5	1/2 DEFENSE DOWN
D-HALF DEA	800	5	1/2 ACC+EVA DOWN
D-BEAM	1000	5	1/2 BEAM
D-FIRE	1000	5	1/2 FIRE
D-ICE	1000	5	1/2 ICE
D-LIGHTNING	1000	5	1/2 LIGHTNING
D-REVENGE	1200	1	SHORT REVENGE
D-BLOCK A	2200	2	NULL ATTACK DOWN
D-BLOCK D	2200	2	NULL D-DOWN
D-BLOCK DEA	2200	2	NULL ACC+EVA DOWN
D-CLEAN	2300	1	SE CHARGE
D-FRAME II	2500	4	HP +6000
D-EN I	2800	3	EN +50
D-CHARGE	3000	2	CHARGE RECOVERY+
D-NULLIFY EFFECT	3000	3	NULL DOWN SE
D-REVENGE+	3000	2	INCREASE REVENGE
D-COUNTER+	4000	2	INCREASE COUNTER
D-EN II	5000	6	EN +100
D-FRAME III	5600	6	HP +10000
D-COUNTER	8000	1	SHORT COUNTER
D-TREASURE II	8000	4	LARGE RARE ITEM
D-EXP I	N/A	4	SMALL EXP+
D-EN III	N/A	8	EN +200
D-EXP II	N/A	6	LARGE EXP+
D-HALF PHYSICAL	N/A	7	1/2 PHYSICAL
D-NULLIFY EVADE	N/A	4	NULL E-EVADE
D-SP I	N/A	4	SMALL SP+
D-TYPE M	N/A	2	TYPE M CRITICAL
D-NULLIFY GUARD	N/A	2	NULL E-GUARD
D-ANIMA	N/A	3	INCREASE ANIMA GAUGE RATE
D-SP II	N/A	6	LARGE SP+
D-TYPE G	N/A	2	TYPE G CRITICAL

INTRODUCTION
ARCHIVES
CHARACTERS
TACTICAL FILES
EQUIPMENT
THREAT ASSESSMENT
REGIONAL ANALYSIS
WALKTHROUGH/DATA

THREAT ASSESSMENT

With the use of the Analyze Ether, or using the inexpensive Analyze Balls, your group can easily find out a great deal of information about normal enemies, enemy E.S.s and other craft, Gnosis, and bosses. Use this chapter as a compendium of information about all foes in the game.

27-SERIES ASURA

HP	4000
EP	199
BL	90
INFO	BIOLOGICAL
TGT	???
EXP	4200
SP	20
G	1200
N ITEM	MED KIT L
R ITEM	MED KIT DX
S ITEM	SKILL UPGRADE A
STRONG	NONE
WEAK	BEAM
ABSORBED	NONE
NULL	POISON

AG-01

HP	750
EP	0
BL	90
INFO	MACHINE
TGT	RANDOM
EXP	100
SP	2
G	80
N ITEM	JUNKED CIRCUIT
R ITEM	ETHER CORE
S ITEM	JUNKED CIRCUIT
STRONG	ICE
WEAK	LIGHTNING
ABSORBED	NONE
NULL	POISON

AG-02

HP	3800
EP	0
BL	150
INFO	MACHINE
TGT	BREAK KILLER
EXP	260
SP	3
G	1000
N ITEM	ETHER CORE
R ITEM	SKILL UPGRADE B
S ITEM	JUNKED CIRCUIT
STRONG	ICE
WEAK	FIRE, LIGHTNING
ABSORBED	NONE
NULL	POISON

AG-03

HP	3200
EP	0
BL	150
INFO	MACHINE
TGT	BREAK KILLER
EXP	250
SP	3
G	800
N ITEM	ETHER CORE
R ITEM	SKILL UPGRADE B
S ITEM	NONE
STRONG	ICE
WEAK	FIRE, LIGHTNING
ABSORBED	NONE
NULL	POISON

AG-03 SPX

HP	4500
EP	0
BL	150
INFO	MACHINE
TGT	BREAK KILLER
EXP	300
SP	4
G	1000
N ITEM	ETHER CORE
R ITEM	BLUE STAR
S ITEM	JUNKED CIRCUIT
STRONG	ICE
WEAK	LIGHTNING, BEAM
ABSORBED	NONE
NULL	POISON

AI APAEC

HP	2600
EP	121
BL	60
INFO	GNOSIS
TGT	BREAK KILLER
EXP	235
SP	4
G	420
N ITEM	WHITE FRAGMENT
R ITEM	UNKNOWN BRACELET
S ITEM	ANTI-CRYSTAL
STRONG	ICE
WEAK	FIRE, LIGHTNING
ABSORBED	NONE
NULL	NONE

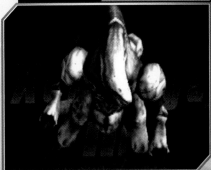

AIAKOS

HP	1800
EP	291
BL	45
INFO	GNOSIS
TGT	RANDOM
EXP	220
SP	4
G	450
N ITEM	WHITE FRAGMENT
R ITEM	SOUL COLLECTOR
S ITEM	ANTI-CRYSTAL
STRONG	FIRE
WEAK	LIGHTNING, BEAM
ABSORBED	NONE
NULL	POISON

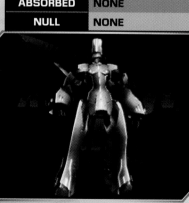

ALUDRA CALF

HP	4500
EP	200
BL	270
INFO	GNOSIS
TGT	???
EXP	885
SP	10
G	260
N ITEM	DECODER 09
R ITEM	NONE
S ITEM	WHITE FRAGMENT
STRONG	NONE
WEAK	BEAM
ABSORBED	NONE
NULL	POISON

ANATHEMA

HP	7300
INFO	MACHINE
TGT	HP KILLER
EXP	265
SP	5
G	340
N ITEM	ETHER CORE
R ITEM	NANO REPAIR DX
STRONG	NONE
WEAK	FIRE
ABSORBED	NONE
NULL	NONE

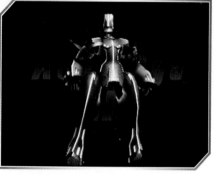

ANATHEMA OFFICER

HP	12000
INFO	MACHINE
TGT	HP KILLER
EXP	282
SP	5
G	600
N ITEM	ETHER CORE
R ITEM	D-EXP II
STRONG	NONE
WEAK	NONE
ABSORBED	NONE
NULL	NONE

ARMAROS

HP	7900
EP	388
BL	180
INFO	GNOSIS
TGT	BREAK KILLER
EXP	450
SP	5
G	2000
N ITEM	SEPHIROTIC CANE
R ITEM	POWER LEECH
S ITEM	CRYSTAL OF SPITE
STRONG	PHYSICAL
WEAK	BEAM
ABSORBED	NONE
NULL	NONE

ASHMED BAPUZ

HP	7500
INFO	GNOSIS
TGT	RANDOM
EXP	235
SP	4
G	320
N ITEM	WHITE FRAGMENT
R ITEM	CRYSTAL OF SPITE
STRONG	PHYSICAL, FIRE
WEAK	LIGHTNING, BEAM
ABSORBED	NONE
NULL	NONE

ASTERION

HP	315
EP	86
BL	30
INFO	BIOLOGICAL
TGT	RECOVERY KILLER
EXP	90
SP	2
G	20
N ITEM	MED KIT S
R ITEM	MED KIT M
S ITEM	MED KIT S
STRONG	LIGHTNING
WEAK	FIRE
ABSORBED	NONE
NULL	POISON

ASTERION REVISED

HP	560
EP	145
BL	30
INFO	BIOLOGICAL
TGT	RECOVERY KILLER
EXP	198
SP	3
G	50
N ITEM	ANTIDOTE
R ITEM	MED KIT M
S ITEM	MED KIT S
STRONG	LIGHTNING
WEAK	FIRE
ABSORBED	NONE
NULL	POISON

AZAZEL

HP	8100
EP	478
BL	150
INFO	GNOSIS
TGT	RANDOM
EXP	450
SP	5
G	2000
N ITEM	SEPHIROTIC CANE
R ITEM	EVANGELIST
S ITEM	CRYSTAL OF SPITE
STRONG	FIRE, ICE, LIGHTNING
WEAK	NONE
ABSORBED	NONE
NULL	NONE

BERSERK REALIAN A

HP	680
EP	47
BL	30
INFO	BIOLOGICAL (HUMAN)
TGT	RANDOM
EXP	180
SP	3
G	42
N ITEM	I.D. PLATE
R ITEM	DOG TAG
S ITEM	MED KIT S
STRONG	NONE
WEAK	BEAM
ABSORBED	NONE
NULL	NONE

BERSERK REALIAN B

HP	590
EP	42
BL	30
INFO	BIOLOGICAL (HUMAN)
TGT	RANDOM
EXP	180
SP	3
G	42
N ITEM	I.D. PLATE
R ITEM	DOG TAG
S ITEM	MED KIT S
STRONG	NONE
WEAK	ICE
ABSORBED	NONE
NULL	NONE

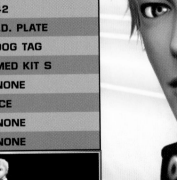

BLACK TESTAMENT

HP	10000
EP	500
BL	600
INFO	BIOLOGICAL (HUMAN)
TGT	???
EXP	3700
SP	15
G	1300
N ITEM	ETHER PACK M
R ITEM	ETHER PACK L
S ITEM	VENOM RING
STRONG	ICE, BEAM
WEAK	FIRE
ABSORBED	NONE
NULL	LIGHTNING, POISON, SEAL ETHER, SEAL BOOST, REFLECT DAMAGE

BLUE TESTAMENT

HP	14500
EP	700
BL	600
INFO	BIOLOGICAL
TGT	???
EXP	11500
SP	20
G	3000
N ITEM	GUSTAV RING
R ITEM	NONE
S ITEM	UNION NECK
STRONG	ICE
WEAK	FIRE
ABSORBED	NONE
NULL	POISON, SEAL ETHER, SEAL BOOST

BYPRODUCT #A156

HP	820
EP	78
BL	60
INFO	BIOLOGICAL
TGT	RANDOM
EXP	120
SP	2
G	28
N ITEM	ANTIDOTE
R ITEM	EVA UPGRADE
S ITEM	ANTIDOTE
STRONG	NONE
WEAK	ICE
ABSORBED	NONE
NULL	FIRE

BYPRODUCT #A283

HP	620
EP	91
BL	60
INFO	BIOLOGICAL
TGT	BREAK KILLER
EXP	118
SP	2
G	28
N ITEM	REMOVER
R ITEM	DEX UPGRADE
S ITEM	REMOVER
STRONG	NONE
WEAK	BEAM
ABSORBED	NONE
NULL	LIGHTNING

CARNICOS I

HP	800
EP	0
BL	90
INFO	MACHINE
TGT	RANDOM
EXP	150
SP	2
G	22
N ITEM	SCRAP IRON
R ITEM	JUNKED CIRCUIT
S ITEM	SCRAP IRON
STRONG	FIRE
WEAK	ICE, LIGHTNING
ABSORBED	NONE
NULL	POISON

CARNICOS II

HP	1100
EP	0
BL	90
INFO	MACHINE
TGT	RANDOM
EXP	170
SP	2
G	35
N ITEM	SCRAP IRON
R ITEM	JUNKED CIRCUIT
S ITEM	SCRAP IRON
STRONG	ICE
WEAK	FIRE, LIGHTNING
ABSORBED	NONE
NULL	POISON

CERA 6 S

HP	6000
INFO	MACHINE
TGT	HP KILLER
EXP	250
SP	5
G	320
N ITEM	ETHER CORE
R ITEM	NANO REPAIR M
STRONG	NONE
WEAK	NONE
ABSORBED	NONE
NULL	NONE

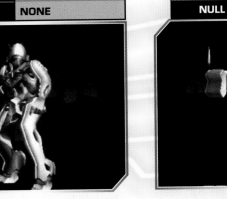

CERA 7 S

HP	5000
INFO	MACHINE
TGT	RANDOM
EXP	250
SP	5
G	310
N ITEM	ETHER CORE
R ITEM	DOWN REPAIR
STRONG	NONE
WEAK	LIGHTNING
ABSORBED	NONE
NULL	NONE

CITRINE

HP	29000
EP	220
BL	400
INFO	BIOLOGICAL (HUMAN)
TGT	???
EXP	13000
SP	20
G	10000
N ITEM	WEAPON DEVELOPMENT AREA KEY
R ITEM	NONE
S ITEM	CRESCENT MOON
STRONG	FIRE
WEAK	BEAM
ABSORBED	NONE
NULL	POISON

COMBAT REALIAN A

HP	1000
EP	17
BL	60
INFO	BIOLOGICAL (HUMAN)
TGT	BREAK KILLER
EXP	118
SP	2
G	36
N ITEM	MED KIT S
R ITEM	MED KIT M
S ITEM	FIRE WALL
STRONG	NONE
WEAK	ICE
ABSORBED	NONE
NULL	NONE

COMBAT REALIAN B

HP	760
EP	14
BL	60
INFO	BIOLOGICAL (HUMAN)
TGT	BREAK KILLER
EXP	115
SP	2
G	36
N ITEM	MED KIT S
R ITEM	MED KIT M
S ITEM	THUNDER WALL
STRONG	NONE
WEAK	FIRE
ABSORBED	NONE
NULL	NONE

INTRODUCTION
ARCHIVES
CHARACTERS
TACTICAL FILES
EQUIPMENT
THREAT ASSESSMENT
REGIONAL ANALYSIS
SUPPLEMENTAL DATA

CRUSTATA

HP	4100
EP	166
BL	90
INFO	GNOSIS
TGT	RANDOM
EXP	223
SP	5
G	330
N ITEM	MED KIT M
R ITEM	NULLIFIER
S ITEM	MED KIT S
STRONG	BEAM
WEAK	FIRE
ABSORBED	ICE
NULL	NONE

DEION

HP	3000
EP	170
BL	90
INFO	GNOSIS
TGT	RECOVERY KILLER
EXP	230
SP	4
G	400
N ITEM	WHITE FRAGMENT
R ITEM	IMPERIAL
S ITEM	ANTI-CRYSTAL
STRONG	BEAM
WEAK	FIRE, ICE
ABSORBED	LIGHTNING
NULL	POISON

DMITRI YURIEV

HP	46000
EP	770
BL	700
INFO	BIOLOGICAL (HUMAN)
TGT	???
EXP	15000
SP	30
G	10000
N ITEM	GOD'S EXPERIENCE
R ITEM	NONE
S ITEM	GENERAL'S BRACELET
STRONG	FIRE, ICE, LIGHTNING
WEAK	NONE
ABSORBED	NONE
NULL	POISON, SEAL ETHER, SEAL BOOST, REFLECT DAMAGE

DOMO-ALPHA

HP	880
EP	0
BL	60
INFO	MACHINE
TGT	RECOVERY KILLER
EXP	142
SP	2
G	18
N ITEM	SCRAP IRON
R ITEM	ETHER PACK S
S ITEM	JUNKED CIRCUIT
STRONG	ICE
WEAK	FIRE, LIGHTNING
ABSORBED	NONE
NULL	POISON

DOMO-BETA

HP	1100
EP	0
BL	60
INFO	MACHINE
TGT	BREAK KILLER
EXP	143
SP	2
G	20
N ITEM	SCRAP IRON
R ITEM	ETHER PACK S
S ITEM	JUNKED CIRCUIT
STRONG	FIRE
WEAK	ICE, LIGHTNING
ABSORBED	NONE
NULL	POISON

E2 HAUSER

HP	2500
EP	0
BL	120
INFO	MACHINE
TGT	RANDOM
EXP	210
SP	3
G	120
N ITEM	SCRAP IRON
R ITEM	JUNKED CIRCUIT
S ITEM	NONE
STRONG	ICE
WEAK	LIGHTNING
ABSORBED	NONE
NULL	POISON

INTRODUCTION
ARCHIVES
CHARACTERS
TACTICAL FILES
EQUIPMENT
THREAT ASSESSMENT
REGIONAL ANALYSIS
SUPPLEMENTAL DATA

ERDE KAISER SIGMA

HP	100000
EP	999
BL	999
INFO	MACHINE
TGT	???
EXP	60000
SP	1000
G	20000
N ITEM	GUSTAV WRIST
R ITEM	NONE
S ITEM	NONE
STRONG	NONE
WEAK	BEAM
ABSORBED	NONE
NULL	POISON, SEAL ETHER, SEAL BOOST, REFLECT DAMAGE

E.S. DAN

HP	800000
INFO	MACHINE
TGT	???
EXP	23000
SP	40
G	12000
N ITEM	D-EN III
R ITEM	NONE
STRONG	NONE
WEAK	NONE
ABSORBED	NONE
NULL	NONE

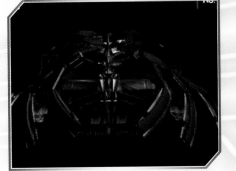

E.S. GAD

HP	280000
INFO	MACHINE
TGT	???
EXP	15000
SP	40
G	4500
N ITEM	D-NULLIFY EVADE
R ITEM	NONE
STRONG	NONE
WEAK	LIGHTNING
ABSORBED	NONE
NULL	NONE

E.S. ISSACHAR

HP	500000
INFO	MACHINE
TGT	???
EXP	17000
SP	40
G	10000
N ITEM	C-US10
R ITEM	NONE
STRONG	NONE
WEAK	NONE
ABSORBED	NONE
NULL	NONE

E.S. JOSEPH

HP	350000
INFO	MACHINE
TGT	???
EXP	15000
SP	40
G	4500
N ITEM	D-HALF PHYSICAL
R ITEM	NONE
STRONG	NONE
WEAK	FIRE
ABSORBED	NONE
NULL	NONE

E.S. LEVI

HP	900000
INFO	MACHINE
TGT	???
EXP	28000
SP	40
G	14000
N ITEM	D-TYPE M
R ITEM	NONE
STRONG	NONE
WEAK	NONE
ABSORBED	NONE
NULL	NONE

E.S. NAPHTALI

HP	85000
INFO	MACHINE
TGT	???
EXP	1900
SP	10
G	580
N ITEM	D-COUNTER
R ITEM	NONE
STRONG	NONE
WEAK	NONE
ABSORBED	NONE
NULL	NONE

FEDERATION SOLDIER A

HP	230
EP	7
BL	30
INFO	BIOLOGICAL (HUMAN)
TGT	RANDOM
EXP	40
SP	1
G	20
N ITEM	MED KIT S
R ITEM	MED KIT M
S ITEM	I.D. PLATE
STRONG	NONE
WEAK	ICE
ABSORBED	NONE
NULL	NONE

FEDERATION SOLDIER B

HP	150
EP	4
BL	30
INFO	BIOLOGICAL (HUMAN)
TGT	BREAK KILLER
EXP	40
SP	1
G	20
N ITEM	MED KIT S
R ITEM	MED KIT M
S ITEM	I.D. PLATE
STRONG	NONE
WEAK	FIRE
ABSORBED	NONE
NULL	NONE

GADREEL

HP	4900
EP	234
BL	60
INFO	GNOSIS
TGT	RANDOM
EXP	250
SP	5
G	550
N ITEM	CRYSTAL OF SPITE
R ITEM	SKILL UPGRADE C
S ITEM	MED KIT M
STRONG	LIGHTNING
WEAK	ICE
ABSORBED	BEAM
NULL	POISON

GOBLIN

HP	850
EP	66
BL	90
INFO	GNOSIS
TGT	RANDOM
EXP	84
SP	1
G	50
N ITEM	SALT PILLAR
R ITEM	ANTI-CRYSTAL
S ITEM	SALT PILLAR
STRONG	NONE
WEAK	LIGHTNING
ABSORBED	NONE
NULL	NONE

GREMLIN

HP	600
EP	198
BL	60
INFO	GNOSIS
TGT	RANDOM
EXP	88
SP	1
G	45
N ITEM	SALT PILLAR
R ITEM	ANTI-CRYSTAL
S ITEM	SALT PILLAR
STRONG	ICE
WEAK	FIRE
ABSORBED	NONE
NULL	NONE

IBLIS

HP	5300
EP	263
BL	60
INFO	GNOSIS
TGT	RECOVERY KILLER
EXP	260
SP	5
G	550
N ITEM	CRYSTAL OF SPITE
R ITEM	SKILL UPGRADE C
S ITEM	MED KIT M
STRONG	ICE
WEAK	FIRE
ABSORBED	BEAM
NULL	NONE

KAZFA JINA

HP	4000
EP	97
BL	120
INFO	GNOSIS
TGT	RANDOM
EXP	256
SP	4
G	880
N ITEM	WHITE FRAGMENT
R ITEM	CORAL STONE
S ITEM	ANTI-CRYSTAL
STRONG	NONE
WEAK	ICE, BEAM
ABSORBED	NONE
NULL	FIRE

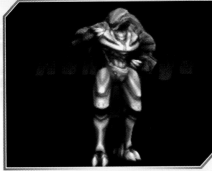

LEUPOLD

HP	6000
EP	0
BL	480
INFO	MACHINE
TGT	???
EXP	3500
SP	15
G	550
N ITEM	REJUVENATOR M
R ITEM	REJUVENATOR L
S ITEM	ETHER PACK M
STRONG	FIRE
WEAK	ICE, LIGHTNING
ABSORBED	NONE
NULL	POISON

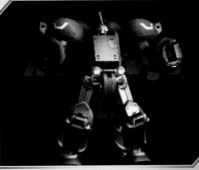

LEVIAT

HP	5800
INFO	MACHINE
TGT	RANDOM
EXP	265
SP	5
G	300
N ITEM	ETHER CORE
R ITEM	HALF REPAIR
STRONG	NONE
WEAK	FIRE, BEAM
ABSORBED	NONE
NULL	NONE

LEVIAT OFFICER

HP	9500
INFO	MACHINE
TGT	HP KILLER
EXP	280
SP	5
G	550
N ITEM	ETHER CORE
R ITEM	D-SP II
STRONG	NONE
WEAK	NONE
ABSORBED	NONE
NULL	NONE

MAI

HP	6000
EP	70
BL	300
INFO	BIOLOGICAL (HUMAN)
TGT	???
EXP	3500
SP	15
G	620
N ITEM	DECODER 11
R ITEM	NONE
S ITEM	KAJIC NECK
STRONG	LIGHTNING
WEAK	NONE
ABSORBED	NONE
NULL	POISON, HEAT

MANTICORE

HP	250
EP	99
BL	30
INFO	GNOSIS
TGT	RECOVERY KILLER
EXP	79
SP	1
G	40
N ITEM	SALT PILLAR
R ITEM	ETHER PACK S
S ITEM	SALT PILLAR
STRONG	NONE
WEAK	FIRE
ABSORBED	NONE
NULL	POISON

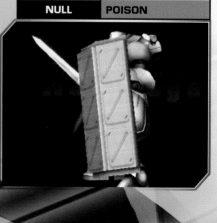

MARANATHA

HP	7500
INFO	MACHINE
TGT	RANDOM
EXP	265
SP	5
G	320
N ITEM	ETHER CORE
R ITEM	ALL REPAIR
STRONG	NONE
WEAK	BEAM
ABSORBED	NONE
NULL	NONE

MERCURIO GM

HP	3300
EP	0
BL	150
INFO	MACHINE
TGT	RANDOM
EXP	244
SP	3
G	380
N ITEM	JUNKED CIRCUIT
R ITEM	ETHER CORE
S ITEM	NONE
STRONG	FIRE
WEAK	ICE, BEAM
ABSORBED	NONE
NULL	POISON

MERCURIO GS

HP	2700
EP	0
BL	150
INFO	MACHINE
TGT	BREAK KILLER
EXP	240
SP	3
G	380
N ITEM	JUNKED CIRCUIT
R ITEM	ETHER CORE
S ITEM	NONE
STRONG	FIRE
WEAK	LIGHTNING, BEAM
ABSORBED	NONE
NULL	POISON

NATUS FLAMMA

HP	230000
INFO	GNOSIS
TGT	???
EXP	13250
SP	30
G	8000
N ITEM	ZF-RYBEUS
R ITEM	NONE
STRONG	FIRE
WEAK	NONE
ABSORBED	NONE
NULL	NONE

NATUS GLACIES

HP	250000
INFO	GNOSIS
TGT	???
EXP	13250
SP	30
G	8000
N ITEM	AF-STEALTH II
R ITEM	NONE
STRONG	ICE
WEAK	NONE
ABSORBED	NONE
NULL	NONE

NATUS LUMEN

HP	225000
INFO	GNOSIS
TGT	???
EXP	13250
SP	30
G	8000
N ITEM	RF-ACALA
R ITEM	NONE
STRONG	BEAM
WEAK	NONE
ABSORBED	NONE
NULL	NONE

NATUS TELLUS

HP	250000
INFO	GNOSIS
TGT	???
EXP	13250
SP	30
G	8000
N ITEM	DF-XX
R ITEM	NONE
STRONG	LIGHTNING
WEAK	NONE
ABSORBED	NONE
NULL	NONE

0-78 GRISLY 1

HP	900
EP	0
BL	60
INFO	MACHINE
TGT	RANDOM
EXP	135
SP	2
G	25
N ITEM	SCRAP IRON
R ITEM	JUNKED CIRCUIT
S ITEM	SCRAP IRON
STRONG	NONE
WEAK	LIGHTNING
ABSORBED	NONE
NULL	POISON

0-78 GRISLY 2

HP	1300
EP	0
BL	90
INFO	MACHINE
TGT	RANDOM
EXP	155
SP	3
G	45
N ITEM	SCRAP IRON
R ITEM	JUNKED CIRCUIT
S ITEM	SCRAP IRON
STRONG	NONE
WEAK	LIGHTNING
ABSORBED	NONE
NULL	POISON

OMEGA ID

HP	999999
INFO	MACHINE
TGT	???
EXP	38000
SP	120
G	16000
N ITEM	DECODER 06
R ITEM	NONE
STRONG	NONE
WEAK	LIGHTNING
ABSORBED	NONE
NULL	FIRE

OMEGA METAMPSYCHOSIS

HP	450000
INFO	MACHINE
TGT	???
EXP	20000
SP	30
G	20000
N ITEM	D-ANIMA
R ITEM	NONE
STRONG	NONE
WEAK	NONE
ABSORBED	NONE
NULL	NONE

OMEGA UNIVERSITAS

HP	200000
INFO	MACHINE
TGT	???
EXP	4900
SP	15
G	2600
N ITEM	D-EN I
R ITEM	NONE
STRONG	NONE
WEAK	NONE
ABSORBED	NONE
NULL	NONE

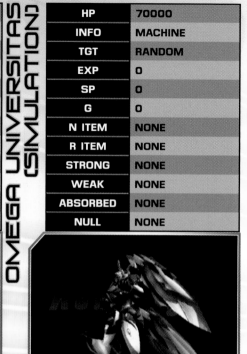

OMEGA UNIVERSITAS (SIMULATION)

HP	70000
INFO	MACHINE
TGT	RANDOM
EXP	0
SP	0
G	0
N ITEM	NONE
R ITEM	NONE
STRONG	NONE
WEAK	NONE
ABSORBED	NONE
NULL	NONE

PELLEGRI

HP	12000
EP	400
BL	300
INFO	BIOLOGICAL (HUMAN)
TGT	???
EXP	5400
SP	15
G	2900
N ITEM	GRAND DESIGN
R ITEM	NONE
S ITEM	DOUBLE VESTMENT
STRONG	FIRE, LIGHTNING
WEAK	ICE
ABSORBED	NONE
NULL	POISON

PELLEGRI'S SOLDIER

HP	4000
EP	44
BL	60
INFO	BIOLOGICAL (HUMAN)
TGT	RECOVERY KILLER
EXP	250
SP	15
G	120
N ITEM	SKILL UPGRADE A
R ITEM	NONE
S ITEM	NONE
STRONG	ICE
WEAK	FIRE, LIGHTNING
ABSORBED	NONE
NULL	NONE

PERUN

HP	6500
EP	294
BL	90
INFO	GNOSIS
TGT	BREAK KILLER
EXP	276
SP	5
G	1200
N ITEM	ETHER PACK S
R ITEM	VELVET BREATH
S ITEM	CRYSTAL OF SPITE
STRONG	NONE
WEAK	BEAM
ABSORBED	LIGHTNING
NULL	NONE

P.S.S. -A

HP	700
EP	25
BL	60
INFO	BIOLOGICAL
TGT	BREAK KILLER
EXP	140
SP	2
G	50
N ITEM	RANK BADGE
R ITEM	SKILL UPGRADE B
S ITEM	MED KIT M
STRONG	NONE
WEAK	ICE, LIGHTNING
ABSORBED	NONE
NULL	NONE

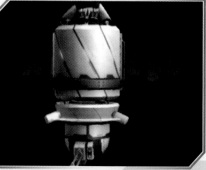

P.S.S. -B

HP	450
EP	17
BL	30
INFO	BIOLOGICAL (HUMAN)
TGT	BREAK KILLER
EXP	130
SP	2
G	45
N ITEM	I.D. PLATE
R ITEM	SKILL UPGRADE A
S ITEM	MED KIT M
STRONG	LIGHTNING
WEAK	NONE
ABSORBED	NONE
NULL	NONE

P.S.S. -C

HP	680
EP	27
BL	30
INFO	BIOLOGICAL (HUMAN)
TGT	RANDOM
EXP	154
SP	2
G	45
N ITEM	RANK BADGE
R ITEM	SKILL UPGRADE B
S ITEM	MED KIT M
STRONG	NONE
WEAK	ICE
ABSORBED	NONE
NULL	NONE

P.S.S. -F

HP	1000
EP	32
BL	45
INFO	BIOLOGICAL (HUMAN)
TGT	BREAK KILLER
EXP	154
SP	2
G	48
N ITEM	RANK BADGE
R ITEM	SKILL UPGRADE B
S ITEM	MED KIT M
STRONG	LIGHTNING
WEAK	BEAM
ABSORBED	NONE
NULL	NONE

P.S.S. -P

HP	520
EP	23
BL	30
INFO	BIOLOGICAL (HUMAN)
TGT	RECOVERY KILLER
EXP	128
SP	2
G	42
N ITEM	I.D. PLATE
R ITEM	SKILL UPGRADE A
S ITEM	MED KIT M
STRONG	LIGHTNING
WEAK	NONE
ABSORBED	NONE
NULL	NONE

P.S.S. P2

HP	590
EP	20
BL	30
INFO	BIOLOGICAL (HUMAN)
TGT	RECOVERY KILLER
EXP	135
SP	2
G	42
N ITEM	I.D. PLATE
R ITEM	SKILL UPGRADE A
S ITEM	MED KIT M
STRONG	NONE
WEAK	FIRE
ABSORBED	NONE
NULL	NONE

RED TESTAMENT

HP	12000
EP	355
BL	150
INFO	BIOLOGICAL
TGT	???
EXP	5000
SP	40
G	0
N ITEM	UNION RING
R ITEM	NONE
S ITEM	WHITE SHIRT
STRONG	NONE
WEAK	NONE
ABSORBED	NONE
NULL	POISON, HEAT

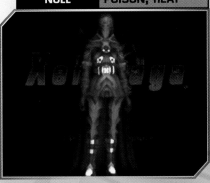

RED TESTAMENT: SECOND FORM

HP	52000
EP	999
BL	780
INFO	BIOLOGICAL
TGT	???
EXP	40000
SP	40
G	18000
N ITEM	KAJIC RING
R ITEM	NONE
S ITEM	VELVET PANNIER
STRONG	ICE, LIGHTNING
WEAK	NONE
ABSORBED	FIRE
NULL	POISON, HEAT, SEAL ETHER, SEAL BOOST, REFLECT DAMAGE

RED TESTAMENT'S ALLY

HP	9000
EP	256
BL	80
INFO	BIOLOGICAL (HUMAN)
TGT	???
EXP	5000
SP	40
G	0
N ITEM	REJUVENATOR DX
R ITEM	NONE
S ITEM	RESEARCH UNIFORM
STRONG	NONE
WEAK	NONE
ABSORBED	NONE
NULL	POISON, HEAT

?

SERRANINAE

HP	3700
EP	108
BL	45
INFO	GNOSIS
TGT	RECOVERY KILLER
EXP	220
SP	5
G	320
N ITEM	MED KIT M
R ITEM	CLEANSER
S ITEM	MED KIT S
STRONG	FIRE
WEAK	ICE
ABSORBED	NONE
NULL	POISON

SIGRDRIFA

HP	3000
EP	140
BL	120
INFO	GNOSIS
TGT	???
EXP	380
SP	10
G	100
N ITEM	NONE
R ITEM	ETHER PACK S
S ITEM	REVIVE M
STRONG	ICE
WEAK	NONE
ABSORBED	NONE
NULL	POISON

STANDARD U.R.T.V.

HP	670
EP	90
BL	45
INFO	BIOLOGICAL
TGT	RECOVERY KILLER
EXP	158
SP	3
G	40
N ITEM	I.D. PLATE
R ITEM	ETHER PACK S
S ITEM	GOD CIRCLE
STRONG	LIGHTNING
WEAK	BEAM
ABSORBED	NONE
NULL	NONE

STOLE ARMA

HP	3000
INFO	MACHINE
TGT	RANDOM
EXP	140
SP	2
G	34
N ITEM	JUNKED CIRCUIT
R ITEM	HALF REPAIR
STRONG	NONE
WEAK	NONE
ABSORBED	NONE
NULL	NONE

STOLE MARINE

HP	3000
INFO	MACHINE
TGT	RANDOM
EXP	140
SP	2
G	32
N ITEM	JUNKED CIRCUIT
R ITEM	HALF REPAIR
STRONG	NONE
WEAK	NONE
ABSORBED	NONE
NULL	NONE

STRIBOG

HP	6400
EP	381
BL	90
INFO	GNOSIS
TGT	BREAK KILLER
EXP	276
SP	5
G	1200
N ITEM	REVIVE M
R ITEM	UNION WRIST
S ITEM	CRYSTAL OF SPITE
STRONG	BEAM
WEAK	FIRE
ABSORBED	ICE
NULL	NONE

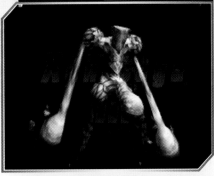

SVAROZIC

HP	6600
EP	322
BL	90
INFO	GNOSIS
TGT	BREAK KILLER
EXP	276
SP	5
G	1200
N ITEM	MED KIT L
R ITEM	KAJIC WRIST
S ITEM	CRYSTAL OF SPITE
STRONG	NONE
WEAK	ICE
ABSORBED	FIRE
NULL	NONE

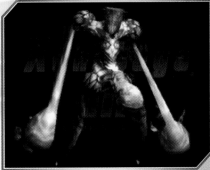

T183 OCULUS

HP	900
INFO	MACHINE
TGT	RANDOM
EXP	63
SP	1
G	30
N ITEM	DOWN REPAIR
R ITEM	JUNKED CIRCUIT
STRONG	NONE
WEAK	NONE
ABSORBED	NONE
NULL	NONE

T190 DENS

HP	1200
INFO	MACHINE
TGT	RANDOM
EXP	63
SP	1
G	30
N ITEM	DOWN REPAIR
R ITEM	JUNKED CIRCUIT
STRONG	NONE
WEAK	NONE
ABSORBED	NONE
NULL	NONE

T-ELOS

HP	7500
EP	250
BL	360
INFO	MACHINE AND HUMAN
TGT	???
EXP	2800
SP	10
G	720
N ITEM	MED KIT L
R ITEM	REVIVE M
S ITEM	GREEN OASIS
STRONG	BEAM
WEAK	LIGHTNING
ABSORBED	NONE
NULL	POISON

INTRODUCTION
ARCHIVES
CHARACTERS
TACTICAL FILES
EQUIPMENT
THREAT ASSESSMENT
REGIONAL ANALYSIS
SUPPLEMENTAL DATA

T-ELOS (LATE GAME)

HP	56000
EP	530
BL	720
INFO	MACHINE AND HUMAN
TGT	???
EXP	32000
SP	40
G	16000
N ITEM	KAP-VEL
R ITEM	NONE
S ITEM	LIFE DEMON
STRONG	FIRE
WEAK	NONE
ABSORBED	NONE
NULL	POISON

U-TIC SOLDIER A

HP	365
EP	14
BL	30
INFO	BIOLOGICAL (HUMAN)
TGT	RANDOM
EXP	80
SP	2
G	30
N ITEM	MED KIT S
R ITEM	REMOVER
S ITEM	I.D. PLATE
STRONG	NONE
WEAK	ICE
ABSORBED	NONE
NULL	NONE

U-TIC SOLDIER B

HP	290
EP	11
BL	30
INFO	BIOLOGICAL (HUMAN)
TGT	BREAK KILLER
EXP	82
SP	2
G	30
N ITEM	MED KIT S
R ITEM	ANTIDOTE
S ITEM	I.D. PLATE
STRONG	NONE
WEAK	FIRE
ABSORBED	NONE
NULL	NONE

V.G.S. EINS

HP	300
EP	0
BL	60
INFO	MACHINE
TGT	RANDOM
EXP	45
SP	1
G	10
N ITEM	SCRAP IRON
R ITEM	MED KIT M
S ITEM	MED KIT S
STRONG	ICE
WEAK	LIGHTING, BEAM
ABSORBED	NONE
NULL	POISON

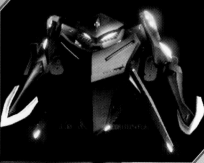

V.G.S. EINS R

HP	2300
EP	0
BL	120
INFO	MACHINE
TGT	RECOVERY KILLER
EXP	220
SP	3
G	300
N ITEM	JUNKED CIRCUIT
R ITEM	MED KIT M
S ITEM	NONE
STRONG	ICE
WEAK	FIRE
ABSORBED	NONE
NULL	POISON

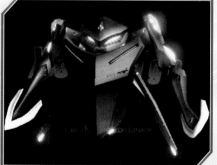

V.G.S. ZWEI

HP	380
EP	0
BL	60
INFO	MACHINE
TGT	BREAK KILLER
EXP	45
SP	1
G	12
N ITEM	SCRAP IRON
R ITEM	MED KIT M
S ITEM	MED KIT S
STRONG	FIRE
WEAK	ICE, BEAM
ABSORBED	NONE
NULL	POISON

V.G.S. ZWEI R

HP	2800
EP	0
BL	120
INFO	MACHINE
TGT	RANDOM
EXP	221
SP	3
G	350
N ITEM	JUNKED CIRCUIT
R ITEM	MED KIT M
S ITEM	NONE
STRONG	FIRE
WEAK	ICE
ABSORBED	NONE
NULL	POISON

V.M.P. ELF

HP	85
EP	0
BL	30
INFO	MACHINE
TGT	RANDOM
EXP	43
SP	1
G	12
N ITEM	SCRAP IRON
R ITEM	MED KIT S
S ITEM	MED KIT S
STRONG	LIGHTNING
WEAK	ICE, BEAM
ABSORBED	NONE
NULL	POISON

V.M.P. SECHS

HP	80
EP	0
BL	30
INFO	MACHINE
TGT	RANDOM
EXP	38
SP	1
G	10
N ITEM	SCRAP IRON
R ITEM	MED KIT S
S ITEM	MED KIT S
STRONG	ICE
WEAK	FIRE, LIGHTNING, BEAM
ABSORBED	NONE
NULL	POISON

VRA-2100

HP	4800
INFO	MACHINE
TGT	HP KILLER
EXP	180
SP	3
G	350
N ITEM	ETHER CORE
R ITEM	ALL REPAIR
STRONG	NONE
WEAK	BEAM
ABSORBED	NONE
NULL	NONE

VRA-2100 ST

HP	8000
INFO	MACHINE
TGT	HP KILLER
EXP	225
SP	4
G	280
N ITEM	ETHER CORE
R ITEM	ALL REPAIR
STRONG	FIRE
WEAK	LIGHTNING, BEAM
ABSORBED	NONE
NULL	NONE

VRA-3500

HP	4000
INFO	MACHINE
TGT	RANDOM
EXP	180
SP	3
G	300
N ITEM	ETHER CORE
R ITEM	NANO REPAIR DX
STRONG	NONE
WEAK	FIRE
ABSORBED	NONE
NULL	NONE

INTRODUCTION

ARCHIVES

CHARACTERS

TACTICAL FILES

EQUIPMENT

THREAT ASSESSMENT

REGIONAL ANALYSIS

SUPPLEMENTAL DATA

VRA-3500 ST

HP	5000
INFO	MACHINE
TGT	RANDOM
EXP	220
SP	4
G	270
N ITEM	ETHER CORE
R ITEM	NANO REPAIR DX
STRONG	BEAM
WEAK	FIRE
ABSORBED	NONE
NULL	NONE

VX-7000

HP	850
EP	0
BL	90
INFO	MACHINE
TGT	RANDOM
EXP	100
SP	2
G	90
N ITEM	JUNKED CIRCUIT
R ITEM	ETHER CORE
S ITEM	JUNKED CIRCUIT
STRONG	ICE, BEAM
WEAK	FIRE
ABSORBED	NONE
NULL	POISON

VX-7000 M

HP	3700
EP	0
BL	150
INFO	MACHINE
TGT	RANDOM
EXP	255
SP	3
G	900
N ITEM	ETHER CORE
R ITEM	SKILL UPGRADE B
S ITEM	NONE
STRONG	BEAM
WEAK	FIRE, LIGHTNING
ABSORBED	NONE
NULL	POISON

VX-9000

HP	4300
EP	0
BL	150
INFO	MACHINE
TGT	RANDOM
EXP	270
SP	3
G	1100
N ITEM	ETHER CORE
R ITEM	SKILL UPGRADE B
S ITEM	JUNKED CIRCUIT
STRONG	BEAM
WEAK	FIRE, ICE
ABSORBED	NONE
NULL	POISON

VX-9000 K

HP	5700
EP	0
BL	150
INFO	MACHINE
TGT	RANDOM
EXP	290
SP	4
G	750
N ITEM	ETHER CORE
R ITEM	GREEN STAR
S ITEM	JUNKED CIRCUIT
STRONG	BEAM
WEAK	FIRE, LIGHTNING
ABSORBED	NONE
NULL	POISON

YACUD CANNON

HP	1000
INFO	MACHINE
TGT	RANDOM
EXP	120
SP	2
G	38
N ITEM	SCRAP IRON
R ITEM	NANO REPAIR M
STRONG	NONE
WEAK	NONE
ABSORBED	NONE
NULL	NONE

YACUB CANNON REVISED

HP	2500
INFO	MACHINE
TGT	RANDOM
EXP	243
SP	5
G	250
N ITEM	JUNKED CIRCUIT
R ITEM	ETHER CORE
STRONG	NONE
WEAK	NONE
ABSORBED	NONE
NULL	NONE

YURIEV SOLDIER A

HP	260
EP	10
BL	30
INFO	BIOLOGICAL (HUMAN)
TGT	RANDOM
EXP	43
SP	1
G	25
N ITEM	ANTIDOTE
R ITEM	MED KIT M
S ITEM	I.D. PLATE
STRONG	NONE
WEAK	ICE
ABSORBED	NONE
NULL	NONE

YURIEV SOLDIER B

HP	200
EP	7
BL	30
INFO	BIOLOGICAL (HUMAN)
TGT	BREAK KILLER
EXP	43
SP	1
G	25
N ITEM	REMOVER
R ITEM	MED KIT M
S ITEM	I.D. PLATE
STRONG	NONE
WEAK	FIRE
ABSORBED	NONE
NULL	NONE

ZARATHUSTRA

HP	70000
EP	999
BL	999
INFO	MACHINE
TGT	???
EXP	0
SP	0
G	0
N ITEM	NONE
R ITEM	NONE
S ITEM	NONE
STRONG	FIRE, ICE, LIGHTNING, BEAM
WEAK	NONE
ABSORBED	NONE
NULL	POISON, HEAT, SEAL ETHER, SEAL BOOST, REFLECT DAMAGE

ZOLFO RG

HP	2900
EP	0
BL	150
INFO	MACHINE
TGT	RECOVERY KILLER
EXP	244
SP	3
G	400
N ITEM	JUNKED CIRCUIT
R ITEM	ETHER CORE
S ITEM	NONE
STRONG	FIRE
WEAK	ICE, LIGHTNING
ABSORBED	NONE
NULL	POISON

ZOLFO RS

HP	2400
EP	0
BL	150
INFO	MACHINE
TGT	RANDOM
EXP	242
SP	3
G	400
N ITEM	JUNKED CIRCUIT
R ITEM	ETHER CORE
S ITEM	NONE
STRONG	FIRE
WEAK	ICE, BEAM
ABSORBED	NONE
NULL	POISON

INTRODUCTION

ARCHIVES

CHARACTERS

TACTICAL FILES

EQUIPMENT

THREAT ASSESSMENT

REGIONAL ANALYSIS

SUPPLEMENTAL DATA

KOS-MOS

INTRODUCTION

ARCHIVES

CHARACTERS

TACTICAL FILES

EQUIPMENT

THREAT ASSESSMENT

REGIONAL ANALYSIS

SUPPLEMENTAL DATA

REGIONAL ANALYSIS

This section offers a vast array of scanned intelligence regarding every area and monster in the game. Through amazing advances in neutral networking, our computer systems are able to predict where all foes, traps, points of interest, and treasure are located. Those are presented here, along with any appropriate actions that need to be taken by your party.

A VISIT TO VECTOR

There are too many things left unexplained for Shion. Though there have been victories in the past she feels like Vector, and even her own father, have left too many ghosts and half-truths in their wake. Not only has Shion left Vector (the company that helped her create the amazing KOS-MOS), but she is now actively investigating their records. Though illegal, she is undaunted by the risks. With the help of several allies, she has come to the S-Line Division, where Vector keeps many of its records of greatest importance.

Shion, Miyuki, Doctus, and Canaan fly into the area, fighting their way through a number of enemies. After making a successful and relatively safe landing, Doctus parts with the group, leaving the other three to infiltrate on foot. Canaan can take hits much better than the others, Miyuki is very effective at frustrating foes, and Shion is (as always) a magnificent support character.

VECTOR S-LINE DIVISION: SECTOR 1

POINTS OF INTEREST	
1	ELECTRIC GATE
2	SIMPLE PUZZLE
3	SEGMENT ADDRESS 8
4	SIDE CORRIDOR
5	COLOR PUZZLE

ITEMS	
1	50G
2	SEGMENT ADDRESS 8
3	ANALYZE BALL
4	100G
5	NANO REPAIR M
6	300G
7	ANTIDOTE
8	ANALYZE BALL

ENEMIES
NONE

After landing, the group is placed under your control. Use the analog stick to move toward the yellow **Save Point** that is nearby. These are locations where you can record your progress through the game and recover from damage taken by the group.

Past that point, down the only hallway, is an electric gate that cannot be passed. To destroy this, press ◉. This locks onto targets in the world and allows your group to interact with them. Shion destroys the gate in this fashion and clears the way.

Use this technique to activate the two electric devices past the gateway. Doing so unlocks the far doorway and allows the group to advance into the building ahead. There, you find out that it is possible to switch between targets using  and . The small puzzle ahead gives you a chance to really try this out; switch between targets to destroy the large container first, then use the light blue platform before activating the red one. This clears the way (if you make a mistake, use the console in front to reset the puzzle).

Break all of the containers as you go, as there are extra items to be found out there. Toward the end of the hall, the first of these is discovered (50G, free of charge).

Take the door that opens into the next hallway, on the right. As you move through, take a look at the Segment Address that is locked away on the upper side of the passage. This cannot be opened until you find a Decoder that corresponds to **Segment Address 08**. That box has Tears River, though you won't be able to get it until after you gain access to the EVS later in the game.

More treats are along the small area that breaks off to the right before the major room at the end of the hall. Take this and destroy everything as you go (400G, an Analyze Ball, and a Nano Repair M await). The fun ends when you blast your way back into the main corridor. Walk into the large room ahead.

Inside the room, there are tougher breakable containers that require several shots each (there is one on each side of the chamber). Destroy them, then move to the center of the room for a puzzle. Remember the order of the colors that appear when the group enters the circle beyond. These are randomly generated, so it's just a matter of memory. There will only be four colors, yet there are five banners that spin around the group, so be doubly sure not to hit the wrong banner. Press ● as the corresponding colors pass by, using the same order that you saw initially. The console on the walkway resets the puzzle if you make a mistake. The next sector opens once you succeed!

INTRODUCTION
ARCHIVES
CHARACTERS
TACTICAL FILES
EQUIPMENT
THREAT ASSESSMENT
REGIONAL ANALYSIS
SUPPLEMENTAL DATA

VECTOR S-LINE DIVISION: SECTOR 2

POINTS OF INTEREST	
NONE	

ITEMS	
1	MED KIT S
2	MED KIT M
3	REMOVER
4	300G
5	NANO REPAIR M

ENEMIES	
1	V.M.P. SECH

Use the **Save Point** near the base of the transportation system, then walk to the left side of the new sector. The side walkway turns to the right, leading toward an obvious mechanical guard unit. It's time to learn how to get things done, so run on over to it and start the fight.

This first fight is extremely simple. The two V.M.P. Sechs are very weak, do little damage, and are meant to be rolled over. Just use normal attacks on them and study how the bar in the upper-left informs you of your group's attack timing in comparison to enemy actions.

If you were hurt in the fight at all, return to the original path and take the route to the left instead (a container over there has a Med Kit S). Though the path forms a dead end, this is a quick fix for any health issues.

Past the V.M.P. Sechs' area, the way left is blocked, the path forward has another fight, and the right route has a couple of items in containers (a Med Kit M and a Remover, which is used to restore proper abilities when an ally is negatively afflicted).

The second Sechs fight is even easier than the first, as you are probably more comfortable with what is going on. This time, try to take out the first Sech quickly, then use the Boost system to squeeze a free attack in before the second Sech even has a turn.

Use Boost by holding down ⬛ or ⬛, then press the button that corresponds to the character that you want to have attack next.

Two more fights follow, as your group learns about back attacks. Back attacks offer an immense advantage in lesser encounters, and it's almost always worth a few moments of preparation time if you think that such an ambush can succeed. In this area, the next Sech group is always going to have its back facing your direction, and the final group patrols in a circle (making it a very simple attack to jump them as well). Take the transporter down to Sector 3 when you are finished with collecting the treasure here.

VECTOR S-LINE DIVISION: SECTOR 3

POINTS OF INTEREST	
1	GREEN TERMINAL
2	YELLOW TERMINAL
3	PURPLE TERMINAL
4	RED TERMINAL

ITEMS	
1	UPDATE FILE 01
2	100G
3	ANTIDOTE
4	REVIVE M
5	MED KIT S

ENEMIES	
1	V.M.P. ELF
2	V.M.P. SECH

Don't worry about the bridges here; though thin, there is no way that anyone in your group is going to be careless enough to fall off. Move to the left, then down into the main portion of the area. Explore to the right first, using the terminal there to raise a green bridge. Keep an eye out for **Update File 01**, an optional additional to your Database that is part of a mission that spans the entire game. Crossing the new portion of the bridge, you get into a fight (this time with one Sech and a slightly tougher Elf). Past these, there is a chest for 100G.

Explore south of the green bridge too, and look for a second bridge terminal. This one raises a yellow bridge on the left side of the area.

INTRODUCTION
ARCHIVES
CHARACTERS
TACTICAL FILES
EQUIPMENT
THREAT ASSESSMENT
REGIONAL ANALYSIS
SUPPLEMENTAL DATA

THE DANGERS OF BREAKING

It's a lot of fun to break all of the containers in the area, but some of them have enemies that trigger when the box/item is destroyed. Instead of treasure, you end up with an encounter. Ultimately, this leads to more experience and treasure, so it's not such a bad thing. However, be certain to keep health as high as possible at all times (you never know when a fight is coming).

The yellow bridge on the left takes the group down to the base of the map then around to the far right. It's a long route, but there are only empty containers in your way for most of the trip. At the end, there is a purple station that raises two sections of bridgework.

Before trying to take the closer purple bridge, toward the end of the map, return to the yellow terminal. From there, seek the secondary portion of purple bridge that was formed; this is very close by. The new bridge gets your group to a chest with a Revive M; these are somewhat rare for now, so it's extremely good to have around. A red terminal there adds another bridge to connect the left and right areas with a shorter walk.

Move to the upper-right side of the map and use the transporter to descend another level.

VECTOR S-LINE DIVISION: SECTOR 4

POINTS OF INTEREST	
NONE	

ITEMS	
1	TRAP X 10
2	ETHER PACK S

ENEMIES	
1	V.M.P. ELF
2	V.M.P. SECH

Walk toward the containers ahead, and don't be too alarmed when the way closes behind you. Nobody was turning back either way, and these mechanical guards aren't posing much of a threat to you.

Notice that the containers have a couple sets of Traps inside them. This is a good thing! The guards ahead have to face your group at a major disadvantage; this time, the system walks you through the traps. For the future, use ▨ + ⬤ to set a trap, and ⬤ to detonate them. This aids in the next fight by avoiding enemy back attacks, increasing your starting Boost, and by granting early initiative to your characters instead of your enemies.

When you obliterate the encounter, it opens the doors ahead. There is a circle on the other side of the door that is guarded by several groups (some Vech/Elf encounters, while others are double Elf encounters). In all cases, the fights are so easy that the traps are only needed if you want to practice your skills. Otherwise, race around the circle in the opposite direction from the patrollers and clean them up. Be sure to keep using either Boost for fights where the enemies never get an attack, or save up two Boosts for a Special Attack and some increased experience. Before leaving, clear the center fight and take the Ether Pack S from the chest there.

VECTOR S-LINE DIVISION: SECTOR 5

POINTS OF INTEREST	
1	SECONDARY SECURITY TERMINALS
2	PRIMARY SECURITY TERMINAL

ITEMS
NONE

ENEMIES	
1	SIGRDRIFA (BOSS)

Save and let your group rest at the **Save Point**, then take a look around at the bottom of the S-Line Division. It's a beautiful place to have a server, certainly. Take the short-range transporters on the left and right sides to disable both **Secondary Security Terminals**, then come back to the center and use the **Primary Security Terminal** at the top side to bring the rest of the measures down. This is a quick process, and you finish by accessing the central server from the main terminal. Get inside there and use the only console to get what you came for.

Bosses have a tendency to notice when happy players are busy stealing knowledge, so stay sharp. Sure enough, there is a powerful creature lurking about in the data flow. Without more than a few moments of warning, Sigrdrifa comes down and starts the first boss encounter of Xenosaga III!

SIGRDRIFA

HP:	3000
EP:	140
BL:	120
INFO:	GNOSIS
TGT:	???
EXP:	380
SP:	10
G:	100
N ITEM:	NONE
R ITEM:	ETHER PACK S
S ITEM:	REVIVE M
STRONG:	ICE
WEAK:	NONE
ABSORBED:	NONE
NULL:	POISON

This boss fight isn't too rough. The Save Point earlier put everyone in good shape in terms of health and ether points, so you have a lot to work with here. The tutorial pops up again to explain a bit about how enemies think; some of them attack randomly, others try to kill off healers, or your weakest group members. Still others do everything they can do put your people past their Break Limit.

EFFECTS OF BREAK STATUS

TARGET IS UNABLE TO ACT FOR TWO TURNS

NO BOOSTS CAN BE USED ON THE TARGET DURING THIS TIME

EVADE/GUARD IS IMPOSSIBLE

COUNTERATTACKS/REVENGE ALSO UNUSABLE

CRITICAL HITS LANDS FAR MORE OFTEN AGAINST THE TARGET

AT THE END OF THE BREAK PERIOD, THE TARGET'S BREAK GAUGE RETURNS TO ZERO

Sigrdrifa's early attacks are intended to put Shion into some real trouble. She'll accrue Break points quickly, and Break Mode is very bad news (more damage taken, no actions for your turns, and so forth). Avoid this by using Canaan's Heat Ether to taunt Sigrdrifa away from Shion after she has taken a hit or two.

Don't use your Boost lightly. Save it up while dealing as much damage as you can with Techniques. Miyuki is especially good here, because she can add quite a bit to your enemy's Break points, pushing him into the corner.

By the time the Break hits, your group should have two or three Boosts as well. Use these while Sigrdrifa's defense is broken; he'll take tons of damage and be unable to respond. Shion's Special Attack, when used at this time, is easily able to do over 400 damage. Not bad for a single attack, especially against an enemy with only 3,000 HPs!

Repeat this process a second time, but be ready for Sigrdrifa to lay on a lot more damage in the second half of the fight. Area attacks are used heavily, but unless you are slow to bring him down healing isn't very important. That said, don't be shy about healing if you start to drop down to 100 health or lower.

PEDEA ISLAND

Shion is back on Pedea Island now, in the flesh. She can explore by heading down the larger part of the beach to the right of where she begins; there is a **Save Point** not far away. To get back to Shion's little place, take the lower path back at the left side, then answer the PC message that Shion receives.

Approaching the palm trees on the beach brings up your targeting systems. Blast the trees to knock coconuts from the trees. Destroy the coconuts for extra items (including money and a Med Kit). Then, along the rocks to the north, there is a destroyable area with a Skill Upgrade A as well.

Many scenes follow, and this ends the tutorial phase of the game. Game as desired, and get ready to move into the main storyline.

MORE THAN MEETS THE EYE

Pedea Island has many hidden items. You find some of them now, if you search well, and quite a few are revealed later (once you return in the EVS).

On the right side of the island, through the water, there is a section of rocks around a small cave area. Search for a destroyable rock there; there is a door behind the rocks, and the Dark Professor's lab is discovered inside. Come there late in the game to face Erde Kaiser Sigma. If you look on the right side of the Dark Professor's base, there is a chair with a down arrow on it. Use that to access the secret base lower level. Segment Address 03 is down there. Update File 02 is as well.

If you wade into the water, notice that there are two suspicious rock pillars. One of these is south from a huge depression underneath the water. Destroy that pillar to reveal a box with Decoder 08.

Return to the island via EVS, and search by the small building where Shion has her computer. There is a chest with Shion's Swimsuit. This powerful item is quite good for criticals!

DURING THE APPROACH (E.S. COMBAT TUTORIAL)

With the extended dialogue scenes coming to a close, the action shifts to MOMO, Ziggy, chaos, Jin, and Jr. While moving to examine an area mentioned in the data stolen from Vector, Ormus craft close to engage the Elsa. This marks the beginning of your first E.S. battle.

Initially, the fighting is against six lesser craft that can't hold a candle to any of your advanced E.S.s. These can be defeated with any basic attack, so it's fun to shift around and see what several of the actions look like. Once there is only a single foe remaining, take the time to Charge all of your E.S.s to full strength. After this ends, you receive several Nano Repair M units and one or two Half Repairs.

E.S. BATTLE COMMANDS

NAME	FUNCTION
ATTACK	PERFORMS A STANDARD ATTACK, USING CRAFT ENERGY UNTIL DEPLETED
ANIMA	AWAKENS ANIMA AND USES SPECIAL ATTACKS; THE CRAFT MUST ACCUMULATE ANIMA BEFORE USING THESE
ITEM	USES A CONSUMABLE ITEM
CHARGE	RESTORES 15% OF THE CRAFT'S TOTAL HEALTH AND GUARDS UNTIL THE NEXT TURN BEGINS
ESCAPE	ATTEMPTS TO LEAVE THE BATTLE, THOUGH STORY/BOSS BATTLES CANNOT BE AVOIDED

E.S. ATTRIBUTES

NAME	PURPOSE
HIT POINTS	FUNCTION JUST LIKE NORMAL CHARACTER HIT POINTS, THOUGH FALLING TO ZERO TAKES THE E.S. OUT OF THE COMBAT FULLY (THEY CANNOT BE REVIVED)
ENERGY	FILLS TO FULL AT THE BEGINNING OF EACH TURN; THESE ARE USED TO UNLEASH A CRAFT'S NORMAL WEAPONS
POWER	THE COMBINATION OF THE PILOT AND CO-PILOT'S STR VALUES; DETERMINES THE PHYSICAL DAMAGE THE CRAFT CAN DEAL IN COMBAT
ARMOR	SUM OF THE PILOT AND CO-PILOT'S VIT VALUES; DECREASES PHYSICAL DAMAGE TAKEN BY THE CRAFT
ETHER ATTACK	THE SUM OF THE PILOT AND CO-PILOT'S EATK VALUES; DETERMINES THE ETHER DAMAGE DONE BY THE CRAFT
ETHER DEFENSE	SUM OF THE PILOT AND CO-PILOT'S EDEF; REDUCES ETHER DAMAGE RECEIVED
DEXTERITY	IS CALCULATED ONLY BY THE MAIN PILOT'S DEX VALUE; INCREASES THE CHANCE OF STRIKING ENEMIES
EVASION	ALSO CALCULATED OFF OF THE MAIN PILOT, BASED FROM THEIR EVA VALUE; IMPROVES THE CHANCE FOR THE CRAFT TO EVADE INCOMING ATTACKS
AGILITY	TAKEN FROM THE PILOT'S AGI; ALLOWS THE CRAFT TO ACT SOONER THAN OTHERS
LUCK	RAISES THE CHANCE TO LAND A CRITICAL HIT OR TO EVADE ATTACKS

ANIMA AWAKENING EFFECTS

AWAKENING LEVEL	EN COST (COMPARED TO STANDARD)	SPECIAL ATTACK LEVEL	DURATION
1	80%	1 (SINGLE-TARGET)	2 TURNS
2	75%	2 (AREA-OF-EFFECT)	3 TURNS
3	75%	3 (SINGLE-TARGET)	4 TURNS

A tougher engagement begins as a much more skilled pilot attacks the group. His E.S. is quite advanced, and it's going to take a great deal more effort to destroy it, or even to chase it off. This foe has many HPs, but that serves as a good way to teach you about the power of Anima.

Engage in normal attacks against the boss until each E.S. hits their individual Anima limit. Then, trigger Anima Awakening Level one and use each craft's special attack to deal massive damage to the target. All three craft doing this should be enough to destroy the enemy's chances for victory. Try to end the battle with one of the Anima special moves for a finishing strike (for bonus experience, skill points, and money).

If any of your craft fall below 3,000 HPs during the battle, go ahead and use Charge to avoid the risk of losing the craft outright. Charge not only heals the E.S.s, but it also places them into a defensive posture until their next turn. This makes it very hard to destroy an E.S. that is recovering health.

FEDERATION ORBITAL SPACE PORT AND FIFTH JERUSALEM

Shion heads out toward Fifth Jerusalem to meet with Allen. When she first lands at the Federation Orbital Space Port, it's a great time to meet and greet people. Walk up to the people in the Space Port and press ● to engage them in conversation. Learn more about the area before moving to the far end of the port and heading down to the planet itself.

Once on Fifth Jerusalem, watch the next few scenes before heading out with Shion. Move to the right side of the station, then out of the Orbital Terminal entirely. From there, take the roads to the south and look for a large red arrow to indicate when the First Business District is located.

FIRST BUSINESS DISTRICT POINTS OF INTEREST

QUINCY'S SELECT SHOP

STREAM CAFE

MÖBIUS HOTEL

PARK

THE MERKABAH SHOWROOM

DON'T FORGET!

SAVE AND SHOP

GET A SEGMENT FILE BY DESTROYING CONTAINERS NEAR THE HOTEL

CHECK OUT THE MERKABAH SHOWROOM AND PLAY HAKOX (GET DECODER 02)

TALK TO ALLEN ON THE FIRST FLOOR OF THE MÖBIUS HOTEL TO ADVANCE THE STORY

After arriving, use **Save Point** at the front of the district, then move deeper in to search for stores and fun items. Quincy's Select Shop is here, and Shion can grab a few toys there with the money that your group has been accumulating.

QUINCY'S SELECT SHOP

ITEM	COST	EQUIPMENT	COST
MED KIT S	100	AUTO MACER	200
REVIVE M	600	DENIM JACKET	110
ANTIDOTE	20	SNAKE EYE	100
ANALYZE BALL	4	SHOCK ABSORBER	100
TRAP	200	RED OASIS	150

INTRODUCTION
ARCHIVES
CHARACTERS
TACTICAL FILES
EQUIPMENT
THREAT ASSESSMENT
REGIONAL ANALYSIS
SUPPLEMENTAL DATA

As long as you can afford it, get some extra Analyze Balls (for times when you don't have a person with Analyze in the group). Purchase the Auto Macer, Denim Jacket, Snake Eye, Shock Absorber, and a Red Oasis. Use the in-store equip screen to put all of these on Shion. A nice upgrade!

Across from the store is a café. Destroy some of their containers for free items: Antidote, Remover, Nano Repair M. Some of the conversations in the café are pretty interesting as well. There is talk of people turning into monsters, and quite a stir about the culinary tastes of the place as well. Café Stream might be dealing in some very rare eggs, talk to Boris at the lower-left side to find out more.

After checking out Café Stream, take the main road north, deeper into the district. The hotel is up there, a park, and many more people. One of them is a man named Theodore, who is trying to clean up some containers. Destroy this cluster of items and he'll give you **A Segment File**. Theodore is also happily willing to explain more about Segment Files and Decoders; what a nifty fellow. He is in front of the Möbius Hotel (if you have any trouble finding him).

If you want a slight detour before meeting Allen, head to the right and wander around the park for a while. Destroying the containers you find leads to getting 100G, and a Down Repair. Then, in the waterways, more containers get you 200G (from the left side), and an item that is hidden behind the water gate. Come back to the park later, in the evening, to destroy a unit above the water gate. This clears the way below to move through the water and destroy a container with a Nano Repair M.

Talk to Isakios, on the right side of the park. He is a database whiz, and he also knows the password for the secret menu in Café Stream (he's forgotten it at the moment, but he really just wants you to come back and visit him later).

On the way back from the park, look for a door on the side of the path (near the guy who likes to talk about the Merkabah). The building there is the Merkabah Showroom, where you can read all sorts of information about the defenses that orbit Fifth Jerusalem. The Merkabah and the Zohar Project are both explained in detail.

Also inside the building is a Hakox Terminal, so you can get some puzzle-playing fun in. Playing through the Tutorial levels for Hakox gets you **Decoder 02**.

The Möbius itself is a ritzy place. So much money is flowing around the place that the destroyable objects there have 50G hidden inside them. Talk to Allen in the lobby area, and watch the next couple of scenes. Afterward, Shion will be in her

hotel room, where she can answer messages from chaos and Doctus. Your database will be updated, and the next place to go is the Café Stream, where chaos is waiting.

Now that you have time to explore the lobby, destroy a few objects for 2 Med Kit S units, 50G, and a Down Repair; then clear the machine on the right side for 10G and some info on the location of the CAT Testing Ground. If you want, hit the park briefly to open the water gate and get a minor item, then walk south to the Café Stream. After the conversation with chaos, the evening will pass.

The next day, head downstairs from your hotel room again. Talk to Allen in the lobby; walk outside with him and move left to leave the district. The CAT Testing Ground is on the right side of the city, so keep taking the roads in that direction until you see the red arrow to indicate that the area is functional.

CAT TESTING GROUND

The CAT Testing Grounds are huge, but most of the area is closed off to you at the moment. With the demonstration just about to begin, there isn't time to explore and see what is going on around here. Instead, walk through the lobby and down the escalators. Use transporters beyond; these will get Shion and Allen to the correct area. From there, walk to the right, take the escalator up, and continue onward to the door on the left side. This is the observation room that you will use for the duration of the experiment. Enjoy the show!

After the battle is over, talk with some of the workers in the room to get their opinions on the demonstration, and look past the controllers on the middle tier. There is a chest there; you can't open it until your group next returns here (it won't be that long). A Van Brace is inside.

Leave the demonstration area and meet Juli. She is in the hallway just outside. Shion automatically has a substantial conversation with her, and she also gets to see the pilot of the new Omega craft that is under development. Before leaving Juli's quarters, pick up the **Decoder 04** that is on the right side of the room, inside a chest. Also, try to interact with the drawing on the floor to get a closer look at it.

Leave Juli's room and use the door at the top end of the hallway to get to the transportation room. A **Save Point** is there, and the transporters are ready to take you to Section 07, where the Vector team is busy figuring out how the test went. Take the transporter; then go along the linear hallways while talking to the staff and security of the area.

By the elevator down into Vector's research area, there is another **Save Point**; take this. Head into Vector's area and see the scene with your old working team, then Shion sets up a dinner appointment for the next evening and heads out of the testing grounds.

INTRODUCTION
ARCHIVES
CHARACTERS
TACTICAL FILES
EQUIPMENT
THREAT ASSESSMENT
REGIONAL ANALYSIS
SUPPLEMENTAL DATA

BACK IN TOWN

Return to the hotel and watch as more of the current situation unfolds. There is quite a lot to view, and Shion's dinner appointment gets a bit disrupted. Instead, the new plan is for her to meet with Allen and Juli the next evening. Once these scenes end, Shion will be in her room at the hotel still, but it will be evening. Use the **Save Point** there, then ride down to the lobby with Allen. The two have an impromptu dinner out, as their main plans were preempted.

When the scenes finish, morning dawns and Shion is on the move again. Leave the hotel, exit the district, and walk north to the Orbital Terminal. Take the elevator back up to the Orbital Station, and walk over to the Durandal's airlock (it's to the right of the one Shion used when she docked).

After a short meeting, everyone decides that it would be best to grab KOS-MOS and use her weapon systems to deal with the problems encountered by the Elsa. The bump in the road is that everyone's going to have to push their way into the CAT Testing Ground again, and this time without a proper invitation.

PROWLING INTO THE CAT

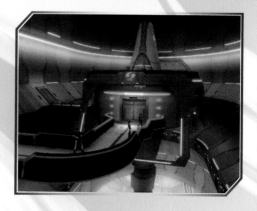

Return to the hotel and speak with Allen to get things started. He'll unlock the Skill System, and he'll give Shion a free 20 Skill Points to play with, in addition to what she's already accrued.

When you want to start the mission, speak with Allen and say that it's okay to have everyone leave on their own. It's best to play with Shion's Skill Points, then to talk to Allen again and head out. A scene cuts to nightfall, when the group meets outside the CAT area. Beneath where you begin, there is a **Save Point** and a Store. Consider spending some extra money to get Shock Absorbers and Red Oasis items

for the couple of people you plan on having in your attack party. Feel free to go into the group menu and use the Formation function to arrange who will be in the actual combat portion of the group (only three can fight at a given time).

SIMPLE STORE

ITEM	COST
MED KIT S	100
REVIVE M	600
ANTIDOTE	20
ANALYZE BALL	4
TRAP	200

EQUIPMENT	COST
AUTO MACER	200
DENIM JACKET	110
SNAKE EYE	100
SHOCK ABSORBER	100
RED OASIS	150

HEALERS IN THE BACK

It's always good to have at least one solid healer outside of the battle party. Use these characters to restore characters to full health after any fighting. This leaves ether point totals high for the characters that are doing the actual fighting. Also, Med Kits drop frequently in a number of areas, and there is no reason to stockpile items that you aren't using. Go ahead and keep your party happy and safe.

OUTSIDE CAT FACILITY AND ENTRANCE STATION

POINTS OF INTEREST	
1	MOVABLE BRIDGES
2	SEGMENT ADDRESS 10
3	TRANSPORTER NUMBER TWO

ITEMS	
1	ANALYZE BALL
2	500G
3	KAP-NAR

ENEMIES	
1	FEDERATION SOLDIER A
2	FEDERATION SOLDIER B

Federation Soldiers are in your way here, but they are very easy to get back attacks against. Wait for them to patrol away from your group, then have at them. Use the early attacks to take down the Federation Soldier Bs first, as they have lower health and are able to deal a fair amount of damage.

Use the walkway on the left side, and turn right when it hits a T-intersection. Use the small, glowing panel to descend on the left side. A container is there to move a bridge into place, and that exposes a red door. Return to the upper part of the left side and take the stairs down at the other end of the walkway. The stairs lead down to a breakable container that shifts another bridge into position once it is destroyed. Use that to unlock the way inside the base. Before heading back up to the beginning and taking the right route (which is now crossable), take out the guard by the red door. This one is **Segment Address 10**. This door won't be opened until well into the story; when you do return for it, KOS-MOS's KAP-NAR armor is found inside.

TRAPS

Use the other bridge, on the right side of the walkways, to reach the door that heads inside the complex. A somewhat understated message over the PA system makes it sound like there are already some problems going on at the CAT facility (unless people go missing all the time).

After a quick walk, the group arrives in the transporter station, not far from the front entrance of the facility. Before taking the transporter that is down from the corridor, head up to the top of the map and open the chest there. 500G awaits for your efforts; go to the transporter afterward and use that to reach the next area.

DEMONSTRATION AREA

POINTS OF INTEREST	
1	DRAWING OF NEPHILUM

ITEMS	
1	VAN BRACE

ENEMIES	
1	FEDERATION SOLDIERS A
2	FEDERATION SOLDIERS B
3	V.G.S. EINS

The patrollers up the stairs from the Demonstration Site Station are able to turn up the heat a bit. The Eins that patrol with them can take more damage and deal fairly well when attacking single group members. Focus on the Federation Soldiers first, for quick victories. Then, team up on the Eins for a solid finish.

Take the left branch of the hall and search the chest from the observation room you were in a couple days ago. A Van Brace is inside. Clear the rest of the hallway when you come out (no reason to miss experience, especially when you are getting used to the system still). Then, move into the large observation room that is across from the stairs.

Walk to the right side of that room and continue along the same path Shion took last time she was in the area. Use the **Save Point** at the next station, then take the transporter to Section 05. Transporter 04 doesn't go anywhere fun at the moment, but 06 takes you to a station with

Containers (100G to be found there). Without a Weapon's Development Area Key you can't go any farther. So, take transporter 05.

WEAPON'S DEVELOPMENT AREA KEY

In the later portion of the game, your characters will run across the Weapon's Development Area Key (it's loot from a boss fight, so you won't be able to miss it). Return here in the EVS after that stage and use it by taking the train to Area 06. Use that key on the console near the large door.

Move into the weapon area and use the next console to simulate a battle with Omega Universitas. That fight is so easy that you can easily blaze through it with your E.S.s. Afterward, however, Omega runs itself through an upgrade cycle. This begins a fight with Omega Id. Read the Supplemental Data chapter for tips on beating this encounter.

GNOSIS STORAGE AREA

POINTS OF INTEREST

1	RESTRAINT UNIT CONTROLS
2	POWER DISTRIBUTION PUZZLE
3	SEGMENT ADDRESS 04
4	ELEVATOR LOCK MECHANISM
5	DOOR CONTROLS

ITEMS

1	50G
2	REMOVER
3	ANTI-CRYSTAL
4	KWP-XI
5	MED KIT M, 100G
6	GARUDA BANGLE
7	G-LEGLE/42
8	HALF-REPAIR

ENEMIES

1	AG-01 X 1
2	FEDERATION SOLDIER A
3	FEDERATION SOLDIER B
4	V.G.S. EINS
5	V.G.S. ZWEI
6	VX-7000 X 1
7	YURIEV SOLDIER A
8	YURIEV SOLDIER B

This is the Gnosis Storage Area. 50G is found in the containers by the side of the area, but the elevators to the Vector Area are your goal. Sadly, it seems that the elevators aren't in the mood to cooperate. Take the smaller lift at the back of the section instead.

The passage stays linear for quite some time; don't use traps on the enemies you face unless you really want to go nuts. Instead, try for back attacks. Even when the fights are not in your favor, the foes won't survive well against concerted attacks.

Eventually, you should spot a glowing lift that goes down and a doorway. Take the doorway, fight a walkway battle, then "Purge the restraint unit!"

Doesn't that always sound like such a good idea? Now take the lift down, and look at the puzzle beneath you. This is a classic puzzle where you want to get all of the cranks into an upward position; hitting any one of them changes the position of adjacent cranks. For a fast win here, try 3,2,1, and 4 (counting from left to right).

Take the lift on the far side of the now-functional bridge once the puzzle is done. Destroy the containers in the area for an Anti-Crystal, and fight the guards you come across. Back attacks are very easy to score, so the battles are quite smooth. Use ether points freely at this point; there will be a Save Point not too far ahead, so it's good to heal with ether points from peripheral characters instead of wasting Med Kits, and have MOMO go to town on V.G.S. foes with her Ether skills.

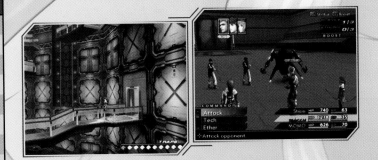

Before using the stairs, take the doorway out into the central area against. Fight the guard there and use the next Restraint Unit Controller to release the mechanism on the other side of the cylinder. Now take the stairs up from the last room. A fight against two V.G.S. systems is ahead; don't be shy about using Beam attacks to finish off these enemies if they get on your nerves.

The rest of the way is linear again. Use the Save Point when you arrive in the next control room, and try not to stress about the little things. A Gnosis here, a Gnosis there; who is going to notice that somebody shut down the Restraint Controls? Could have happened to anyone!

INTRODUCTION

ARCHIVES

CHARACTERS

TACTICAL FILES

EQUIPMENT

THREAT ASSESSMENT

REGIONAL ANALYSIS

SUPPLEMENTAL DATA

Two tougher units have been dispatched in the hall above. The AG-01 requires a bit of a beatdown, and the VX-7000 is truly a nice piece of technology. Ziggy's special attacks are still able to do a massive amount of damage, so build up to those if you have him in the group. If not, Jin and Jr. are good candidates for ripping into these guys. Return to the earlier room and rest at the Save Point if you end up using too much ether points in these encounters.

Keep going as far as the hallway can take you, and destroy the containers when you finally reach a turn. **Segment Address 04** is hidden behind the crates, so that is a pleasant discovery, doubly so because you have the Decoder for this one from the room where you spoke with Juli earlier. The golden chest inside has a KWP-XI.

The same room has a button to activate the elevator system that was stuck before. Use that before continuing, and descend on the lift to grab the chest that you could see earlier but not take from inside the elevator doors (there is a Garuda Bangle to equip to protect one of your characters from Poison effects).

Now, take the door on the right side and keep fighting the enemies in your path. Destroy all containers after clearing out the many guards. There is even a hidden encounter with even more of the new Yuriev Soldiers inside one of the boxes;

these fights often have Eins and Soldiers. As before, take out the softer targets first, then try for a Finishing Move against the Eins.

The best treasure here is to the left of the main container area. Use a red button near a yellow blast wall to gain access to a tiny section of corridor. There is a locked room there with a chest in it. To unlock the room, press the red button on the other side of the wall from the first. This gets you a G-Legle/42 (a very nice energy upgrade for one of your E.S. mechs).

Follow this path to the far right for more treasure, and it eventually leads to a ladder. At the top of the ladder, first go left toward the dead end. Open the hidden chest for a Half Repair. Proceed to the right through a door into a **Save Point**. Feel free to rest there and return to the upper section where some of the enemies respawn. This is a good way to farm some extra money, experience, or points for skills.

Use the elevator above the Save Point to descend to the Vector area. It works in theory!

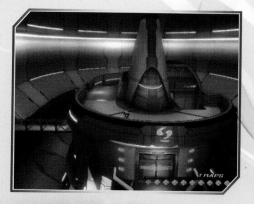

UNDERGROUND HANGER

POINTS OF INTEREST
NONE

ITEMS	
1	ANTI-CRYSTAL
2	ETHER PACK S

ENEMIES	
1	ALUDRA CALF (BOSS)
2	V.G.S. EINS
3	V.G.S. ZWEI X 2

Move left across the hanger area and follow Abel deeper into this underground section of the base. Oddly decrepit, things seem to be falling apart all over the place. Use ● to destroy the debris that gets in your path after crossing the bridge and reaching the room of scrap.

KOS-MOS is sleeping here, and she is reawakened with a bit of work. After a brief reunion, she is integrated into the party. Shift around your formation as needed, then take the large hallway out of the room. If you picked up the KWP-XI earlier, from the Segment Address, equip that on KOS-MOS at this time.

Use the Dumping Elevator to reach the Exercise Area. Absolutely hit the **Save Point** there before continuing; there is a trap prepared with quite a few mechs. VX-7000s are all over the place, and they get back attacks against your group unless you specifically stand to fight them. The enemy mechs won't follow you into the elevator, so you can retreat there during your immunity phase and use your traps before re-engaging to get some pre-emptive attacks.

Heal between fighting, during your brief immunity phase. This allows all characters to focus fire and deal pure damage during the engagements. During the final fight of the series, add as much to your Boost Gauge as possible, and don't use any of it. Rest again at the Save Point when you are done, and put your group in a configuration for a boss fight; one is coming up soon.

INTRODUCTION
ARCHIVES
CHARACTERS
TACTICAL FILES
EQUIPMENT
THREAT ASSESSMENT
REGIONAL ANALYSIS
SUPPLEMENTAL DATA

ALUDRA CALF

HP:	4500
EP:	200
BL:	270
INFO:	GNOSIS
TGT:	???
EXP:	885
SP:	10
G:	260
N ITEM:	DECODER 09
R ITEM:	NONE
S ITEM:	WHITE FRAGMENT
STRONG:	NONE
WEAK:	BEAM
ABSORBED:	NONE
NULL:	POISON

This Gnosis has size on his side, but your group is probably at full HP/EP, so they can stand up to some punishment before getting into any trouble. Beam Bolt I is a solid Ether skill for this fight, as the Gnosis is weak to Beams.

Go ahead and let Shion steal from him at some point, as she can get a White Fragment from doing this. The early fighting is very simple. Keep up on health with one person while the others lay on the damage.

Be certain to hold back a full 3/3 Boost for the period when the Aludra Calf hits one-quarter health. This is when he goes into his enraged phase, and the damage output rises considerably. The entire party runs the risk of hitting their Break Limit here, especially if you aren't careful. Thus, have a good special attack ready, and make every point count. By the same thinking, keep your health at or near full as the boss starts to really drop low on his HPs. That gives you a better buffer against his late-fight attacks.

Toward the end of the fight, when your group is getting hit with constant area-of-effect attacks, be sure to consider changing out those members with low health who are high on their Break Gauge. It's powerful to switch in members with full health who are fresh for the fight. This also allows for ether points to be used more heavily during the early part of the encounter.

INVESTIGATE THE FLOATING LANDMASS

After a narrow escape, the group is ready to try their idea. The Durandal is prepped to fly out to the Elsa's previous position while the main group breaks their way into the anomaly. KOS-MOS has her tertiary weapons system up to the task, and soon everyone gets the opening they need to head inside the event horizon.

The Elsa is indeed on the other side, but getting it back out is going to require effort as well. Because of odd engine troubles, it seems like Shion and the others will have to explore the area before the Elsa can "take off."

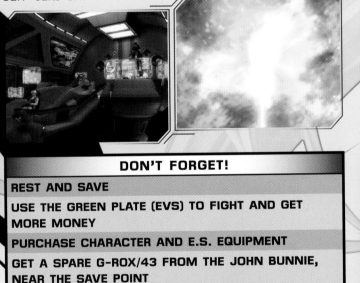

Use the store to upgrade a wide selection of your group's equipment, and stock up on any items that you enjoy using. Holding on to money is rarely as useful as having some high-end equipment, and you are now free to go back into older areas and farm for more money by fighting! This is a superb way to grab enough cash to outfit your E.S. craft with all of the best engines that are available at this time!

Another point of interest on the Elsa is the lounge (on the left side of the ship). They have a Hakox terminal there, and new levels have been added, as well as new characters. Down in the hold, where the E.S. craft are stored, there is a chest with an AF-Scout R piece (to raise E.S. Asher's HP to 15000). Also in that room is **Segment Address 14**; blast the container at the far end of the hanger to reveal this door. Look in the Professor's room for another special door. Behind a container on the right side of the lab area is **Segment Address 09**, with a golden door.

DON'T FORGET!

REST AND SAVE

USE THE GREEN PLATE (EVS) TO FIGHT AND GET MORE MONEY

PURCHASE CHARACTER AND E.S. EQUIPMENT

GET A SPARE G-ROX/43 FROM THE JOHN BUNNIE, NEAR THE SAVE POINT

FIND SEGMENT ADDRESSES 09 AND 14

TAKE THE AF-SCOUT R FROM THE HANGER AREA

SEARCH THE MEN'S QUARTERS FOR SURVIVAL WEAR (JR. OR CHAOS ARMOR)

Before leaving the ship, talk to the crew and notice the extra tabs outside of the bridge. Not only is there a Save Point here, but the blue plate offers an upgraded store, and the green plate lets you go back into previous areas (a wonderful feature, as always).

ELSA STORE

ITEM	COST
MED KIT S	100
MED KIT M	500
REVIVE M	600
ANTIDOTE	20
REMOVER	50
ANTI-CRYSTAL	1000
G VACCINE	500
ANALYZE BALL	4
TRAP	200
NANO REPAIR M	400
DOWN REPAIR	50

E.S. EQUIPMENT	COST
G-ROX/43	480
C-US2	100
D-SENSOR	50

ELSA STORE

EQUIPMENT	COST		EQUIPMENT	COST
AUTO MACER	200		SPEED II VEST	110
BLUE LADY	300		KAP-BEG	150
HINOKA SANJU	200		FIBER VEST	120
QI YAN	300		GRANITE MANTLE	120
DELTA EDGE I	180		LEATHER CHOKER	150
ZERO CRUSHER	210		SNAKE EYE	100
KWAP-PII	300		SHOCK ABSORBER	100
FORCE HAND	190		COBRA BANGLE	100
DESERT EAGLE	190		RARE BRACE	300
LACE TANK TOP	120		RED OASIS	150
METAL CORSET	120		RED STAR	300

BEDROCK LAYER

POINTS OF INTEREST	
1	GEOCRYSTALS
2	SEGMENT ADDRESS 12

ENEMIES	
1	E.S. NAPHTALI (BOSS)
2	T183 OCULUS
3	T190 DENS

ITEMS	
1	DF-V2
2	HALF REPAIR
3	ROUGH GEOCRYSTAL
4	GUARDIAN

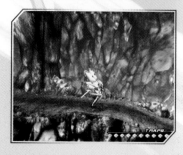

When everything has been collected, take the elevator beneath the men and women's quarter to leave the ship in your group's E.S. craft. As you explore, look for the first group of enemies. Not only is this a fun little fight, but it serves as a tutorial for more advanced E.S. combat. Striking an enemy two or more times in a row leads to a chain; these add accuracy and damage to the attacks, making it possible to hit well even with low accuracy actions.

Characters will continue a chain as long as the enemies aren't able to guard or fully evade the attack. When one enemy is destroyed, the chain continues on to the next enemy (though the damage bonus is reset).

Normally, 5% bonus damage is added to a chain for each consecutive hit. This can add all the way up to dealing as much bonus damage as the normal strike, effectively piling on double damage!

The next aspect occurs with team combos. These are sudden attacks by another craft (cooperative attack) or by both of the other craft in your group (an ambush). These won't occur all the time; there is a chance with each attack you take that a team combo will occur. Attacks with a higher team rating are much more likely to trigger these, and yes, they do continue your chains. Note that ambush combos only have a chance of occurring when your E.S. craft are in Anima Awakening mode.

The enemies in this area won't stand up well to your E.S. craft if you were able to afford the full range of upgrades. With the newer generators, your craft are able to do two attacks per turn, adding quite a sum to their damage output. Go after the T183s first, as they have lower health and can be destroyed with great speed.

The T190s are much better, and they won't usually survive a direct assault either.

Advance along the linear path, destroying the large rock formations as you go. This clears and way and eventually leads the group to an area with geocrystals. Clear the cave of enemies, but don't worry about the crystals quite yet. Instead, take the path on the left and head up the hill. Push the next geocrystal off of the cliff's edge to shatter it into the first crystal below. This does succeed in destroying both geocrystals.

ALWAYS TAKE DOWN AOE CRAFT

The T190 Dens have the area-of-effect attacks. If you can't destroy all the enemies in the first round, destroying the T190 Dens will reduce the damage you take. If you intend to do some charging to restore health, leave a T183 Oculus as the final enemy.

Keep flying up the hill and rest when you reach the Save Point. Your group probably isn't taking any major damage anyway, but it's never a bad thing to record your data. Remember that it's easy to Charge during E.S. battles once there is only a single enemy remaining. This way, you never have to worry about health during random encounters, even if you aren't fully equipped.

The cave beyond the Save Point is rather large. Going from left to right, there are a number of corridors that lead into the mountain. The first passage, on the far left, leads way up and around a blind turn. You eventually reach a small ledge with a chest; this has DF-V2, an upgraded armor frame for the E.S. Dinah! Quite a nice find.

The second passage is reached after destroying the rubble that blocks the way forward. At its apex, this route reaches another geocrystal. Drop this one down on one of the two earlier crystals and notice that an item appears from the resulting blast.

The passage on the right side heads down, around, and later upward again. The peripheral offshoots of the path have extra fights but little treasure; there is a geocrystal part of the way up that just barely misses the crystal below that is blocking the path. At the very top is the geocrystal that hits the spot! As an added bonus, your group automatically returns to the Save Point after destroying the crystal down there.

Before continuing collect the Half Repair from the nearby crystal, then descend and steal the Rough Geocrystal from the debris in the cave below (from the item you saw appear a short time ago). That geocrystal was also blocking a small ledge. Your group can safely leave their E.S.s there, and take a look at **Segment Address 12**! You won't be able to unlock Address 12 until much later in the game, but it has a powerful Guardian weapon (for Shion).

After saving again, take the unblocked route all the way to the very top of the region. There are only a couple more encounters along the way before the group reaches an important cave. Inside, there is a short scene before the party is attacked.

E.S. NAPHTALI

HP:	85000
INFO:	MACHINE
TGT:	???
EXP:	1900
SP:	10
G:	580
N ITEM:	D-COUNTER
R ITEM:	NONE
STRONG:	NONE
WEAK:	NONE
ABSORBED:	NONE
NULL:	NONE

This E.S. fight is somewhat challenging. Though your enemy is alone, they have a very strong E.S., and the area around the craft is constantly affecting the fight too; Anima shifts up or down randomly at the beginning of each character's turn, leading to unpredictability in when you can use Anima Awakening.

Use a full wave of Anima Awakening in the early fight to get a quick start against the Naphtali. Though this isn't necessary, your craft will need Anima for the final quarter of the encounter (and that means holding off on Anima use in the middle fight). Thus, you might as well use everything at the start and regenerate the Anima afterward. Use charge to keep everyone at high health.

Once the Naphtali is down to half health, it will start to deal more damage. Not only will your group begin to see more area-of-effect attacks, on the order of two-thousand damage per E.S., but the Naphtali will unleash a single-target attack at 50% and 25% health that will deal painful damage. A blow of 10,000 HP is entirely possible on the second blast, so keep health high even on your toughest craft.

After the second Buster Launcher, the Naphtali will be low enough on health that a series of three Anima Awakenings will end the fight completely. Try to have the Anima Gauges ready for this sudden burst, to keep from facing the brutal onslaught of area-of-effect attacks (with nearly 3,000 damage per target being possible on bad rounds).

Once the Naphtali collapses, collect a fair sum of experience and give yourself a smile. It's time for some ground work!

ANCIENT TEMPLE

POINTS OF INTEREST

1	BRIDGE TERMINALS

ENEMIES

1	GOBLIN
2	GREMLIN
3	MANTICORE

ITEMS

1	ANTI-CRYSTAL
2	MED KIT S
3	ANTI-CRYSTAL
4	DECODER 01
5	BLUE OASIS
6	ETHER PACK S
7	MED KIT M, REVIVE M, 100G
8	UPDATE FILE 14
9	SKILL UPGRADE A

Walk through the large opening in the cave wall. Inside is the entrance area of an ancient temple. Though cut off from the Elsa for the moment, there is fortunately a **Save Point** here, and a blue plate as well. You won't find any weapon or armor upgrades here, but you can purchase items that weren't affordable before and restock any supplies that were depleted.

Advance into the temple proper, taking the door ahead to a lift that raises a few floors. On the level above, try your group against the Goblin and Manticore that are patrolling. It's very easy to get back attacks against these slow-moving foes, so that is a perk. Break the boxes on the sides of the path for a couple Med Kits. Defeat both groups in the room and take the next lift up at the far end.

TEMPLE STORE

ITEM	COST	EQUIPMENT	COST
MED KIT S	100	AUTO MACER	200
MED KIT M	500	BLUE LADY	300
REVIVE M	600	HINOKA SANJU	200
ANTIDOTE	20	QI YAN	300
REMOVER	50	DELTA EDGE I	180
ANTI-CRYSTAL	1000	ZERO CRUSHER	210
G VACCINE	500	KWAP-PII	300
ANALYZE BALL	4	FORCE HAND	190
TRAP	200	DESERT EAGLE	190
		LACE TANK TOP	120
		METAL CORSET	120
		SPEED II VEST	110
		KAP-BEG	150
		FIBER VEST	120
		GRANITE MANTLE	120
		LEATHER CHOKER	150
		SNAKE EYE	100
		SHOCK ABSORBER	100
		COBRA BANGLE	100
		RARE BRACE	300
		RED OASIS	150
		RED STAR	300

INTRODUCTION

ARCHIVES

CHARACTERS

TACTICAL FILES

EQUIPMENT

THREAT ASSESSMENT

REGIONAL ANALYSIS

SUPPLEMENTAL DATA

In these fights, use early firepower against the Manticores; they fall very quickly compared to the Gremlins and Goblins that come with them. Use Finishing Moves against the Goblins especially, as they are fairly tough enemies and require a lot of punishment otherwise. Their attacks leave characters with a debuff that crystallizes them after three rounds of combat, but that isn't much of an issue in these fights (by that time, the enemies are doomed anyway).

The next tier has many bridges that can shift between two positions. Use the red terminals to change the bridge back and forth while collecting items and destroying the Goblins. Note that one push on each terminal is sufficient to place the bridges in position for getting across to the next lift. You should get the Blue Oasis from the chest on the left side before shifting that bridge (or be sure to shift that terminal back long enough to get the item, as it offers +50 EP).

Take the lift to the next level. This area has more fighting, but the rewards are better as well! Use the nearby terminal to shift the bridges, then clear the left side of the walkways. **Update File 14** is in a chest over there, and there are a few minor items near it. Then, shift the bridges back and take the other route.

Each terminal needs to be used one time throughout the rest of the area, so it's a very simple run. Make sure to destroy the crystal that is near the final terminal, in the north-east corner of the room. There is a Skill Upgrade A inside of it, and those are always useful. After getting that, use the last terminal. Before you exit this level by heading up again, return to the previous floor. On the left side of the that map, with walkways that start in the center, there is a box that you can now reach. That is a very important box because it has **Decoder 01** in it!

THE ARCADIAN RESOURCE

Now that you have this odd item, return to the front entrance of the temple (this can be done in the EVS any time you are on the Elsa). Activate the lower lift by using the Arcadian Resource on the pedestal by the front of the temple. This takes your group down to a lower level that was unavailable to you the first time you came through.

That action triggers a cutscene, after which you are thrown into a bonus dungeon area. Read more about this in the Supplemental Data chapter, when you are ready.

The next two floors are fully linear and only feature a couple fights each. Wipe the floor with the Gnosis there and climb until you find the hole in the wall at the top of the temple.

Above the temple is a place that was only known to exist as a dream within KOS-MOS's unconscious. Smashing the upper-left tombstone reveals stairs down. Follow these and grab a Rejuvenator M. Head back up and break through the stones on the upper-right side of the graveyard and smash your way through the barriers ahead. This clears another underground area; descend into it and examine the burial area. After a short scene, destroy the wall beyond the cross and take the Arcadian Resource from the last part of the tomb.

T-ELOS

T-elos has a high level of evasion, but she won't dish out a lot of damage at first. Use Break attacks to get her about two-thirds of the way through her Break Gauge then cool off on those attacks for a time. Keep health high, as always, and use any buffs for the battle to keep your group ready for the serious stuff. Have Shion steal her Green Oasis if you can, as that grants +300 HPs!

Halfway through the fight, she goes into an increased rate of Boost gain and starts to get ready for a massive attack. Finish off her Break Gauge to stop her from having a good time. Having Ziggy in the group, with his awesome Choke ability, really helps here. This prevents T-elos from doing anything impressive. Not only does she lose her turn preparing for her special attack; it never goes off, so it's time that she never gets back.

If you've held back enough Boost, slam T-elos with that while she is in her Break recovery. The damage will greatly help to conclude the battle, and it's likely that she won't come to until around her 25% mark. At that point, it's a rush to see if you can hit her Break Limit a second time. Even if you don't, it's likely that the fight is yours at this point!

HP:	7500
EP:	250
BL:	360
INFO:	MACHINE AND HUMAN
TGT:	???
EXP:	2800
SP:	10
G:	720
N ITEM:	MED KIT L
R ITEM:	REVIVE M
S ITEM:	GREEN OASIS
STRONG:	BEAM
WEAK:	LIGHTNING
ABSORBED:	NONE
NULL:	POISON

THE FOREST

Shion wakes in a forest, but there isn't much clue as to which forest or how exactly she got there. To the left is a **Save Point** and blue plate to do some buying and selling. Smash the boxes for a Med Kit M, and Med Kit L, then trash the bushes for a D-Treasure I. The gate is locked, so head back to where Shion woke and walk to the right until you meet most of the group, heal, and arrange people for combat, in case there is trouble ahead.

THE FOREST AND THE OLD CHURCH

It's a tad strange farther along the path, because there are U-TIC Soldiers patrolling. Certainly this isn't what you expected, but either way they are going to be a problem. Rush them from behind for easier encounters, and hit the Soldiers first before worrying about the heavier Grisly mechs. Make sure to soften the Grislys before using a Special Attack; this ensures that the attack is a finishing move.

Break the rock on the bottom side of the path, just after the second encounter. This leads to a side trail; a Hero's Bracelet is in a chest at the end of that trail.

The main path continues, with more U-TIC Soldiers along the way. Once things start moving up the hillside, expect to see some other biologic targets as well. Asterions deal a moderate amount of damage, but they go down quickly.

POINTS OF INTEREST	
1	TREE WITH CARNELIAN EGGS

ITEMS	
1	MED KIT S, MED KIT M
2	HERO'S BRACELET
3	REVIVE L
4	REJUVENATOR M
5	WARRIOR'S BRACELET
6	EX SKILL KEY I
7	UPDATE FILE 06

ENEMIES	
1	ASTERION
2	COMBAT REALIAN A
3	COMBAT REALIAN B
4	O-78 GRISLY 1
5	U-TIC SOLDIER A
6	U-TIC SOLDIER B

Continue up the path and destroy the rock on the right side to reach another item box. This one has a Rejuvenator M in it. Only another few moments of walking and the group will come to a dead end. Search for a portion of rock on the cliff wall that can be destroyed, then climb to the top of the internal tunnel.

After taking a better look around, Shion and Jin figure out where the group might be. Follow the path and watch for Asterions that come out of the waterfall when you try to cross the great, fallen tree over the river. Kill these Asterions and blow apart the branches of the tree that keep you from reaching the item box nearby (with a Warrior's Bracelet). Beware, hitting the branch under the chest drops it into the water below! If that happens, you won't be able to get the chest again without leaving the area and coming all the way back.

On the other side of the tree is a **Save Point**. Take the path at the bottom of the screen; this leads down to the falls, and you can safely pass behind the water. The chest there has the EX Skill Key I, an item of immense power. Go ahead and unlock these skills and take a look at what you can start saving points for. Truly nice.

The pleasant walk through the forest ends when gunshots are heard in the distance. Not willing to ignore this, the group closes in and sees that Combat Realians are attacking two Federation troops, though one of those men is already doomed. Being good folks, Shion and the rest jump into the fray. Take down the Combat Realian B first, as he has only three-quarters of the other's health. Ultimately, it's an easy fight, then you get to talk to the Federation soldier. He's quite a charmer. To get him to safety, stay on the same route. **Update File 06** is on the way and only takes a second to grab.

Also, keep an eye on the north side of the trail. There is a section of bushes that can quickly be pushed aside.

They reveal a tree; press ● to destroy its large branch, then collect the three Carnelian Eggs that fall. They are worth money when sold at the store.

It's not much farther to a church where the wounded soldier can be tended. There you speak with the inhabitants and learn that a ship landed to the east, near some caves. The description of the vessel makes it sound like it might be the Elsa.

Leave the church entirely and use the road to the left to head out. Once you reach the large-area map, take the trail to the south-east and look for the red arrow. That is the Dabrye Mine. Enter there.

DABRYE MINE

POINTS OF INTEREST

1	SEGMENT ADDRESS 01
2	WILD ROLLER COASTER

ENEMIES

1	BYPRODUCT #A156
2	BYPRODUCT #A283
3	MAI AND LEUPOLD (BOSSES)
4	U-TIC SOLDIER A
5	U-TIC SOLDIER B

ITEMS

1	SKILL UPGRADE A
2	MED KIT M
3	200G
4	3000G
5	G-LEGLE/56
6	500G
7	1000G X 2
8	ETHER PACK M
9	WITCH'S EYE
10	UPDATE FILE 07

The Dabrye Mine has seen many better days, and U-TIC troops are apparently all over the place. After speaking to the mine supervisor, you discover that a lone girl with an auto-tech is trying to thwart U-TIC in the mines.

Considering how your group feels about U-TIC, there is no reason not to help out if you can.

INTRODUCTION
ARCHIVES
CHARACTERS
TACTICAL FILES
EQUIPMENT
THREAT ASSESSMENT
REGIONAL ANALYSIS
SUPPLEMENTAL DATA

Search the left side of the area, near the **Save Point** and the blue plate. There is a small, almost hidden, staircase with a Skill Upgrade A inside a container. Moving the crane on the right side gets a Med Kit M, and a container by the Save Point has 200G in it.

The next cavern, on the right side, is quite large. It is a descending spiral, and there are monsters and treasures everywhere. Destroy all of the limestone pillars for quite a sum of wealth (multiple ones have 1000G). Then, before you reach the bottom, destroy a suspicious looking section on the left wall to uncover a secret passage. This leads to **Segment Address 01**. If you grabbed Decoder 01 from the Floating Landmass (first floor of the puzzle section in the temple), this door can already be opened.

DABRYE MINE STORE	
ITEM	**COST**
MED KIT S	100
MED KIT M	500
REVIVE M	600
SEVEN MOONS	300
ANTIDOTE	20
REMOVER	50
ANTI-CRYSTAL	1000
G VACCINE	500
ANALYZE BALL	4
TRAP	200

EQUIPMENT	COST
AUTO MACER	200
BLUE LADY	300
HINOKA SANJU	200
QI YAN	300
DELTA EDGE I	180
ZERO CRUSHER	210
KWAP-PII	300
FORCE HAND	190
DESERT EAGLE	190
LACE TANK TOP	120
METAL CORSET	120
SPEED II VEST	110
KAP-BEG	150
FIBER VEST	120
GRANITE MANTLE	120
LEATHER CHOKER	150
SNAKE EYE	100
SHOCK ABSORBER	100
COBRA BANGLE	100
RARE BRACE	300
RED OASIS	150
RED STAR	300

Destroy the rocks blocking the mine after saving, then check inside. There are biological monsters wandering the place, and a few wounded folks getting some rest at the top. The Byproducts that wander around are slow and easy to ambush, but they are tough. Despite the configuration of their groups, you want to hit the A283s first, even though they "look" tougher. In truth, they are faster to kill and deal area-of-effect damage if left to their own devices.

Take the short ledge on the left side first, as there is a chest with 3000G in it! Turn around and take the right route next, where there are more Byproducts to fight. When passing a large pillar around the next turn, use ● to hit it repeatedly. Destroy every section of the pillar to uncover a treasure chest. Once the base of the pillar is gone, the chest should be quite recoverable; it has a G-Legle/56 generator.

THE CRANE GAME

There are actually several rewards for playing with the Crane. Each time, your group needs to guess the proper timing for the arm so that it smashes into the box. You leave the area, return, and a new box (with a new reward will be there). You cannot get the ultimate reward until after the encounter with Mai at the end of the mine. This is where MOMO's Swimsuit is found.

A Witch's Eye is within. At the bottom of the main cavern is a chest with a simple Ether Pack M.

The passage at the bottom of the cavern leads to a much-valued **Save Point**, and there is a W.R.C. Unit there. This stands for Wild Roller Coaster, and it's a heck of a way to get around the old mine. You use the left analog stick to accelerate or brake while riding the coaster and the group boards it by moving to the right side of the ledge. Go ahead and let loose while going down; it's a great view if you aren't afraid of heights.

Move through the passage at the bottom of the line and prepare your group for a boss battle.

MAI AND LEUPOLD

MAI'S STATS	
	6000
	70
	300
	BIOLOGICAL (HUMAN)
	???
	3500
	15
	620
M:	DECODER 11
M:	NONE
M:	KAJIC NECK
NG:	LIGHTNING
K:	NONE
RBED:	NONE
	POISON, HEAT

LEUPOLD'S STATS	
HP:	6000
EP:	0
BL:	480
INFO:	MACHINE
TGT:	???
EXP:	3500
SP:	15
G:	550
N ITEM:	REJUVENATOR M
R ITEM:	REJUVENATOR L
S ITEM:	ETHER PACK M
STRONG:	FIRE
WEAK:	ICE, LIGHTNING
ABSORBED:	NONE
NULL:	POISON

This fight is against two bosses at the same time, and that makes it more strategically complicated. It seems like Mai is the more sensible early target, as she takes a great deal more damage per hit (thus she'll go down more easily). Yet, Leupold is going to go nuts when Mai collapses. Tricky, eh?

First, wound both targets while building up your Boost Gauge and getting any buffing done that is needed. Steal from Mai to get her Kajic Neck, and push both foes to a higher point on their Break Gauges.

Until the fight starts to ramp up, you won't need to choose which target to take down first. Wounding them both during the easy phase just makes everything better later on. But, once Mai starts to buff the two of them, it starts to get painful having both targets around.

The better path is probably to take Leupold out first, despite the increased time fighting against two enemies. That said, Mai is a very fast girl to drop, and if you can handle the enraged Leupold, the fight does become simpler. Basically, decide based on your current group's needs. If you need the fight to be less chaotic, take out Mai first. If you are worried about being wiped out directly, play the safe route and go for Leupold.

Either way, Mai is destroyed by raising her Break Gauge quickly (her limit isn't very high). After that, a single special attack will do brutal damage to her, especially as her vitality is already poor.

For Leupold, try to pile on anti-machine attacks. His Break Limit is much higher, so it's better to find attacks that do substantial damage outright. MOMO on lightning attacks, Jin on anti-machine strikes, and Shion or chaos to heal is a decent idea.

Note that Mai will return to the front of the mine area after her defeat. If you find information about her father (in, for example, a Labyrinthos computer), bring it back to Mai. She'll reward you with Decoder 15.

Walk through the next cave and take **Update File 07** from the item box in there. Enter the Elsa when you are ready, and watch the scenes with the crew.

GETTING TO KNOW MILTIA

Back on the Elsa, talk to MOMO in the quarters where Shion wakes, then leave and take the elevator down to B1 (to the right of the women's quarters). Everyone is waiting in the Gun Room, barely down the corridor on level B1.

After the meeting, look at the Professor's area on B1 at the golden door that you discovered last time. You now have the Decoder for that door (gained in the battle against Mai). Use that on the door and collect the EK Device! This teaches you the ether skill: Erde Kaiser. Also notice that the plates on the main deck have been updated with new areas and new store items, but these aren't of direct importance because you don't have your group around at the moment.

Being Shion, it wouldn't be right to sit around the Elsa and do nothing while the Professor tries to figure everything out. Head out and leave the Elsa's cave. There is a fast path to the city that Shion finds outside, so that takes her straight in without any problems. Use the roads to the west.

MILTIA

DON'T FORGET!

SHOP FOR NEW ITEMS

TRY YOUR LUCK WITH COUPONS

GET UPDATE FILE 08 FROM A CHEST, EAST SIDE

GET FEDERAL REPORT 01 FROM A CONSOLE, WEST SIDE

GET FEDERAL REPORT 06 FROM A TRASH CAN, WEST SIDE

GET FEDERAL REPORT 02 FROM A CONSOLE, NORTH SIDE

GET UPDATE FILE 09 FROM A CHEST, 5TH FLOOR, 2ND ROOM

INTRODUCTION
ARCHIVES
CHARACTERS
TACTICAL FILES
EQUIPMENT
THREAT ASSESSMENT
REGIONAL ANALYSIS
SUPPLEMENTAL DATA

Once you reach town, there are a number of activities. Check out the ice cream store on the left, use the **Save Point** on the right, buy some tickets, or use Quincy's Select Shop.

HARAMIYA ICE CREAM

ITEM	PRICE
LEMON ICE CREAM	80
BERRY ICE CREAM	480
MELON ICE CREAM	1000

QUINCY'S SELECT STORE

ITEM	COST
MED KIT S	100
MED KIT M	500
REVIVE M	600
NULLIFIER	1000
SEVEN MOONS	300
ANTIDOTE	20
REMOVER	50
ANTI-CRYSTAL	1000
G VACCINE	500
ANALYZE BALL	4
TRAP	200

EQUIPMENT	COST
AUTO MACER	200
BLUE LADY	300
RED CANCER	600
HINOKA SANJU	200
QI YAN	300
VB-RAIN	670
DELTA EDGE I	180
COMPOUND VII	580
ZERO CRUSHER	210
RANGER HUNT	610
KWAP-PII	300
KWP-XII	700
FORCE HAND	190
PSYCHO DRIVER	590
DESERT EAGLE	190
LEGACY OF ZARA	590
LACE TANK TOP	120
METAL CORSET	120
GRAMPUS PANNIER	370

EQUIPMENT	COST
BOLERO CAPE	370
GRANITE MANTLE	120
HAZE ROBE	400
SPEED II VEST	110
SPEED III VEST	380
KAP-BEG	150
KAP-CLE	450
FIBER VEST	120
TECHTRON CLOTH	380
NEO PROTECTOR	380
BULLET NECK	600
LEATHER CHOKER	150
CYLINDER NECK	300
OPEN HEART	450
RED CRYSTAL	300
SNAKE EYE	100
SHOCK ABSORBER	100
FIRE WALL	1000
THUNDER WALL	1000
ICE WALL	1000
BEAM WALL	1000
COBRA BANGLE	100
RARE BRACE	300
RED STAR	300
VELVET RING	600
CRIMSON RING	300
YELLOW RING	300
COBALT RING	300
SILVER RING	300

Head back the way you came and destroy the plants to the left to reveal a ladder down. This brings you to the fountain control. Playing with the fountain settings and choosing Pattern C forces a piece off and back onto the walkway. Head back through the tunnels and grab the Skill Upgrade C.

Money is easy to spend in town. You can drop 500G on tickets for the **Coupon Raffle**, near the Save Point (Try 68, 37, and 12 for good luck). There are also binoculars that let you look around the city for 100G, and those aren't too far down the road.

Head to the left of the center arches, then climb up them. Blast the Realian to get it out of the way to see a short scene.

On the eastern side of the city, is a building on the right section of the map. Blast through its door and head up the inside of the structure. An item box with **Update File 08** is there. Continue to the top of the building for some Berry Ice Cream; drop a trap at the base of the pole where the cat is walking. Use the trap to stun the kitty then quickly tap ⊚ to grab the balloon it has stolen. The child there gives you two cones of Berry Ice Cream in return.

Stop when you find the vending machines and the second set of binoculars in the region. Search the trashcans nearby (they are small, grey, and easy to miss). Inside the one on the left is **Federal Report 06**.

To find the **Federal Report 01**, look on the western block of the city. Past the guard post on the lower tier, there is a door near two talking women. Destroy the door, head through the passage there, and blast a console on the other side. The Report was inside of the console. By destroying other consoles in the area, you find various items: Nano Repair DX, Rejuvenator M, Half Repair.

Travel to the north side of town by going up the stairs on the west side and using the path past the U-TIC soldiers; they won't bother you. In the next area, talk to a number of people to learn about the current mood of the city.

After speaking with Bailey, an older worker from the mines, destroy the consoles nearby for **Federal Report 02** and a C-US3G.

After getting these free items, walk to the left side of the map and leave the area. There is another section of city nearby; enter that and take a look at the impressive Special Research Facility there. Walk up to the building to trigger the next plot event. Step inside after talking to the guard.

THE HOSPITAL

Walk through the lobby of the "hospital" and see another scene with a U-TIC soldier. Use the **Save Point** nearby afterwards, then move to the left side and destroy a cart there. A Skill Upgrade B is hidden inside. An Ether Pack M is on the right side, in the ceiling light.

Take the elevator up to the fourth floor. There isn't anything impressive available on the other floors yet, though you can stop by the fifth and poke your head around if you like.

Central Management is on the fourth floor, where you can talk to quite a few people. Head to the northern corridor, and take the first door you find. The Observer Communications Console is there; the business district gate entrance password is 5150, as you learn. Suou's Memo is also found there. The second such lab, down the corridor, starts a plot event.

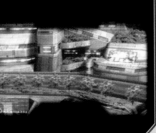

PRAYER BEADS

To use the 5150 code you just received, look on the larger city map while walking around; it is possible to move to the eastern side of town, even though there aren't any red arrows over there. Do this and you will soon see a large chest in that region. Move toward it and enter 5150 when asked for the gate code to the business district. The box beyond has Prayer Beads, which are needed in the distant future for Jin's final weapon.

Not far to the south from that location is another somewhat-hidden road. Look for a second chest, and open that one to discover Jr's Swimsuit.

Run to the left side of the main corridor afterward for more scenes. Return to Joachim's lab, talk with him, and head up to the fifth floor. You can now pass by the Control Room on the fifth floor and enter the main section of the floor. Shion and Allen get to find out more about the tests that are going on at the facility as well.

The first room along the fifth floor corridor has a chest that you can't get quite yet (you need to wait until people clear out of the room later). The second room has **Update File 09**. A plot event starts when Shion enters the fourth room, at the end of the hallway.

After talking with people in the room, escort the young girl who arrives outside so that she can pick some flowers. The scene there is brief, after which Shion should move out of the northern area and continue on toward the church. The scenes continue from there, and the chapter soon comes to a close.

ON THE ELSA

The scenes run their course, and Shion ends up back at the Elsa. Examine the two Federal Reports by logging into the blue computer terminal in the Professor's area. The online store has also been updated, and a third tier of Hakox missions are available as well. In truth, the online store has the same items it did earlier, just like the store in town, but you now have your buddies around and can buy them items without having to guess whether something is a good upgrade or not. Grab everything you want, equip the fun stuff, and save the game. If you have the cash, take a few extra rings for extra properties to physical attacks; these come in handy from time to time. Speaking of which, put Crimson Rings on a couple of your attackers (e.g. Jin, Jr., Ziggy).

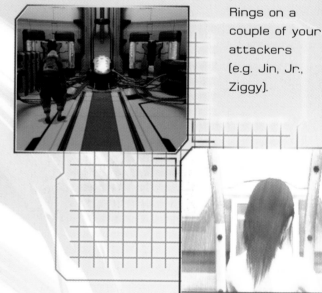

Play some Hakox for a time, then take a break from it to trigger the next plot event. This leads to an impressive event and the initiation of a boss fight!

BLACK TESTAMENT

HP:	10000
EP:	500
BL:	600
INFO:	BIOLOGICAL (HUMAN)
TGT:	???
EXP:	3700
SP:	15
G:	1300
N ITEM:	ETHER PACK M
R ITEM:	ETHER PACK L
S ITEM:	VENOM RING
STRONG:	ICE, BEAM
WEAK:	FIRE
ABSORBED:	NONE
NULL:	LIGHTNING, POISON, SEAL ETHER, SEAL BOOST, REFLECT DAMAGE

The Black Testament is going to test your group considerably. Not only does this enemy have quite a sum of health, but his various attacks are able to do either substantial area-of-effect damage to the group or massive single-target damage. Either way, a very solid healer will be needed in the second half of the fight.

Early on, get that nifty Venom Ring stolen from Black Testament. Don't buff your party with those expensive Offensive/Defensive type of spells. Black Testament can dispel these in a single turn, and the entire group will lose the benefit. Instead, save these for a later stage of the fight, when getting this monster to lose a turn debuffing the group is almost worthwhile all by itself.

Don't rely on Break attacks to get the job done. After the halfway point, Black Testament uses Stand Keeper is make Break damage ineffective. Because he also has an extremely-high Break Limit, it's better to rely on high-damage attacks.

Stick with your melee types for most of the fight and let them spend their ether points freely. Not only do you need these characters for their anti-biological attacks; you are going to want to save EPs on your ether-based characters (especially MOMO). The reason is obvious when Black Testament uses Abyss Walker around one-quarter health. This ability makes him immune to physical damage for a considerable period. Shift in your best healer and your best ether-damage characters and have them go to town. Anything with fire is especially useful.

Absolutely rely on medium level healing. Don't fall behind on this guy, because his late-stage area-of-effect poison attacks are cruelty given form. If you saved MOMO for the later portion of the fight, her energy points should last even under a high healing load.

Try to end the fight with a finishing strike. This is always a good idea, but the time investment of this fight makes it a real shame if you can't pull off the bonus here.

INTRODUCTION
ARCHIVES
CHARACTERS
TACTICAL FILES
EQUIPMENT
THREAT ASSESSMENT
ADDITIONAL ANALYSIS
SUPPLEMENTAL DATA

GETTING INTO LABYRINTHOS

POINTS OF INTEREST	
1	SEGMENT ADDRESS 15
2	CENTRAL ELEVATOR 2
3	CONTAINER RECEIVING SYSTEM
4	SECURITY B CARD

ITEMS	
1	MED KIT S
2	MED KIT M
3	HINOKA KAGURA
4	MED KIT S
5	UPDATE FILE 10
6	JIN'S SWIMSUIT
7	D-FRAME I
8	500G, ETHER PACK M, NULLIFIER, MED KIT M, NANO REPAIR M
9	REVIVE L
10	200G
11	D-NULLIFY GUARD
12	REVIVE M

ENEMIES	
1	CARNICOS I
2	DOMO-ALPHA
3	O-78 GRISLY 2
4	P.S.S. A
5	P.S.S. B
6	U-TIC SOLDIER A
7	U-TIC SOLDIER B

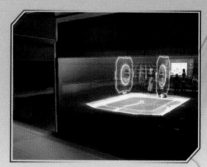

It's a fairly standard configuration, though it helps to use anti-machine or fire/lightning attacks if you like to bring down the Domos with extra speed.

Beyond the gates is the lift, Central Elevator 1. Take that into the main portion of Labyrinthos. The security level of the guards is quickly upgraded, and your group is likely to face far more resistance. Expect to find P.S.S. soldiers and occasional O-78 Grislys inside. Ice and anti-biological weaponry are quite effective here. Or, if you want to be really naughty, try out the Erde Kaiser that your group learned way back when (it's so much fun against the groups of four enemies).

Ignore the central doorway and use the gateway on the right side to get past the blocked routes. On the left side, when you come from the back, **Segment Address 15** is found. Blast open the containers there to expose it.

Hinoka Kagura is found inside Segment Address 15. By finding the information about Mai's father (in the upper floors of the hospital) and taking it to her, you gain the Decoder for this door. The weapon is a sword for Jin.

After resting and preparing, leave the Elsa again and go back into the city. Pass the normal districts and head all the way to the end of the line. The group wants to enter Labyrinthos!

The plan for getting in is pretty straight forward; charge the gates. In the first fight, take down the U-TIC Soldiers first (B, then A), and finish the fight with the Domo.

Take the double doors at the far end of the room. The walkways ahead have blocked passages, but your characters can blast through the walls on either side of the walkway.

Walk to the right and go into the large ductwork. The rooms ahead lead to a scene, and you see a room with an Area 13 marking. You cannot use that door now, so the other door in that room is your goal. Clear the hallway ahead, then exit from the left side.

This takes the group back out into the main chamber. Use the **Save Point** on the left side of the room, and also examine the blue plate if you need any supplies (the inventory is identical to what you see on the Elsa during this period).

FREE REST

With such a nice Save Point here and so many good fights nearby, it would be a shame to conserve EPs. Use heavy-hitting area-of-effect attacks to destroy the large patrol groups easily. Then, head back to rest and save after the fighting is over or if you run out of EPs on multiple characters.

There are also rooms on the left side from the central chamber. If you enter this from the door beside the Save Point, the first room you reach has two item boxes. **Update File 10** is inside. Jin's Swimsuit is as well!

Exit that room and follow the hallway until it reaches an elevator; down below is a room with D-Frame I. The second room in the basement is guarded by sleeping soldiers; pass them and destroy all containers for light items and money (though you end up fighting the guards because of the noise).

Go all the way down the hallway and into a larger room. Move toward the camera to find a Revive L.

At the very bottom of that section, if you go all the way out to the main room again, there is an entrance to an ammo containment area. The puzzle here is easy, but it might take a second to realize that you have to do everything by hand (it looks like a crane puzzle, but it isn't). Destroying an ammo crate causes any ammo crates immediately beside it to be pushed away.

The containers on the upper side of the room need to be destroyed in such a way that a final container gets pushed onto the green squares before being destroyed. This ensures that the two doors are going to be opened properly. Go after the left door first, to get a item box with a D-Nullify Guard in it. Then, move forward through the right door. At any time, you can use the terminal nearby to restore the containers, resetting the puzzle.

INTRODUCTION

ARCHIVES

CHARACTERS

TACTICAL FILES

EQUIPMENT

THREAT ASSESSMENT

REGIONAL ANALYSIS

SUPPLEMENTAL DATA

LEFT DOOR
UPPER-RIGHT CONTAINER
CONTAINER PUSHED BY THE BLAST
CONTAINER ON THE LEFT
CONTAINER ON THE GREEN SQUARE, LEFT SIDE

RIGHT DOOR
UPPER RIGHT CONTAINER
CONTAINER DOWN AND LEFT FROM THERE
CONTAINER ON BOTTOM-RIGHT SIDE
CONTAINER ON UPPER-RIGHT GREEN SQUARE

This lets the group continue into the complex. Exit the ammo room and keep walking until you hit the next scene. Watch that, then back out into the hallway where it began. Follow the only way forward until you spot two familiar faces walking above, and examine the room they left behind. After another scene, take the **Security B Card** from the left side of the room. Use the elevator that the researchers took a moment ago for a shortcut up toward the top floor of the central chamber (where you started). Save again, then take the elevator down.

LOWER LABS

POINTS OF INTEREST	
1	CENTRAL ELEVATOR 3
2	LANDING SITE

ITEMS	
1	CLEANSER
2	ETHER PACK S
3	CLEANSER
4	MED KIT L
5	MED KIT L
6	NANO REPAIR DX
7	CLEANSER
8	HALF REPAIR
9	ALL REPAIR

ENEMIES	
1	CARNICOS I
2	P.S.S. A
3	P.S.S. B
4	P.S.S. P
5	STOLE ARMA
6	STOLE MARINE
7	YACUD CANNON

The elevator leads to a train depot; blast the crates to the left and grab the Cleanser before boarding the train. Then, ride the car to the far side of the base. There aren't any side passages here, so it's mostly a direct fight as your group moves toward the next room and another elevator.

It won't be long at all until you reach the target of your intrusion. Watch the scenes that unfold, then follow the only way forward. Use the **Save Point** before passing through into the actual chamber with the Vessels of Anima that you need.

The group preps their E.S.s and is soon on the move in style. There is simply no way to steal a selection of Vessels of Anima without being noticed, and that means that the chase is on. Don't forget to equip any E.S. items that you have found recently. If nothing else, you likely have a that G-Legle/56 that you found!

ANIMA CHANGES

Your E.S.s can now charge to Anima level two, giving the craft new special attacks to use in battle. Use these higher-end special attacks only for large groups, as they are not in any way needed for the riff-raff of the area.

Another point of interest is the Anima gain for E.S. Asher. That E.S. has been equipped with the Professor's homemade generator. Though powerful, that system won't allow Anima abilities. For this reason, you may want to have E.S. Asher go into the reserve group and let E.S. Reuben take to the front lines.

Move through the complex. Don't bother disembarking at the first dock as the door is locked. Marine and Arma groups are in the way at first; these are high damage but low health targets that can be dealt with easily if you don't let them get the drop on you with back attacks. If a second enemy unit is trying to attack you and you are invulnerable after a previous engagement, don't run. The enemy craft move faster than yours and will get a back attack. With most fights, it's quite useful to destroy all but the last craft then charge for a turn to get a fair amount of health back. This precludes the use of Nano Repairs.

After a few rooms of this, the group comes to a **Save Point**. That area has similar enemies, but it also adds the Yacud Cannons; those enemies are quickly destroyed, and should be taken out before Marine or Arma crafts!

And now for a major treat; there is a blue plate by the Save Point. This store has upgrades for almost every slot of every E.S. in your group. Go nuts, buy new frames, generators, weapons, CPUs, and disks. Equip it all and use the Save Point again to restore the E.S.s to their full potential. Getting D-Frames and D-Kill Rs are especially useful. For the upcoming boss battle at the end of the area, the D-Kill Rs are very nice!

INTRODUCTION

ARCHIVES

CHARACTERS

TACTICAL FILES

EQUIPMENT

THREAT ASSESSMENT

REGIONAL ANALYSIS

SUPPLEMENTAL DATA

LABYRINTHOS STORE

ITEM	COST
MED KIT S	100
MED KIT M	500
REVIVE M	600
NULLIFIER	1000
SEVEN MOONS	300
ANTIDOTE	20
REMOVER	50
ANTI-CRYSTAL	1000
G VACCINE	500
ANALYZE BALL	4
TRAP	200
NANO REPAIR M	400
HALF REPAIR	1500
DOWN REPAIR	50

E.S. EQUIPMENT	COST
STING RAY II	300
ST SWIFT HG	300
TYPE II – GALE	600
DAWNING MOON	1000
G90 ASSAULT	300
SG-M20	400
LINDWURM	300
EM FADEN	400
VOLANS G	300
ARF-R5	350
G PHALANX	320
AF-HUNTER	460
ZF-UPARA	460
DF-V2 R	460
RF-FLAME	460
RF-SHADOW	800
G-ROX/43	480
G-ROX/56	1200
C-US2	100
C-US3	150
D-SENSOR	50
D-GUARD	200
D-KILL C	300
D-KILL R	300
D-TREASURE I	500
D-FRAME I	750

LABYRINTHOS STORE

EQUIPMENT	COST	EQUIPMENT	COST
AUTO MACER	200	KAP-BEG	150
BLUE LADY	300	KAP-CLE	450
RED CANCER	600	FIBER VEST	120
HINOKA SANJU	200	TECHTRON CLOTH	380
QI YAN	300	NEO PROTECTOR	380
VB-RAIN	670	BULLET NECK	600
DELTA EDGE I	180	LEATHER CHOKER	150
COMPOUND VII	580	CYLINDER NECK	300
ZERO CRUSHER	210	OPEN HEART	450
RANGER HUNT	610	RED CRYSTAL	300
KWAP-PII	300	SNAKE EYE	100
KWP-XII	700	SHOCK ABSORBER	100
FORCE HAND	190	FIRE WALL	1000
PSYCHO DRIVER	590	THUNDER WALL	1000
DESERT EAGLE	190	ICE WALL	1000
LEGACY OF ZARA	590	BEAM WALL	1000
LACE TANK TOP	120	COBRA BANGLE	100
METAL CORSET	120	RARE BRACE	300
GRAMPUS PANNIER	370	RED STAR	300
BOLERO CAPE	370	VELVET RING	600
GRANITE MANTLE	120	CRIMSON RING	300
HAZE ROBE	400	YELLOW RING	300
SPEED II VEST	110	COBALT RING	300
SPEED III VEST	380	SILVER RING	300

Destroy the doors at the top of the ramps and explore the nooks above while fighting the enemies there. With the addition of new equipment, the battles here have gone from fun plus challenging to fun plus slaughter!

By flying to the top of the ramp, you trigger a scene and a boss fight with your E.S. craft. A mobile weapon is ready to counter your escape.

INTRODUCTION

ARCHIVES

CHARACTERS

TACTICAL FILES

EQUIPMENT

THREAT ASSESSMENT

SCENARIO ANALYSIS

SUPPLEMENTAL DATA

OMEGA UNIVERSITAS

HP:	200000
INFO:	MACHINE
TGT:	???
EXP:	4900
SP:	15
G:	2600
N ITEM:	D-EN I
R ITEM:	NONE
STRONG:	NONE
WEAK:	NONE
ABSORBED:	NONE
NULL:	NONE

Omega Universitas isn't too scary a foe, especially if you have D-Kill Rs equipped. These prevent the boss from interrupting longer groups of normal attacks. Not only does this avoid damage for your E.S.s, but it also allows everyone to gain Anima much faster because they are getting more hits in successfully.

Remember to have E.S. Asher out of the fight, so that nobody is without Anima. Use Anima Awakening early on for easy damage, then regenerate Anima through the rest of the encounter (to be used for a rush of damage at the end). This makes the encounter much shorter and is still quite safe.

Once Universitas gets close to 50% health, the craft will use Black Wave to raise its attack power. This will occur later as well, at 25% health, and possibly again in the final stages of the fight. Once this starts, expect to start seeing the boss's real attacks.

Ether Wave and Ether Wave II (seen after the second Black Wave), are light area-of-effect strikes that are not the biggest threat. Rather, the single-target Martial Ring and Super Martial Ring are the ones to fear. These contribute brutal damage against lone E.S.s.

Charge to keep health strong, and use Nano Repairs as needed, and hold the big guns back for the last 20%. Three Anima Awakenings, even if some aren't back to level two will be enough to blast through the remainder of Omega Universitas' HPs.

THE THIRD DESCENT OPERATION

The Federation is starting its major push against the capital of Miltia. Things are going to get really chaotic in a short period, and the group is prepared to take advantage of that. While onboard the Elsa, save, purchase any necessary supplies, and do any work in the EVS Simulator that you want. When ready, leave the Elsa and head back into the city.

This time, your group has to walk through the normal districts. Nobody tries to stop you or give you trouble, but there is a scene on the way out from the northern district. Watch this, then wait for the story to advance. The group regains control at Labyrinthos, where many people are disrupted due to the current Descent Operation.

LABYRINTHOS RESCUE

POINTS OF INTEREST	
1	CENTRAL ELEVATOR 1
2	SEGMENT ADDRESS 05
3	STAFF ROOM

ITEMS	
1	ROSARIO OF GRIEF
2	ETHER PACK S
3	REVIVE M
4	MED KIT L
5	REJUVENATOR M
6	DECODER 13
7	MED KIT DX
8	ETHER PACK S, REJUVENATOR M
9	STAFF ROOM ACCESS KEY, MED KIT DX

ENEMIES	
1	CARNICOS II
2	DOMO ALPHA
3	O-78 GRISLY 2
4	P.S.S. –C
5	P.S.S. –P2
6	PELLEGRI'S SOLDIERS AND PELLEGRI (BOSS)
7	U-TIC SOLDIER A
8	U-TIC SOLDIER B

There are groups of mechs and soldiers all over the place now, in anticipation of the attack. Fight these if you wish, and walk forward into Labyrinthos. You cannot access the elevator to reach the other areas of the building at this time anyway.

INTRODUCTION

ARCHIVES

CHARACTERS

TACTICAL FILES

EQUIPMENT

THREAT ASSESSMENT

REGIONAL ANALYSIS

SUPPLEMENTAL DATA

Use Central Elevator 1 to return to Labyrinthos. This time, take the door at the center of the area and defeat the two P.S.S. groups inside the room. There is a chest with the Rosario of Grief, an item that adds extra EP.

Otherwise, continue into the area just as you did the first time. The difference is that the Area 13 door a few rooms away is now unlocked. Note that you can move past the door, use the Save Point from the last incursion, or even take Central Elevator 2 if you wish. After having whatever fun you wish, use the Area 13 doorway and continue to the south.

There are fun fights in here, with many biological and mechanical targets. Segment Address 05 is revealed at the bottom of the hallway by destroying two containers against the inside wall of the turn. Left from that is a hallway with a Save Point that is worth using. The gate below that is blocked, and the Staff Room is locked. For now, exit the area by taking the door you just used and walk down the stairs outside.

Climb down and into the lower hall. From there, destroy the containers on the left to expose another door. This one gets your group a chest with a Rejuvenator M. Exit and use the lower passage next; this opens into a room with many tight routes through cramped storage rooms. Search these for minor items in containers and a chest with Decoder 13. The P.S.S. groups in the room are easy kills, especially in high damage parties. If you really wish to get the drop on them, note the fact that many of them face a given section of hallway (so taking the long route to their backs is useful for easier hits).

Use the stairway on the right side to get out of the area. Your goal is close, but there isn't much time; the Song of Nephilim is going to be used soon. Follow the left side of the hallway when it splits later, and move along that until you see the Save Point from earlier. Use the terminal near the gate to open the way. You can save now, and regain quite a bit of HPs/EPs.

The Staff Room Key is down the lower of the two passageways on the right side of this area. Destroy the containers there to get it, then unlock the room. Inside, on the console desk, is an important PDA that updates your database. With all of the problems taken care of, walk along the final section of corridor on the right side. A boss fight is waiting, so keep all health full!

PELLEGRI AND HER SOLDIERS

The two soldiers at Pellegri's side make this boss fight sound more than a bit scary, but it's not as bad as some of the ones you've already faced. And if you have the Erde Kaiser ability this is just amusing to watch.

Use area-of-effect attacks early on (especially Erde Kaiser, with its ability to send Pellegri's Soldiers past their Break Limit very quickly). Kill off both of these tough foes first. Neither of them pose too much of a threat to the party, but you won't want them around later on, when Pellegri gets uppity.

After the bodyguards are knocked out, steal the Double Vestment from Pellegri if you can (Jr. and some of the others can learn Rare Steal from the EX-A skill group, so you might have a few people with steal at this time). It's a slugfest after that point.

Try to get Pellegri's Break Gauge toward its high end as she nears the 50% health mark. She'll use Overtaker to get fast Boost and prepare special attacks after that point. Her Impulsion area-of-effect strike is nothing to worry about, but Megiddo Rosarium is a single-target slap that can take out weaker characters very easily. Consider tipping her past her Break Limit if you get behind in the healing. Otherwise, save that ace for the final push.

Once down around 30% health, Pellegri enters consecutive attack mode. It's very good to have characters fast enough to go early in each combat round, because a successful hit knocks her out of this. Jin is quite good for such a role. For that matter, Jin is a great character for this fight in any event, as he is able to keep quite a sum of damage coming at Pellegri throughout the engagement.

With a final push, try out your special moves and eliminate Pellegri. She wasn't too tough a boss, but the fight sure was fun!

PELLEGRI'S SOLDIERS (X2)	
HP:	4000
EP:	44
BL:	60
INFO:	BIOLOGICAL (HUMAN)
TGT:	RECOVERY KILLER
EXP:	250
SP:	15
G:	120
N ITEM:	SKILL UPGRADE A
R ITEM:	NONE
S ITEM:	NONE
STRONG:	ICE
WEAK:	FIRE, LIGHTNING
ABSORBED:	NONE
NULL:	NONE

PELLEGRI	
HP:	12000
EP:	400
BL:	300
INFO:	BIOLOGICAL (HUMAN)
TGT:	???
EXP:	5400
SP:	15
G:	2900
N ITEM:	GRAND DESIGN
R ITEM:	NONE
S ITEM:	DOUBLE VESTMENT
STRONG:	FIRE, LIGHTNING
WEAK:	ICE
ABSORBED:	NONE
NULL:	NONE

MILTIA IN FLAMES

POINTS OF INTEREST	
1	ONLINE STORE

ITEMS	
1	FEDERAL REPORT 04
2	SKILL UPGRADE A
3	ALL REPAIR
4	SKILL UPGRADE B
5	HALF COAT
6	FEDERAL REPORT 03
7	FEDERAL REPORT 05
8	TALISMAN

ENEMIES	
1	E2 HAUSER
2	FEDERATION SOLDIER A
3	FEDERATION SOLDIER B
4	U-TIC SOLDIER A
5	U-TIC SOLDIER B
6	ZOLFO RG

The area outside the hospital, as well as the rest of the city, is crawling with soldiers. You are free to use the Save Point inside the hospital, and to return to it later as well (if you use too much of your resources fighting everyone in sight). Many of the soldiers' groups can be avoided, but there are many skill points to be gained by taking on these clusters. Most of the fights have three or four targets, don't take long to best, and are quite rewarding. Thus, this is a good place to farm for a short time.

Your group cannot skip back to the Elsa. It's a long haul through Federation and U-TIC troops to get there. Take the same path through the city that you've used before, but in reverse. Avoid using high-cost techniques and ether attacks unless you want to use ether packs or swap characters, as you will run out of EP before you get to your next save plate.

Be sure to destroy everything you come across as there are a couple Skill Upgrades to find in the rubble and a Half Coat (armor for chaos/Jr.) in the raised area near the U-TIC transport.

Federal Report 04 is in the lower portion of the northern district. Destroy a container on the left side, after coming down the staircase. To the east, in the next map, is **Federal Report 03**; you get that after destroying a U-TIC transport that lands nearby. For yet another one, **Federal Report 05** is given to you by a collapsed soldier by the Green Motor sign a bit down the road. Searching containers on that right side soon reveals a Talisman as well (+800 HPs for its user).

When the road divides, stick to the right for a Save Point and access to Quincy's Select Store.

QUINCY'S SELECT STORE	
ITEM	COST
MED KIT S	100
MED KIT M	500
REVIVE M	600
NULLIFIER	1000
SEVEN MOONS	300
ANTIDOTE	20
REMOVER	50
ANTI-CRYSTAL	1000
G VACCINE	500
ANALYZE BALL	4
TRAP	200

QUINCY'S SELECT STORE

EQUIPMENT	COST	EQUIPMENT	COST
RED CANCER	600	BRIGAND	1050
TOLL BUNKER	1800	BULLET NECK	600
VB-RAIN	670	CYLINDER NECK	300
VB-FALL	2000	DOG TAG	600
COMPOUND VII	580	OPEN HEART	450
DELTA EDGE II	1600	RED CRYSTAL	300
RANGER HUNT	610	SNAKE EYE	100
ROCK STAR	2000	PANTHER EYE	1200
KWP-XII	700	SHOCK ABSORBER	100
KWP-XIII	2100	FIRE WALL	1000
PSYCHO DRIVER	590	THUNDER WALL	1000
MEDES DRIVER	1700	ICE WALL	1000
LEGACY OF ZARA	590	BEAM WALL	1000
PHANTOM SILVER	1800	COBRA BANGLE	100
GRAMPUS PANNIER	370	QUEEN JACK	700
BOLERO CAPE	370	KING JACK	700
PLATINUM BUSTIER	1000	VAN BRACE	700
KAJIC CAPE	1000	RARE BRACE	300
GRANITE MANTLE	120	RED STAR	300
HAZE ROBE	400	VELVET RING	600
MOONLIGHT ROBE	1200	CRIMSON RING	300
SPEED III VEST	380	YELLOW RING	300
GUSTAV VEST	1000	COBALT RING	300
GUSTAV ARMOR	1300	SILVER RING	300
KAP-CLE	450	FLAME AVATAR	900
KAP-COS	1300	LIGHTNING AVATAR	900
TECHTRON CLOTH	380	ICE AVATAR	900
NEO PROTECTOR	380	BEAM AVATAR	900
DOUBLE RIDERS	1050		

After resting and saving, purchase a full range of weapon, armor, and accessory upgrades. The store has truly outdone itself, and all of the excess money that your group has accumulated will drift into a meager supply. To bolster that, sell off some of your barter items to the store.

You can leave the city now, without fear of losing any opportunities. There is a very cool scene as Shion and the others move toward the church. Enter the church when the cutscenes end, then fight the Berserk Realians in a trivial encounter. More scenes follow, concluding with a superb boss encounter.

THE BLUE TESTAMENT

HP:	14500
EP:	700
BL:	600
INFO:	BIOLOGICAL
TGT:	???
EXP:	11500
SP:	20
G:	3000
N ITEM:	GUSTAV RING
R ITEM:	NONE
S ITEM:	UNION NECK
STRONG:	ICE
WEAK:	FIRE
ABSORBED:	NONE
NULL:	POISON, SEAL ETHER, SEAL BOOST

Because the Blue Testament isn't joking around, he'll use Overtaker immediately. This means that the rate of Boost accrual for the Blue Testament is extremely high even during the early portions of the encounter.

None-the-less, take the time to steal the Union Neck from him. This item is so wonderful that nobody wants to miss it; the item gives your group +1 to their maximum Boost. That is wonderful for normal encounters and boss fights. Love it forever.

Next, abuse some good Break attacks to prepare a push for later. The Blue Testament doesn't take that much damage in the grand scheme of things, but his output is enough in the second half that it's very wise to have this Break scheme ready to go.

Once the Blue Testament hits half health, he'll use Offensive periodically, then unleash major special attacks. Victim's Hail isn't something you'll see every round or two, but its rarity is not enough to diminish its reputation. Most likely, the entire group will be pushed to their Break Limit and wounded by this area-of-effect nightmare. By the time you recover, major healing *will* be needed.

Thus, have a skilled group healer already out and ready to cast before the Blue Testament uses his special ability. Better yet, slap Erde Kaiser on him to deal heavy Break damage, then try a second-level special attack for a finishing move. Properly equipped and with only minor level building, Jin's best special attack can comfortably deal well over 4,000 damage. Right there, that is almost 30% of the Blue Testament's health.

It is certainly suggested that you have at least one of your highest HP character out for the entirety of the fight. Ziggy, even if he never did a point of damage, would ensure that one good rush by the Blue Testament couldn't spell a total wipeout for your party.

BACK TO THE HOSPITAL

POINTS OF INTEREST	
1	TRANSPORT CONVEYOR SWITCHES

ITEMS	
1	D-TREASURE I
2	MED KIT L
3	MED KIT M
4	SKILL UPGRADE A
5	CLEANSER
6	SKILL UPGRADE A
7	ASSAULT VEST
8	D-TYPE G
9	FEDERAL REPORT 08
10	FEDERAL REPORT 07
11	MED KIT DX
12	SKILL UPGRADE C

ENEMIES	
1	FEDERATION SOLDIER A
2	FEDERATION SOLDIER B
3	MERCURIO GM
4	STANDARD U.R.T.V.
5	U-TIC SOLDIER A
6	U-TIC SOLDIER B

The story follows Shion to the back door of the Labyrinthos facility. Use the **Save Point** and the blue plate to respectively save, rest, and replenish any lost items. Be certain to equip the powerful Gustav Ring and Union Neck you recently received, then destroy the bushes on the left side of the outdoor area. There is a chest with a D-Treasure I hidden way back there.

Inside, the corridor has minor items hidden in containers. Use the terminal on the left side to activate the left conveyor belt (a container with a cleanser comes down the line).

The U-TIC Soldiers are still holding off the Federation rush in this discrete location. It doesn't hurt that they have Mercurio mechs; they take a beating. Use special moves to either take out both U-TIC Soldiers in one blow, as with KOS-MOS's X-Buster, or save the Boost points for finishing off the Mercurio GMs.

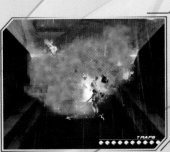 

The second conveyor chamber has a couple different groups of enemies (there are two sets of Standard U.R.T.V.s). These are not simple Realians that can be tossed aside; they attack very quickly, hit hard, and should be dealt with using fast area-of-effect strikes to eliminate entire groups before they can let their damage add up.

The two conveyor belts in that section are activated with separate terminals (both are on the right). Use these, then destroy the container that stops on the upper-right part of the map. Inside that container is a chest with an Assault Vest; Ziggy is *very* happy to have that.

After the conveyor area, the party goes topside again. There are several treats to find in this ruined part of town, and the battles are top notch for gaining skill points, so long as you have fair area-of-effect potential. Look on the right side of the burning area for both a D-Type G, and **Federal Report 08**. If you are having trouble getting to these, start at the stairs by the Federation Soldiers, climb down the right side, and destroy the rubble beneath you. That gets you close to the loot. On the other side of the map, in the very corner, is **Federal Report 07**.

Leave via the right side of the map, and move to the area in front of Labyrinthos again. Each time you are here, this place gets a little bit more beaten up. The Federation hasn't been able to take and hold this area yet, but U-TIC has a minimal grip

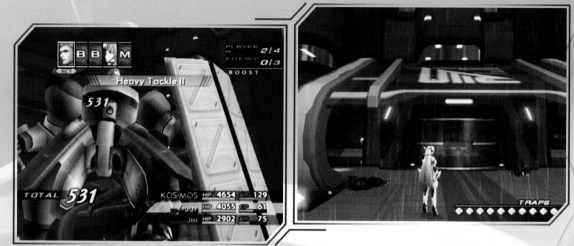

at best. Fight through the groups out front, and search the parking lot to the left before going inside (a Skill Upgrade C offers 100 free points if you blow up the large transport there).

Use the **Save Point** inside the lobby of the building. The store next to it has nothing new, but it's still a convenient location to sell.

SAVING THE FAMILY

POINTS OF INTEREST	
1	SEGMENT ADDRESS 07
2	REALIAN UNIT MONITOR
3	MARKY (FUNCTIONAL REALIAN)
4	IGGY (FUNCTIONAL REALIAN)
5	DEEDEE (FUNCTIONAL REALIAN)
6	OBSERVER COMMUNICATIONS CONSOLE (5150 CODE)
7	SPRINKLER ACTIVATION SYSTEM
8	SECURITY MANAGEMENT SYSTEM

ENEMIES	
1	27-SERIES ASURA
2	ASTERION REVISED
3	BERSERK REALIAN A
4	BERSERK REALIAN B
5	BYPRODUCT #B156
6	BYPRODUCT #B283

ITEMS	
1	YASOMA SANJU
2	REVIVE M
3	ETHER PACK L
4	DECODER 07
5	COERCION RING
6	REJUVENATOR L
7	MED KIT L, 2000G, HP UPGRADE
8	SKILL UPGRADE B
9	DECODER 05
10	C-US5G
11	REJUVENATOR DX

Before blasting open the door to the emergency stairway, look in the elevator room. There is a fight with Realians and an Asterion Revised in there, but Jin gets a Yasoma Sanju from the chest they guard. This weapon is a tad lower on direct damage, but its improvement to his Break Limit and Luck is quite noteworthy. If you are already shooting for a build with many criticals (and wearing his Swimsuit), then this is ideal.

Now you should break into the emergency stair area and move up. Use ● to put out the fire on the steps, and continue up to the second floor. A Revive M is in a container there, and the ceiling light breaks open and drops a chest into the room; a fight comes with it, but you receive an Ether Pack L as a reward.

Along the second-floor hallway, the first door gets you into a lab that hasn't been ransacked yet. Loria is still in there, and she wants a complete version of the Federal Report. She'll give you **Decoder 07** in exchange.

Outside, destroy the debris a few feet down from there, along the wall. This exposed **Segment Address 07**! Because you likely just got the Decoder for this door, open it and grab the Coercion Ring. The barricade past that protects you from the Realians in the hall, but you aren't a chicken. Destroy the barricade, and notice that this act temporarily freezes some of the Realians in place. Go for back attacks!

FINISHING THE FEDERAL REPORTS

You now have all of the Federal Reports, which means that you should update them next time you are on the Elsa. Go to the Professor's area on the ship and use the console in front of the glowing, blue "S" and read each file. When they are all done, you receive Update File 03.

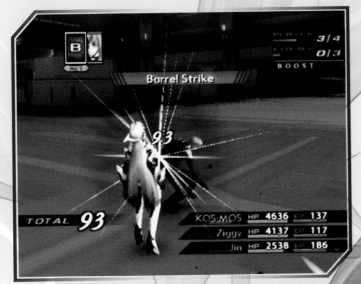

INTRODUCTION
ARCHIVES
CHARACTERS
TACTICAL FILES
EQUIPMENT
THREAT ASSESSMENT
REGIONAL ANALYSIS
SUPPLEMENTAL DATA

After clearing everyone, look in the second room along the hall that isn't destroyed. Save Rosley, a scientist in there, then use the Realian Unit Monitor next to him; this provides details on which Realian models are going berserk. Additionally, the console provides news footage from out in the city.

The final door, at the base of the corridor, leads to an alternate emergency stair section. Climb the stairs, and put out another fire above the third floor. Enter the fourth floor at the top of the steps, and begin trashing all of the enemies up there as well.

Inside the room at the top of the floor are many Realians undergoing calibration. Some of these are berserk, others are not. For the maximum value of experience and skill points, break all containers. To receive only the bonus items from freeing the three functional Realians, only break containers with non-malfunctioning model numbers. Or, if you don't feel like comparing the numbers, just break these containers: bottom-left, upper-middle, upper-right. The best item you receive for helping these Realians is an HP Upgrade.

Use the other doorway, on the left side of the room, to enter the main passage again. Move around the wreckage and walk to the room below. Press the red bottom on the floor to open the door to the surgery room, and fight

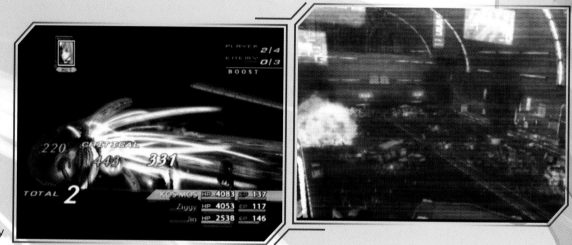

the Realian inside. If you are fast enough to save the doctor, he rewards you with an EP Upgrade! A Skill Upgrade B and **Decoder 05** are within also; now you can open Segment Address 05, in the lower parts of Labyrinthos.

The left end of the floor has a raging fire that is still in progress. Weave through the flames and use the Sprinkler Activation System by the elevator. This saves the two Realians that were in the blaze; the lower Realian rewards you with an Ether Pack S. The other goes nuts and attacks you.

Use the stairs on the left side, but search the lower portion first. There is a very nice CPU in a chest farther down; once you have that, ascend the stairs and look for the fifth floor. A **Save Point** is floating just outside the doors to this final landing, and that probably looks pretty good after the long chain of fights that got you up there.

Once on the fifth floor, use the Security Management System console, behind the desks. This triggers a fight, but it is needed to open the hallway on the right. Walk down the hallway, and search the first room for the Rejuvenator DX if you wish (it triggers more fighting, but at least it spites the guy who used to guard the darn chest).

At the very end of the hallway is a door; moving beyond there triggers a scene, then a fight against the much-heralded 27-Series Asura Realians. They aren't exactly pretty, but they'll try to get the job done against you. One of their biggest tricks is that they deliver a heavy amount of Break damage with their attacks. Erde Kaiser is a good starting move, to keep the Realians pinned with their own Break problems. Try area-of-effect attacks as follow-ups. Everyone with special attacks that hit the entire enemy group is going to have a lot of fun here, with KOS-MOS being the best candidate, with X-Buster. You can also steal Upgrade A, if you are willing to take the time. Done correctly, you can finish the enemies off together, leading to a wonderful bonus in experience. It's not too bad at all!

Extended scenes follow, leading to the end of the chapter.

INTRODUCTION

ARCHIVES

CHARACTERS

TACTICAL FILES

EQUIPMENT

THREAT ASSESSMENT

REGIONAL ANALYSIS

SUPPLEMENTAL DATA

Things are safe, for the moment, and everyone is back on the Elsa. Take the opportunity to save and use the updated store. There are many fine equipment choices and E.S. equipment pieces to purchase, and you likely have the money to get what you want.

UPDATED ELSA STORE

ITEM	COST	E.S. EQUIPMENT	COST	EQUIPMENT	COST	EQUIPMENT	COST
MED KIT S	100	EM FADEN R	2100	TOLL BUNKER	1800	RED CRYSTAL	300
MED KIT M	500	VOLANS G	300	VIPER BUNKER	3400	SUN CRY	1800
REVIVE M	600	ARF-R5	350	VB-FALL	2000	SNAKE EYE	100
NULLIFIER	1000	G PHALANX	320	VB-FLAME	3500	PANTHER EYE	1200
SEVEN MOONS	300	ARF-R7	2000	DELTA EDGE II	1600	SHOCK ABSORBER	100
CLEANSER	1000	G PHALANX II	1800	ADONA SHOOTER	3200	FIRE WALL	1000
ANTIDOTE	20	SR SHAULA A	2200	ROCK STAR	2000	THUNDER WALL	1000
REMOVER	50	ZF-UPARA	460	BREAK KNUCKLE	3200	ICE WALL	1000
ANTI-CRYSTAL	1000	ZF-GARNET	2500	KWP-XIII	2100	BEAM WALL	1000
G VACCINE	500	DF-V2 R	460	KWP-XIV	3800	COBRA BANGLE	100
ANALYZE BALL	4	DF-V3	2500	MEDES DRIVER	1700	QUEEN JACK	700
TRAP	200	RF-FLAME	460	TIMAEUS	3200	KING JACK	700
NANO REPAIR M	400	RF-SHADOW	800	PHANTOM SILVER	1800	GOD CIRCLE	1700
HALF REPAIR	1500	RF-TIGER	2500	BLOOD M40	3300	IMPERIAL	1700
DOWN REPAIR	50	G-ROX/56	1200	PLATINUM BUSTIER	1000	SOUL COLLECTOR	1700
		G-ROX/63	2000	KAJIC CAPE	1000	VAN BRACE	700
		C-US3	150	VELVET BOLERO	2000	RARE BRACE	300
E.S. EQUIPMENT	**COST**	C-US4	1000	BUTTERFLY SUIT	2000	UNKNOWN BRACELET	1400
STING RAY II	300	C-US5	1500	MOONLIGHT ROBE	1200	GREEN STAR	2600
ST SWIFT HG	300	D-SENSOR	50	RAPTOR ROBE	2100	VELVET RING	600
AIRD-E	3000	D-GUARD	200	GUSTAV VEST	1000	CRIMSON RING	300
TYPE II – GALE	600	D-KILL C	300	GUSTAV ARMOR	1300	YELLOW RING	300
DAWNING MOON	1000	D-KILL R	300	PROTECT GEAR	2100	COBALT RING	300
SHIRANUI	2200	D-TREASURE I	500	KAP-COS	1300	SILVER RING	300
MISTY MOON	3400	D-FRAME I	750	KAP-GLA	2300	FLAME AVATAR	900
G90 ASSAULT	300	D-HALF A	800	DOUBLE RIDERS	1050	LIGHTNING AVATAR	900
SG-M20	400	D-HALF D	800	BRIGAND	1050	ICE AVATAR	900
SG-M30P	1600	D-HALF DEA	800	RIGID LEATHER	2200	BEAM AVATAR	900
TEMPEST	2200	D-REVENGE	1200	BULLET NECK	600	COUNTER RING	1800
LINDWURM	300	D-FRAME II	2500	CYLINDER NECK	300	REVENGE RING	1800
EM FADEN	400			DOG TAG	600	RUTHLESS RING	1800
LINDWURM M2	1600			OPEN HEART	450		
SCHWALBE F	1800			CROSS CHOKER	1600		

INTRODUCTION

ARCHIVES

CHARACTERS

TACTICAL FILES

EQUIPMENT

THREAT ASSESSMENT

REGIONAL ANALYSIS

SUPPLEMENTAL DATA

DON'T FORGET!

SAVE, SHOP, AND EQUIP NEW GEAR

RETURN TO LABYRINTHOS IN THE EVS FOR SEGMENT ADDRESS 05 (ERDE KAISER FURY)

PLAY THE NEW MISSIONS FOR HAKOX

TALK TO THE CAPTAIN WHEN YOU WANT TO LEAVE THE ELSA

This is a good time to look back through previous areas. All of the Miltia area is up for grabs in the U.M.N. This is wonderful for grabbing more money, heading into Labyrinthos to open **Segment Address 05**, and finding anything that you missed earlier. To reach Segment Address 05, travel back to Labyrinthos in the simulator; walk all the way back to the Area 13, and look at the bottom portion of that region. The golden door you revealed earlier will still be there, and it has an EK Fury! This teaches the Erde Kaiser Fury skill to your characters.

There are also new levels of Hakox for you to play, if you are interested.

Check on your E.S.s to make sure that they are ready for more action, then talk to the Captain and let him know that everyone is good to go for the next mission. With any luck, you won't get blown out of the sky while trying to cross a field of fire from Federation capital ships, Ormus craft, and Gnosis. Piece of cake.

THE MERKABAH

POINTS OF INTEREST	
1	LOCK MECHANISMS
2	SHAFT STOP SWITCH
3	HONEYCOMB PROTECT TERMINAL
4	SEGMENT ADDRESS 11

ENEMIES	
1	AG-03
2	VRA-2100
3	VRA-3500
4	VX-7000 M
5	YURIEV SOLDIER A
6	YURIEV SOLDIER B

ITEMS	
1	EX SKILL KEY II
2	D-CLEAN
3	DOWN REPAIR
4	HALF REPAIR
5	DECODER 10
6	DECODER 12
7	SWEET PAIN
8	NANO REPAIR DX, NANO REPAIR M DOWN REPAIR, 1000G
9	SKILL UPGRADE C
10	MED KIT L, MED KIT M
11	MED KIT DX, 1000G X 2, MED KIT L
12	DECODER 12

Fly into the Merkabah; there is only limited control, so you won't need to worry about messing things up. After a surprisingly simple landing, the party is set to advance into the warship. Note that you can exit the Merkabah from this point and return to the Elsa, if that is needed.

With your newly-upgraded E.S.s, these enemy VRAs won't be more than a speed bump. Destroy all three of the guards in the area, and fly to the left where there is an item box. Inside is the EX Skill Key II, one of the most important items that you could possibly discover. Use this immediately, and look at the new possibilities for each character. Spend any immediate points that are too tempting to resist, then leave the room using the central doorway.

The engine system in the next area needs to be stopped, but there isn't an immediate need to disembark. Instead, fly to the left doorway and explore that area first. Take the conveyor belt up through the room, and press to the right to jump off at each stop. The first stop leads to a chest with a D-Clean (an E.S. disk that is very powerful against status effects).

The third stop on the conveyor belt leads around and up to the next tier of the central room. A button up there releases the lock on the lower door (the one you passed earlier, when first entering the central chamber). Now that the way is clear, take the right door to head on a path that gets you back down to the first tier.

Go to the center of the main room and disembark. There is a **Save Point** there, and a door that is now open. The elevator inside sends the group up quite a distance, to the top of the engine system.

There are four lock mechanisms at each end of this great hall. Travel to the lower end first, and avoid the Yuriev patrollers if you aren't looking for a fight. The place is so huge that nothing has much of a chance to get near you unless you actively annoy the patrollers. Blast all four of the locks at that end, then head up to the top. Use the conveyor belt for a fast trip back to the center.

On the other end, look in the cubbies on the left side as you go up. **Decoder 10** is there, ripe for the taking. It might be better to avoid the two patrols, as neither are worth much, and they are slow to destroy.

Whether you fight or slip past, trash the four locks at that end as well. This enables the Shaft Stop Switch. Return to your E.S.s and fly to the top of the shaft again. Use the red button in the center (that is the Shaft Stop Switch). On the right side, the Core Maintenance Lift is now usable, so take that as a shortcut.

Disembark a second time, travel to the top of the shaft, and use the door at the top of the area. The Honeycomb area is ahead of the group now. Advance, use the Terminal there, and take a look around. Follow the chain of small rooms around the left portion of the honeycomb; these eventually lead to a room with **Decoder 12** (in a box).

INTRODUCTION

ARCHIVES

CHARACTERS

TACTICAL FILES

EQUIPMENT

THREAT ASSESSMENT

REGIONAL ANALYSIS

SUPPLEMENTAL DATA

Other than that the upper-right path, from the start of the honeycomb, is the only important route. This leads to both **Segment Address 11**, and to the way out. Segment Address 11 can be opened immediately, and Sweet Pain is found inside.

And now for the bad news; until you get the fields to deactivate, this area cannot be traversed. Return to your mechs, and fly to the top of the shaft with the Core Maintenance Lift. At this time, the two passages at the bottom of the screen are open. Use the exit on the lower-left, then push past the minor craft in the next area. Take the lift down to the second floor, and return to the central chamber.

Use the door at the top of the area. When you start to see the little power pods, you know that you are in the right place for smashing! Trash everything you see, then take the lower-right exit from the central chamber after you come back. A tiny lift inside takes your group up to level three. These lifts keep going up, and there is a box with a Skill Upgrade C on the fourth floor.

With all of the loot from the area in your hands now, and the power pods destroyed, head all the way back to the honeycomb area. Destroy each and

every pod at the center of those rooms, then use the doorway on the top side of the region once you are done.

Follow the lone tube up to the core reactor and enjoy the conversations with the man there. You'll get quite a bit of useful information, but not all of it is good news. As such, you'll find yourself back on the Elsa before long, with new problems to face.

Before rushing off, use the Save Point, buy/sell, and take a trip in the EVS to get the treasure from Segment Addresses 10 and 12. When those fun chores are out of the way, talk to the captain to begin the next mission.

RETURNING TO THE MERKABAH

In the future, you can (and should) use the EVS system on the Elsa to return to the Merkabah. There are more goodies to find there, and it's a fun trip. When you do this, follow the group's original path to the core area: disembark, ride up the elevator, head to the top of the shaft area and through to the honeycomb. From there, move to the north and reach the core area. There is a button to press at the far end of the core area that unlocks an E.S.-sized entrance to the core.

Return to your E.S.s and use the door on the second floor of the shaft to reach the core again, this time in your craft.

In the core area, there are boxes with Update File 11 and G-Ignis I.

DURANDAL

POINTS OF INTEREST

1	SEGMENT ADDRESS 06
2	CENTRAL MANAGEMENT CONTROLS

ITEMS

1	MED KIT DX
2	MED KIT L (X2)
3	REJUVENATOR L
4	BLUE STAR
5	ETHER PACK M
6	REJUVENATOR L
7	UPDATE FILE 12

ENEMIES

1	AG-02
2	CITRINE (BOSS)
3	FEDERATION SOLDIER A
4	FEDERATION SOLDIER B
5	V.G.S. EINS R
6	V.G.S. ZWEI R
7	VX-9000
8	YURIEV SOLDIER A
9	YURIEV SOLDIER B

On the left side is a golden door (**Segment Address 06**). Not much else is found in the Park currently. Once you have Decoder 06, from  the brutal Omega Id encounter, you can unlock this door. Dark Erde Kaiser is learned as a result, from the Erde Kaiser Dark Device.

Your group is located in a docking area of the Durandal. If you want to return to the Elsa, use the airlocks on the right side of the screen at any point. Otherwise, walk left and use the train system. The areas available are as follows: Isolation Area, Park, Bridge, Third Residential Area.

The Isolation Area has almost nothing that can access yet, so that is better left for later. The Bridge has **Update File 12**, but that area too is mostly sealed off.

If you go to the Park, expect to face fairly soft Yuriev forces that are supplemented with powerful mechs. Walk to the top of the terminal area, fighting the Yuriev troops, and enter the next section of the Park.

The Third Residential Area is a nice destination, because it has a **Save Point**. There is a central corridor leading into the heart of the region; take that after the initial foes are cleared, and notice that the first door you come to is locked by Central Management. The best path to take would be one that gets you to Central Management as quickly as possible.

Advance to the junction, then head up from there. Take a right at the T-intersection, and fight past the continuing guards along the way. Don't hold back on ether use, considering that there is a Save Point not that far off.

INTRODUCTION

ARCHIVES

CHARACTERS

TACTICAL FILES

EQUIPMENT

THREAT ASSESSMENT

REGIONAL ANALYSIS

SUPPLEMENTAL DATA

Don't take the side passages, and instead move steadily left once you get up the ramp. The controls for Central Management are past a doorway there, and those unlock everything. When leaving Central Management, know that the upper route has three rooms, with the middle one containing a Blue Star. The lower route is simply a faster way to get back to where you were a short time ago. Explore all of the side passages on the way down through the junction, but the lower-right path is the really important one. There are people in there that you want to talk to, and they are only guarded by a single squad of enemies.

After freeing those buddies, walk to the left and enter the large chamber at the end of the hall. The rooms around the periphery aren't important at all, bearing almost no treasure. However, the chamber at the base of the steps has the other set of prisoners that you need to free. Take care of that, then return to the Save Point. After resting, travel to the Isolation Area.

Prepare yourself for a boss fight while entering the Isolation Area. After a few empty rooms, a scene will play, and the fun starts immediately after.

CITRINE

HP:	29000
EP:	220
BL:	400
INFO:	BIOLOGICAL (HUMAN)
TGT:	???
EXP:	13000
SP:	20
G:	10000
N ITEM:	WEAPON DEVELOPMENT AREA KEY
R ITEM:	NONE
S ITEM:	CRESCENT MOON
STRONG:	FIRE
WEAK:	BEAM
ABSORBED:	NONE
NULL:	POISON

Citrine starts the fight off with a daunting move; she uses Mystique to seal your group's ether attacks. Yet, this will wear off in time, and her basic attacks do so little damage that you shouldn't be overly concerned.

Instead, activate your buffs, start to pile on Break attacks, and deal general damage. Citrine's Break Limit isn't that high for her level (and in comparison to your group's current level of output). Thus, it won't be too bad at all to Break her a couple of times during this encounter; even without abusing Erde Kaiser.

Don't forget to steal from Citrine. Her Crescent Moon is a necklace that improves SP gained! That isn't an effect that you see very often, so it's really not something that you want to miss out on.

After the halfway point, Citrine threatens the party with becoming disabled if anyone falls beneath 666 HPs. The mental waves needed to maintain this can be stopped if you Break Citrine. Thus, if you still don't have any healers ready to go and anyone's health is low, just tip her over the Break Limit.

At really low health (around 25%), Citrine uses a truly unfair power; she sets all group HPs to 666. You have choices: Break her then, change group members to people at full health, or Boost and get a couple good healing spells off quickly.

All told, this lady just can't stand up to your party. She was just a foolishly-chosen delaying tactic. Now it's time to see if the gambit paid off for your enemies.

ABEL'S ARK

With everyone back on the Elsa again, there is quite a bit to do and fret about. But stay calm; there are still many things to try. As a reward for your hard efforts, the store has been updated with many new items. There are boss E.S. fights in the not-so-distant future; that makes it doubly important to upgrade now and keep a strong eye out for things that might be good for your specializations. No matter what, stock up on D-Charges. Those disks are amazing (they increase the amount of HPs recovered per turn when you use charge). Load one of these disks onto every E.S., and watch boss fights turn into easy mode.

UPDATED ELSA STORE

ITEM	COST	E.S. EQUIPMENT	COST	E.S. EQUIPMENT	COST
MED KIT S	100	V18 ASSAULT II	3900	RF-XUAN WU	3700
MED KIT M	500	AIRD-E	3000	G-ROX/63	2000
REVIVE M	600	ST2-SWIFT	2400	G-ROX/80	3000
NULLIFIER	1000	AIRD-E+	4000	C-US4	1000
SEVEN MOONS	300	AIRD-C II	4200	C-US5	1500
CLEANSER	1000	S SIFT FX	2400	C-US6	2000
ANTIDOTE	20	SHIRANUI	2200	C-US7	2500
REMOVER	50	MISTY MOON	3400	D-SENSOR	50
ANTI-CRYSTAL	1000	FOUR HEAVENS	4400	D-GUARD	200
G VACCINE	500	NEW MOON	5000	D-KILL C	300
ANALYZE BALL	4	TEMPEST GP	2400	D-KILL R	300
TRAP	200	DRACHE	4100	D-TREASURE I	500
NANO REPAIR M	400	LINDWURM M2	1600	D-FRAME I	750
HALF REPAIR	1500	SCHWALBE F	1800	D-HALF A	800
DOWN REPAIR	50	EM FADEN R	2100	D-HALF D	800
		G PHALANX II	1800	D-HALF DEA	800
		SR SHAULA A	2200	D-FIRE	1000
		SR SHAULA R2	2500	D-LIGHTNING	1000
		DORADE RK-3	4200	D-ICE	1000
		AF-COMMANDO	2500	D-BEAM	1000
		AF-COMMANDO T	3700	D-REVENGE	1200
		ZF-GARNET	2500	D-CLEAN	2300
		ZF-TURMALI	3700	D-FRAME II	2500
		ZF-TOPAZ	4500	D-EN I	2800
		DF-V3	2500	D-CHARGE	3000
		DF-V4	3700	D-REVENGE+	3000
		RF-TIGER	2500		

UPDATED ELSA STORE

EQUIPMENT	COST	EQUIPMENT	COST
VIPER BUNKER	3400	EAGLE EYE	4500
COMBAT LADY	5300	STEEL BANGLE	300000
VB-FLAME	3500	TITANIUM BANGLE	300000
SHEN YAN	5600	SHOCK ABSORBER	100
ADONA SHOOTER	3200	FIRE WALL	1000
COMPOUND VIII	5200	THUNDER WALL	1000
BREAK KNUCKLE	3200	ICE WALL	1000
BLUE NAIL	5000	BEAM WALL	1000
KWP-XIV	3800	COBRA BANGLE	100
KWP-XV	5800	QUEEN JACK	700
TIMAEUS	3200	KING JACK	700
KRITIAS	5200	GOD CIRCLE	1700
BLOOD M40	3300	IMPERIAL	1700
BLACK RELIC	5400	SOUL COLLECTOR	1700
VELVET BOLERO	2000	VAN BRACE	700
BUTTERFLY SUIT	2000	RARE BRACE	300
DRAGON BUSTIER	3400	UNKNOWN BRACELET	1400
GORGON COAT	3400	GROSS SOUL	3000
RAPTOR ROBE	2100	DRAGON HEAD	3000
HEAVEN'S ROBE	3500	GREEN STAR	2600
WARLORD'S MANTLE	3500	VELVET RING	600
PROTECT GEAR	2100	CRIMSON RING	300
ZIG-MUSCLE	3700	YELLOW RING	300
ZIG-SKELETAL	3700	COBALT RING	300
KAP-GLA	2300	SILVER RING	300
KAP-SAL	3800	FLAME AVATAR	900
RIGID LEATHER	2200	LIGHTNING AVATAR	900
VECTOR CROSS	3500	ICE AVATAR	900
BULLET NECK	600	BEAM AVATAR	900
ROSARIO OF LOVE	6000	COUNTER RING	1800
CYLINDER NECK	300	REVENGE RING	1800
DOG TAG	600	RUTHLESS RING	1800
OPEN HEART	450	ACALA'S PULSE	3000
CROSS CHOKER	1600	HAMMURABI SPELL	3000
RED CRYSTAL	300	LOST KINGDOM	3000
SUN CRY	1800		
PANTHER EYE	1200		

The final stage of Hakox is available for the mighty puzzle-solvers of Xenosaga III. Take a break from the battle and crack those tough stages. When you've had your fill, talk to the captain and watch the scenes before the Elsa heads out (or in, as the case may be). Use the weapon-loading elevator to leave the Elsa via your E.S.s.

ENTERING THE ARK

POINTS OF INTEREST	
NONE	

ITEMS	
1	D-BEAM
2	ETHER PACK L
3	EX SKILL KEY III

ENEMIES	
1	ASHMED BAPUZ
2	VRA-2100 ST
3	VRA-3500 ST

Take the crystal on the right side of the map first. There are mechs over there, but they are much easier to obliterate! Destroy VRA-3500 STs first, as they are soft beyond belief. The tougher 2100 are better to finish against.

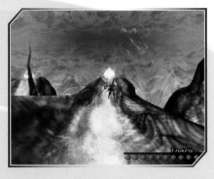

It's very useful to build Anima off of the VRA encounters, and to use Anima Awakening to take down larger groups of the Ashmed Bapuz Gnosis (they are far more of a threat, and it's a huge skill point boost to rip them all up in one shot with E.S. Reuben's level two special attack).

Though the path through the area looks confusing, it's almost linear. There are side branches with minor treasure (the notable piece being the **EX Skill Key III**), but you can't get far off of the route without hitting a dead end. That is a very good thing! Just explore slowly, hit every encounter, and enjoy the huge amount of skill points and money that come in here.

After several teleporter fields, your group will be slightly stuck. There are four globes circling a spire, and those globes must be disabled for you to proceed. Use the **Save Point** and blue plate in that area, as needed.

Fly out into the open space where the globes are spinning, and let one of them run into you. This teleports the group out of their E.S.s and into the inner portion of the sphere.

After reaching "ground" of Abel's Ark, fly to the crystal ahead of your craft and use ● to activate it. These are teleporters that take you between different sections of the Ark. Go through two of these, then take on your first encounter of Gnosis defenders. It won't take people long to realize that the Gnosis here are very good at dealing damage, but they can't survive for long against your upgraded E.S.s. Use heavy attacks (especially Beam or Lightning ones) against these Gnosis to bring them down, and Charge to replenish HPs when the fight is almost over.

THE BLUE SPHERE

POINTS OF INTEREST	
1	SEGMENT ADDRESS 13

ITEMS	
1	COAT HARDY
2	DECODER 14
3	SAGE'S RING

ENEMIES	
1	AI APAEC
2	AIAKOS
3	DEION
4	KAZFA JINA
5	NATUS LUMEN (BOSS)

The blue sphere starts with a shift landscape that must be traversed carefully. Move against the tilt of the ground, and be ready for the rocking to shift rhythmically. Stay along the center to avoid falling into the many pits that line both sides of the passage. There are side sections of land that seem useless on both sides of the narrow ledge; let yourself slide down the second one on the left. There is a box there, with **Decoder 14** inside of it. Next time you are on the Elsa, open Segment Address 14 to get the Iron Maiden (search the E.S. Bay for that door). Then, just before the end of the area, slip to the right and look for the box with a Sage's Ring. Afterward, use the teleporter at the end, and walk across the empty space beyond.

The fights are slow ones, with the enemies having quite a few tricks to pull out. Try to build up Boost points and use them with area-of-effect attacks that exploit enemy weaknesses. For instance, Ziggy's Hind attack works very well in Deion fights, while KOS-MOS's X-Buster is strong against the Kazfa Jina.

Walk forward, then right to continue revealing blocks. When in doubt, move while pressing both forward and to one side to check for peripheral passages in the strange area. Use the teleporter on the far side of the map.

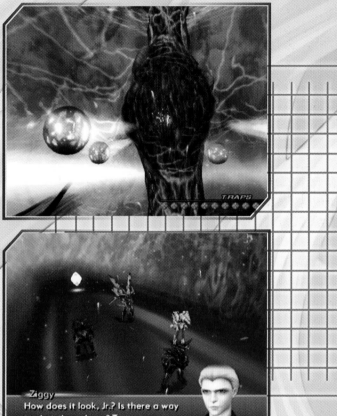

Ziggy
How does it look, Jr.? Is there a way to shut them down?

In the next area, complete the fights while trying to get to the left side. There is a box there with a Coat Hardy, a good armor upgrade for chaos or Jr. Then, there are two teleporters from that map. To the right is an area with **Segment Address 13**. Pick up the Dragon Eye inside there! Return to the last chamber and take the northern route this time.

Use the Save Point beyond the next teleporter. It sounds like there is a big fight about to occur. Take a short flight toward the center of the room, and you'll find out if that hunch is accurate. If you read ahead, it becomes clear that anti-counter disks are good to put on your craft right now, and any beam weapons that can be removed in favor of other damage types would also make things easier.

INTRODUCTION

ARCHIVES

CHARACTERS

TACTICAL FILES

EQUIPMENT

THREAT ASSESSMENT

REGIONAL ANALYSIS

SUPPLEMENTAL DATA

NATUS LUMEN

HP:	225000
INFO:	GNOSIS
TGT:	???
EXP:	13250
SP:	30
G:	8000
N ITEM:	RF-ACALA
R ITEM:	NONE
STRONG:	BEAM
WEAK:	NONE
ABSORBED:	NONE
NULL:	NONE

If your E.S.s are fully upgraded, this fight won't hurt very much. Use heavy Anima Awakening attacks from your best people for the primary damage, and watch Natus Lumen start to melt.

The biggest problem in this match is that Natus Lumen has a Strength against Beams. That is tough on the E.S. Zebulun, but it's even worse on the E.S. Dinah. It's better to shift the Dinah out of the rotation for this fight.

Because this boss has a very strong Counter ability, you never want to miss (not like you want to miss anyway). Try to rely on high accuracy attacks whenever you can afford to.

Using your tertiary attacks to begin a chain works well as they have high accuracy, cost little, and hit multiple times. This stacks a nice accuracy bonus for your more powerful attacks (that tend to have lower accuracy) at the end of the chain.

Natus Lumen likes to go into sniper mode in the mid and late battle. Using accurate attacks and Anima Awakening ensure that he'll never get anything good out of this technique.

The E.S. Reuben gets a huge frame upgrade for beating this battle. Considering that the Reuben is one of your best damage dealers for these engagements, this is certainly a piece of good fortune.

Save again when you have won the fight, then take the teleporter back to the main area. It's time to grab another sphere.

THE GREEN SPHERE

POINTS OF INTEREST	
1	SEGMENT ADDRESS 02

ITEMS	
1	G-IGNIS III

ENEMIES	
1	AG-03 SPX
2	AI APAEC
3	DEION
4	KAZFA JINA
5	NATUS GLACIES (BOSS)
6	VX-9000 K
7	YURIEV SOLDIER A
8	YURIEV SOLDIER B

The first room of the green sphere is very easy, and it only has two small fights. Walk forward and use ● to hit the crystal on the main spire. This causes the spire to rise, and the teleporter you want is at the bottom of the area, attached to the pillar itself. So the trick is to keep hitting the top crystal until it's as high as it can go, then *run* to the base of the pillar as quickly as possible to use the teleporter before it descends back into the water.

The second room has two pillars of the same type. Use the second pillar that you come to, and make your way down the long spiral. There are a couple tough fights to face, with the massively-upgraded VX-9000 Ks to give you trouble. Destroy them with much ferocity, their Break potential and overall damage are fearsome.

When you use the teleporter on the rightmost pillar, it takes you to a minor area with a couple Gnosis encounters. **Segment Address 02** is there, and G-Ignis III is inside. Collect this and equip it on your favorite E.S., then return to deal with the first pillar from the main room. Repeat the process, and enter the last room of the Green Sphere.

Use the **Save Point**, and steel yourself for another boss fight! This time, the enemy is going to have Revenge instead of Counter, so set your disks appropriately before entering the engagement.

NATUS GLACIES

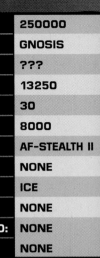

	250000
	GNOSIS
	???
	13250
	30
	8000
	AF-STEALTH II
	NONE
:	ICE
	NONE
D:	NONE
	NONE

Natus Glacies is all about HP. This boss takes many hits to bring down, and its constant use of revenge is quite a pain if you don't use D-Kill R to eliminate both the returning damage and the potential to stop your chains.

Circle of Water and Circle of Iron are counterattack stances that are used by Natus Glacies. Neither of these affects the fight too heavily, as the use of proper disks and charge for minor repairs makes this negligible.

The same can be said for Ventus Nivalis, the somewhat tough area-of-effect attack that Natus Glacies uses. It can easily be countered with the use of charge because it's not going to even come close to destroying anyone outright, and it isn't used often.

...ead, all of the sweat and fear for the match goes into the final two or three rounds. ...us Glacies uses Inferno around 25% health to boost its attack power greatly, and after ...t it is able to deliver 25-30k damage in a single burst. Ouch! If you want to play it safe ...e, save almost all Anima for most of the fight, and use everything as soon as Inferno ...es into play. Three of your craft, using Anima Awakening level 2, can certainly destroy ...us Glacies before these super bursts come to fruition.

...erwise, it's a damage race that you are facing. Even with enhanced charge, your E.S.s ...'t keep up with that much of a single-target output. Instead, use items to accomplish ...repairs.

...e to record your progress and repair your beloved craft, then choose the next sphere.

PINK SPHERE

POINTS OF INTEREST	
NONE	

ITEMS	
1	MED KIT DX
2	ETHER PACK M
3	NANO REPAIR DX
4	ZF-SMARAKATA
5	NULLIFIER
6	UPDATE FILE 13
7 °	CLEANSER
8	NANO REPAIR DX
9	NULLIFIER
10	G-LEGLE/85

ENEMIES	
1	ASHMED BAPUZ
2	NATUS FLAMME (BOSS)
3	VRA-2100 ST
4	VRA-3500 ST

Use the pink crystal, and fight the Bapuz group on the other side. Look for an orange block on the edge of the walkway, and use that to knock it across the gap. This becomes a bridge for anyone using the far route. Explore and have another fight if you like, but eventually you have to return to the main chamber and use the yellow crystal. There is another bridge to shift there, and that opens the way from the pink crystal to the next tier.

Like the first tier, there are four crystals to choose from in the central chamber. Use the green crystal first, as it quickly leads to a bridge section that must be pushed across the gap. Then, take the yellow crystal to put the next bridge piece in place. The white crystal is third in the list, and moving that section completes the bridge.

The pink crystal is last on the list, and that takes you to a place where the group can actually use the walkway that they have been building. Walk onto the bridge and take the path on the left to get a G-Legle/85 for one of your mechs. Follow by using the only remaining path to exit the tier.

As before, there is a **Save Point** just before the end.

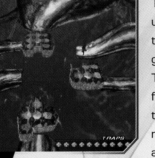

This is an E.S. area, unlike the last two spheres your group has used. Take the teleporter from the first tier of the large mushroom-like area, then see that you have a selection of teleporters to choose from on the other side.

Take the green crystal if you want a Zebulun armor frame (the ZF-Smarakata), but the ZF-Topaz from the store is better. Using the white crystal is a better idea, as it has **Update File 13**, and that is certainly good to pick up.

INTRODUCTION ARCHIVES CHARACTERS TACTICAL FILES EQUIPMENT THREAT ASSESSMENT REGIONAL ANALYSIS SUPPLEMENTAL DATA

NATUS FLAMMA

HP:	230000
INFO:	GNOSIS
TGT:	???
EXP:	13250
SP:	30
G:	8000
N ITEM:	ZF-RYBEUS
R ITEM:	NONE
STRONG:	FIRE
WEAK:	NONE
ABSORBED:	NONE
NULL:	NONE

Natus Flamma doesn't have revenge or counter, but its evasion is fairly high. If your group is somewhat low level for the area still, that is going to make it a slower fight. This foe plans to dish out quite a heavy serving of pain. His single-target Unda-Duo and later Unda Septum II are only modest in what they can do. Instead, Flucticulus I and II are more frightening, with area-of-effect damage.

Frequently, you receive a message that there will be an explosion in three turns. The F Mine blows up and ends up dealing a massive hit to a single target, but an E.S. with the clean disk can charge to heal itself and remove the effect. Otherwise, use a Down Repair to take care of this problem.

At lower health, Flamma actives Chaos Eye, to act as a soul down for all characters. After that point, you'll encounter his most aggressive attacks.

Keep one of your E.S.s at a full Anima bar until the end, to act as a rear-loaded damage dealer. Use the other two E.S.s, in alternation, to lay on Anima attacks throughout the mid-battle. If you don't bring this Gnosis down quickly enough, he uses a 35k heal to put himself back in the fight.

After the fight ends, you receive a third frame upgrade. This one is for the Zebulun.

Save and head out to the final sphere!

INTRODUCTION

ARCHIVES

CHARACTERS

TACTICAL FILES

EQUIPMENT

THREAT ASSESSMENT

REGIONAL ANALYSIS

SUPPLEMENTAL DATA

YELLOW SPHERE

POINTS OF INTEREST	
NONE	

ITEMS	
1	NANO REPAIR M
2	MED KIT DX
3	ETHER PACK S
4	C-US9G
5	1000G
6	D-EN I
7	YASOMA KAGURA

ENEMIES	
1	AI APAEC
2	AIAKOS
3	ASHMED BAPUZ
4	KAZFA JINA
5	NATUS TELLUS (BOSS)
6	VRA-2100 ST
7	VRA-3500 ST

The yellow sphere is another section where the party remains in their E.S.s. Destroy the many wandering targets, and enjoy the open space of this section. Quite a few of the lights can be destroyed for minor items, and a box on the upper-left side has a C-US9G upgrade. Otherwise, it's a totally linear route. Use the teleporter from the upper-right path to reach the next section.

You cannot pass through the main tunnel in the next area; at first, there is a purple substance blocking the way. To destroy it, use either crystal on the left side. This switches you out of your E.S.s. You appear in a very similar area. Your characters can destroy the pink crystalline substance, and that removes the obstacle in both areas (for your characters and for the E.S.s).

Use the crystals to switch back to your E.S.s and advance. Destroy the green obstacles that are farther along the corridor. Return to the character side (using a crystal that is ahead and on the left side), and blast more pink obstacles. Switch and search the left corridor on the E.S. side for a box with D-EN I.

In the large room at the end of the tunnel, use these methods to destroy the pink and green obstacles. In character form, search the back-right portion of the map for Yasoma Kagura, a new Jin blade.

The upper-left corridor leads to the **Save Point** and the boss fight. Light up those anti-revenge disks, improved charge, and remove any lightning weaponry from your lineup of weapons.

NATUS TELLUS

HP:	250000
INFO:	GNOSIS
TGT:	???
EXP:	13250
SP:	30
G:	8000
N ITEM:	DF-XX
R ITEM:	NONE
STRONG:	LIGHTNING
WEAK:	NONE
ABSORBED:	NONE
NULL:	NONE

Natus Tellus is not too hard to deal with, especially if you have negated his revenge potential. His Procella and later Tempestas attacks are fairly low on their damage. Nimbus I and II (its area-of-effect attack and upgraded version), are also somewhat minor.

Tellus' Chaos Eye is able to deliver a reactive skin down effect, but it doesn't make a huge difference to the group. The sheer number of armor frame upgrades that the group has gained by fighting the others mean that Tellus is facing an uphill struggle.

If you have the Reuben in your party, remember to avoid using his level two Anima Awakening special attack (the level two one is lightning based). Instead, use Anima Awakenings to have the Reuben go nuts with multiple sword attacks. If the Reuben is equipped with the G-Ignis III engine, it's possible to deal three sword attacks per round during this mode.

Late in the fight, the Tellus increases its physical capabilities by 35%. Use all Anima at this time to destroy the Tellus and score a finishing move.

INSIDE THE SPIRE

Save the game again after exiting the sphere, and fly out to the central spire. Use the E.S.s to break into the spire. This triggers a major scene, and another boss fight soon follows.

DMITRI YURIEV

HP:	46000
EP:	770
BL:	700
INFO:	BIOLOGICAL (HUMAN)
TGT:	???
EXP:	15000
SP:	30
G:	10000
N ITEM:	GOD'S EXPERIENCE
R ITEM:	NONE
S ITEM:	GENERAL'S BRACELET
STRONG:	FIRE, ICE, LIGHTNING
WEAK:	NONE
ABSORBED:	NONE
NULL:	POISON, SEAL ETHER, SEAL BOOST, REFLECT DAMAGE

The fight against Dmitri is one of the more complex and interesting battles in the game. Your overall goal is to deal damage to Dmitri while holding back his ability to gain Boost. Not only is Boost a bad thing for enemies to have anyway, but in this case Omega Metempsychosis is the one able to wield Boost that is gained in this battle. When Dmitri gets to 3/3 Boost, Omega Metempsychosis gets to make attacks.

Dmitri's big ace is that he has a Telekinetic Wave that deals area-of-effect damage to the group and delivers tons of Break damage as well. None of your anti-Break people can keep up with this. So, have Ziggy or KOS-MOS use Heat and encourage Dmitri to use his pathetic single-target attacks. This won't work all of the time, but it helps.

Once Dmitri gets up to 3/3 Boost, Omega Metempsychosis uses Infinitum to blast a couple of characters for fairly high damage. He pulls out this nasty trick at 30% health as well, regardless of his Boost status. This gets even uglier, and you'll be forced to heal instead of do anti-Break work unless you can shut down Dmitri's Boost.

At 25%, Yuriev increases the strength of his waves. This is the time to pull out all of the stops. Unleash a wave of Erde Kaiser or heavy Break attacks, then use every bit of Boost to try and knock off this vicious foe.

Note that you can take a long-haul strategy with Dmitri and do many things to prevent his Break moves from succeeding. Us more Break Heals, have one person dedicated to casting Heat each round (preferably, a person who appears close to Dmitri in the rotation), and watch as he fails to accrue Boost. Though this style is slower, it allows groups of lower level to fight safely through this tough encounter.

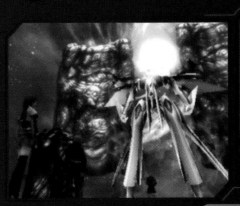

OMEGA METEMPSYCHOSIS

HP:	450000
INFO:	MACHINE
TGT:	???
EXP:	20000
SP:	30
G:	20000
N ITEM:	D-ANIMA
R ITEM:	NONE
STRONG:	NONE
WEAK:	NONE
ABSORBED:	NONE
NULL:	NONE

Though this fight chains into the last, there is little fear of losing. The Omega Metempsychosis battle is much easier than the ground fight, and it's also quite a bit of fun. Your craft can now gain up to three levels of Anima, making the ultimate attacks available for your E.S.s.

Both Sanctio and Visc are meager single-target attacks that Omega Metempsychosis uses often. It's only the area-of-effect attacks that you need to worry about. For the early part of the fight, these aren't so bad. However, Omega Metempsychosis has Anima Awakening powers that are deeply frightening.

The first time this comes up, your group can stop the special attack by dealing two special attacks of your own. Use simple, level one special attacks to do this at a very minimal cost. You'll be able to make up for this quickly and still have a fast rush to make up your Anima.

The second time Omega Metempsychosis goes for a special attack, things won't go so well. When the craft's HP drops to near 25%, be sure to charge everyone to full strength. The blast that ensures is enough to nearly level all of your people, so it's quite unsafe to be below 80% of your HP total.

Once that happens, you are over the hump. Unload with high-end Anima Awakening attacks, and watch the fireworks.

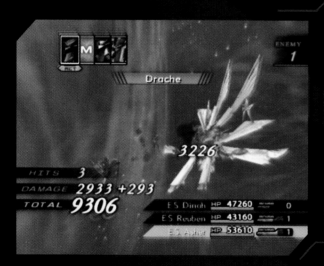

MICHTAM

After everything has developed, the group returns to the Elsa. Many peripheral quests are opened at this time, and there are powerful equipment pieces to be found throughout the world. Shion can talk to Miyuki using the monitor to the right of the Save Point, and her final weapon quest is gained there. Check out the store for items of all sorts as well. See the Supplemental Data chapter for a thorough run through of peripheral missions and other late-game goodies.

For instance, now is a good time to get Jin's final sword. You grabbed the Prayer Beads from Miltia earlier (they are mentioned in the walkthrough and into the Supplemental Data chapter). Purchase a VB-Crimson, then give the Prayer Beads and an unequipped VB-Crimson to Panache in the men's quarters. You receive VB-Dawn and Nine Stones.

G-VACCINE

The G Vaccine increases you resistance to Gnosis crystallization permanently. Each only costs 500G, while increasing this resistance by 5%. For 10,000G (per character) you can be immune to Gnosis crystallization. chaos has a natural resistance of this type, but no one else does. As the Gnosis fights at the end actually last long enough for this to be an issue, it is worth spending the money to get this done.

UPDATED ELSA STORE	
ITEM	COST
MED KIT S	100
MED KIT M	500
REVIVE M	600
NULLIFIER	1000
CLEANSER	1000
ANTIDOTE	20
REMOVER	50
ANTI-CRYSTAL	1000
G VACCINE	500
ANALYZE BALL	4
TRAP	200
NANO REPAIR M	400
NANO REPAIR DX	1000
HALF REPAIR	1500
ALL REPAIR	3800
DOWN REPAIR	50

INTRODUCTION
ARCHIVES
CHARACTERS
TACTICAL FILES
EQUIPMENT
THREAT ASSESSMENT
REGIONAL ANALYSIS
SUPPLEMENTAL DATA

UPDATED ELSA STORE

EQUIPMENT	COST	EQUIPMENT	COST	EQUIPMENT	COST
COMBAT LADY	5300	KAP-VEN	5900	COBRA BANGLE	100
NIGHT BUNKER	8000	VECTOR CROSS	3500	QUEEN JACK	700
SHEN YAN	5600	NANO CARE COAT	3500	KING JACK	700
VB-CRIMSON	8500	UNION LEATHER	5300	GOD CIRCLE	1700
COMPOUND VIII	5200	LONG HORN	5300	IMPERIAL	1700
BARBIT SHOOTER	7900	BULLET NECK	600	SOUL COLLECTOR	1700
MARKI SHOOTER	8600	ROSARIO OF LOVE	6000	VAN BRACE	700
BLUE NAIL	5000	CYLINDER NECK	300	TEMPEST BEADS	5600
BARBELO KNUCKLE	8600	DOG TAG	600	RARE BRACE	300
KWP-XV	5800	OPEN HEART	450	UNKNOWN BRACELET	1400
KWP-XX	300000	CROSS CHOKER	1600		
KRITIAS	5200	RED CRYSTAL	300	GROSS SOUL	3000
CHAOS LORD	7800	SUN CRY	1800	DRAGON HEAD	3000
BLACK RELIC	5400	PANTHER EYE	1200	RA'S BEADS	100000
VI-SHOT	8200	EAGLE EYE	4500	WISEMAN'S BEADS	450000
DRAGON BUSTIER	3400	STEEL BANGLE	300000	GREEN STAR	2600
GORGON COAT	3400	TITANIUM BANGLE	300000	VELVET RING	600
VELVET PANNIER	5300	PLATINUM BANGLE	300000	FLAME AVATAR	900
KAJIC BLOUSE	5300	SHOCK ABSORBER	100	LIGHTNING AVATAR	900
HEAVEN'S ROBE	3500	FIRE WALL	1000	ICE AVATAR	900
WARLORD'S MANTLE	3500	RESIST FIRE	600000	BEAM AVATAR	900
TRUE JADE	5300	THUNDER WALL	1000	COUNTER RING	1800
ZIG-MUSCLE	3700	RESIST THUNDER	600000	REVENGE RING	1800
ZIG-SKELETAL	3700	ICE WALL	1000	RUTHLESS RING	1800
TOP SECRET SKELETAL	5300	RESIST ICE	600000	PIERCE RING	12000
KAP-SAL	3800	BEAM WALL	1000	BIND RING	15000
KAP-SAN	5900	RESIST BEAM	600000	ACALA'S PULSE	3000
		ROSENCRANTZ	7000	HAMMURABI SPELL	3000
		DOUBLE DEALER	7000	LOST KINGDOM	3000

UPDATED ELSA STORE

E.S. EQUIPMENT	COST	E.S. EQUIPMENT	COST
V18 ASSAULT II	3900	RF-HUANG LONG	14000
STING RAY V	4400	G-ROX/80	3000
V2 ASSAULT II	7500	G-ROX/90	5200
ST2-SWIFT	2400	C-US6	2000
AIRD-E+	4000	C-US7	2500
AIRD-C II	4200	C-US8	3000
SENTIR A-L	8000	C-US9	3500
AIRD-C V	9000	D-SENSOR	50
S SIFE FX	2400	D-GUARD	200
FOUR HEAVENS	4400	D-KILL C	300
NEW MOON	5000	D-KILL R	300
FULL MOON	9000	D-TREASURE I	500
SG-M WOLF	2200	D-FRAME I	750
TEMPEST GP	2400	D-HALF A	800
DRACHE	4100	D-HALF D	800
BZ AVENGER	4600	D-HALF DEA	800
DRACHE-RR	5300	D-FIRE	1000
SC LINDWURM	5000	D-LIGHTNING	1000
SCHWALBE SW	5400	D-ICE	1000
SR SHAULA R2	2500	D-BEAM	1000
DORADE RK-3	4200	D-REVENGE	1200
VOLANS SV	4500	D-CLEAN	2300
DORADE RK-5		D-BLOCK A	2200
ARF RASTABAN	4700	D-BLOCK D	2200
PHALANX XX	4600	D-BLOCK DEA	2200
AF-COMMANDO T	3700	D-FRAME II	2500
AF-STEALTH	8000	D-EN I	2800
AF-GHOST	15000	D-NULLIFY EFFECT	3000
ZF-TURMALI	3700	D-CHARGE	3000
ZF-TOPAZ	4500	D-REVENGE+	3000
ZF-AMADAS	10000	D-COUNTER+	4000
DF-V4	3700	D-EN II	5000
DF-X	8000	D-FRAME III	5600
DF-ORB	12000	D-COUNTER	8000
RF-XUAN WU	3700	D-TREASURE II	8000
RF-VAJRA	8000		

HALLOWED GROUND

POINTS OF INTEREST	
1	DISEMBARKING POINT

ITEMS	
1	1000G
2	NIGHT MOON
3	REJUVENATOR DX
4	DOWN REPAIR
5	5000G
6	D-EXP I

ENEMIES	
1	CERA 6 S
2	CERA 7 S
3	E.S. GAD (BOSS)
4	E.S. ISSACHAR (BOSS)
5	E.S. JOSEPH (BOSS)
6	LEVIAT
7	LEVIAT OFFICER

After buying, selling, equipping, and saving, take the E.S.s out into the field. Michtam is a somber place, but there is a beauty to it as well. Fly through the broken landscape and approach the smoking wreckage that isn't too far away. An early boss fight occurs once you reach that location.

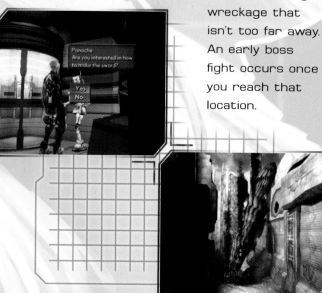

E.S. GAD AND E.S. JOSEPH

GAD	
HP:	280000
INFO:	MACHINE
TGT:	???
EXP:	15000
SP:	40
G:	4500
N ITEM:	D-NULLIFY EVADE
R ITEM:	NONE
STRONG:	NONE
WEAK:	LIGHTNING
ABSORBED:	NONE
NULL:	NONE

JOSEPH	
HP:	350000
INFO:	MACHINE
TGT:	???
EXP:	15000
SP:	40
G:	4500
N ITEM:	D-HALF PHYSICAL
R ITEM:	NONE
STRONG:	NONE
WEAK:	FIRE
ABSORBED:	NONE
NULL:	NONE

Gad and Joseph start off with minor attacks that won't require charge use. In truth, all of their power comes from their use of Anima. While attacking normally, these enemy E.S.s are gaining Anima just like your craft (you can even hear when they gain Anima ranks).

When ready, your opponents will spend one round preparing their Anima special attacks, and they are extremely deadly. To stop them, use a level one Anima Awakening on one of your craft and devote the entire round to attacking with your highest Team weapon. Even if the direct damage is modest, this almost ensures that an ambush will occur. Having all three of your characters attack at the same time does a major amount of free damage, and it stops the Anima charging of the target. You can tell which enemy is charging by watching for the purple glow, and that lets you know who to target for ambushes.

Gad is certainly softer, so his E.S. is the first target to destroy. Weaken both enemy E.S.s until they are closing in on 60% of their full health, then switch to single-target damage and wail on Gad. Get one of your stronger E.S.s up to a level three Anima rating so that you can destroy Gad outright when his HPs fall into the 25%-30% mark. That prevents him from doing much damage at all during his more impressive later-match attack rounds.

This leaves Joseph on his own, and in a dark place. He'll have major Anima to use because of his rage at losing an ally, but you can use the same ambush trick from earlier (doubly effective considering that whoever just knocked out Gad is still in Anima Awakening mode). If you won't have them get another turn in time, use a level one Awakening from another character.

Neither enemy stands any chance against this tactic when used carefully. If you have any trouble, make sure that proper E.S. upgrades were purchased at the Elsa store before heading down to Michtam.

Fly along the main street. Take the small ramp up when you come to it, not far along the path. There is a large piece of rubble to destroy on the right side that hides a box; a Night Moon is inside of it, offering a Large SP+ effect. On the bottom side of the main path is another piece of rubble, just a bit beyond the ramp. Destroy this to reveal a disembarking point.

Hop off of your E.S.s and walk down into the lower map. A box in that area has a Rejuvenator DX, and those sure come in handy. Return to your E.S.s after you get that item.

The northern part of the map has several numbered warehouses. Number three leads deeper into the region, where there is a **Save Point**. Number four has a container with D-EXP I (a disk for improving experience gained in E.S. battle). Go into the third warehouse area, save, and move beyond that into the next region. Another incredible fight is on the way! Consider D-Kill Cs for your active members, as this boss has a decent counter attack. If you need CPU space, remove D-Charge and use Nano Repair DXs and All Repairs during the attack. Be sure to put your new D-Nullify Evade on a low accuracy E.S. to ensure full damage output against upcoming high-evasion bosses. The Reuben is a very good choice for this useful disk.

E.S. ISSACHAR

HP:	500000
INFO:	MACHINE
TGT:	???
EXP:	17000
SP:	40
G:	10000
N ITEM:	C-US10
R ITEM:	NONE
STRONG:	NONE
WEAK:	NONE
ABSORBED:	NONE
NULL:	NONE

The last boss fight was a fun one, but it was kind of a walk in the park. This fight is more like a frantic dash through a deadly warzone. The E.S. Issachar is mean and hateful, being able to deal moderate damage even early in the fight, when most bosses are letting you get your bearings. After the halfway point, it's going to get ugly. The Issachar does not shy away from single-target damage or area-of-effect strikes.

Even worse, the Issachar uses a Magic Sword ability shortly into the encounter. This enables the E.S. to damage the Anima Gauge of targets that are attacked. This isn't as crippling as it sounds, but it is a good reason to convert some of your Anima into old-fashioned damage with a good special attack. The Issachar can't damage Anima that is already spent.

Being another E.S., the Issachar accrues Anima and uses area-of-effect attacks with it. You won't be able to stop her from doing this, and she'll comfortably strike down 40,000 HPs of damage to everyone in the group with Mal'ach Laser. Don't try to charge to recuperate from this; go directly for your better Nano Repairs and use them freely (All Repairs make this a cinch). It's well worthwhile to save the time, since even improved charges take two turns to get a person fully healed after this blast.

In the middle of the fight, your enemy heals her mech for 75,000 HPs. Don't stress out when this happens; she won't be able to do this with any frequency.

Late in the fight, the Issachar gets bonus Anima when struck with special attacks. This is your cue to use Anima for ambushes instead of special attacks with your better team players. Have your best damage dealer save Anima while this is occurring, and use a level three special attack as a finisher when the Issachar is down to 10-15% of its health. If you need to, have all characters use all Anima for special attacks on the same turn, as there is only so much Anima your enemy can store, and you'll hopefully destroy the mech outright.

Return to the last Save Point for an easy repair and a convenient save, then continue to the end of the map. There is only one path, and it leads invariably to the Archon Cathedral off in the distance.

ARCHON CATHEDRAL

POINTS OF INTEREST	
1	DISEMBARKING LOCATIONS
2	EMERGENCY SUB-GENERATOR
3	RESEARCH RESOURCE TRANSPORT ELEVATOR

ITEMS	
1	UPDATE FILE 04
2	HALF REPAIR
3	NANO REPAIR DX
4	GOLD FALL
5	DOWN REPAIR
6	SKILL UPGRADE D

ENEMIES	
1	ANATHEMA
2	CERA 6 S
3	CERA 7 S
4	E.S. DAN (BOSS)
5	LEVIAT
6	LEVIAT OFFICER
7	MARANATHA

Fly through the column of buildings and destroy the statue in the plaza ahead; this takes several shots, but it gets you **Update File 04**, which is worth roughly 4% of the total database. There is an area on the right side, behind some rubble, but that has no items of greater importance (just a Half Repair).

Enter the cathedral via the doors on the right side. These are open and are obvious unlocked. Move to the left once your are inside the cathedral and exit again by the doors on the far bottom-left; there is a small part of the yard that is accessible only from there, and you receive a Gold Fall from a box.

If your E.S.s don't all have their Anima Gauges filled, use the random fights in the area to raise them. Moving back and forth into the cathedral resets several of the fights, making this very easy to do. Save again when you have all E.S.s at full strength and a full Anima charge. Equip your E.S.s with anti-revenge disks and any extra frame disks you can stack on. Then, enter the main hall of the cathedral and approach the middle of the room. This triggers a battle.

E.S. DAN

HP:	800000
INFO:	MACHINE
TGT:	???
EXP:	23000
SP:	40
G:	12000
N ITEM:	D-EN III
R ITEM:	NONE
STRONG:	NONE
WEAK:	NONE
ABSORBED:	NONE
NULL:	NONE

Yes, this fight pushes your E.S. skills even farther. The E.S. Dan has immense health, daunting firepower, and special abilities that are going to frustrate some of your efforts.

First off, E.S. Dan relies on Revenge instead of Counters. If you want to stay as safe as possible, use long-range attacks to avoid this damage. Also, have a spread of damage types ready, so that your group won't depend on any single person or form of damage. The E.S. Dan starts a cycle very early in the fight that prevents elemental damage of one type. Each attack the Dan gets, this element shifts. Have one of your E.S.s equipped with D-Sensor to make monitoring those weaknesses easier.

If the Dan is immune to the type of damage an E.S. does during (immune to Fire during the Reuben's turn for example), use the turn to charge or use an item to restore your HP or those of an ally.

Once you have the E.S. Dan down to 60%, your foe will have enough power to start using Anima Awakening attacks. Top off your health before these, and pray that your E.S.s have enough health to survive. This is especially evil because the Dan does a double attack *on the same round he starts charging!* This double attack is actually worse than the area-of-effect Disrupter that he uses. The single E.S. hit by the double can be destroyed outright in the battle!

The Disrupter is still no laughing matter. Be ready to use an All Repair before his next attack.

Use Nano Repair DX, Half Repairs, and even All Repairs as needed in this fight. Never use a charge if it won't top off your HPs. Even being a few hundred HPs away from full might be enough to spell doom.

Keep in mind the element type of your Anima attacks. These are often different then the primary damage type for a given E.S. (the Reuben deals beam damage at level three, but lightning at level two, physical at level one, but usually does fire damage with normal attacks). Remembering this helps you keep the damage pouring in no mater what the Dan is immune to.

At 40% health or so, the E.S. Dan uses Great Weapon to increase its attack power. After this point, any double attacks and area-of-effect blasts are enough to nearly level the group. Even from full, you might lose people during the set attacks that are done two more times before the Dan falls.

Have your highest HP characters be the ones to save Anima for the final push (these are the least likely members to be destroyed outright). By using Nano Repairs and playing conservatively, it's likely that you'll lose only one or two craft. If you can make it through without a single loss, feel very pleased with your specialization and skills.

Now that the chapel is clear, fly to the back-right side of the room and enter the side chamber. Disembark and take the Skill Upgrade D from the platform. Then, fly to the left side of the chapel and repeat this on the platform there, though your goal is to use the Emergency Sub-Generator to restore power to the region. Use the elevator that activates in the room to descend into the lower complex, beneath the cathedral.

ISOLATED RESEARCH FACILITY

POINTS OF INTEREST	
1	RESEARCH RESOURCE TRANSPORT ELEVATOR
2	DISEMBARKING LOCATIONS
3	LIFTS
4	A-1 GATE SWITCH
5	A-2 GATE SWITCH
6	SOUTH GATE SWITCH
7	DATA ROOM
8	ZOHAR STORAGE ROOM PUZZLE
9	ZOHAR ELEVATOR STARTUP SWITCH
10	L-10 ELEVATOR

ITEMS	
1	NANO REPAIR DX
2	ALL REPAIR
3	D-SP I
4	DELTA EDGE III
5	UPDATE FILE 05
6	LIFE LEECH

ENEMIES	
1	ANATHEMA
2	ANATHEMA OFFICER
3	E.S. LEVI (BOSS)
4	LEVIAT
5	MARANATHA
6	YACUD CANNON REVISED

LIFT PURPOSES	
LIFT	DESTINATION/TREASURE
1	ALL REPAIR CONTAINER
2	SMALL FIGHT
3	NOTHING
4	WAY FORWARD
5	SMALL FIGHT, A-1 GATE SWITCH

The laboratory areas below the cathedral have more guardians, a few scattered containers, and quite a few lifts that lead to different parts of the facility. Use lift number five and disembark at the ledge on the right wall. There is an A-1 Gate Control terminal up the stairs from that landing. After using that, take your E.S.s up and back to lift number four.

Use the disembarking area south of lift four, in the next map, to reach the upper walkways of the facility. These are dominated by massive, quick conveyors. Take the southern route and explore the belts there; destroy the terminal along the edge, look on the right side for a D-SP I, and use the A-2 Gate Switch that is closer to the left side.

Having done this, get back to your E.S.s and go through the open door to the south (this is the A-2 Gate that is now open). Search the first passage you approach to find MOMO's Delta Edge III, and enjoy the **Save Point** and store along the next corridor.

There is also a disembarking point. These lead up and left, to a terminal for the Research Ward South Gate. Use that terminal and head back to your E.S.s, passing a door that is still locked. Take your E.S. to the disembarking point at the top of the hall now. Grab **Update File 05** up there by climbing the steps and using all of the panels in the data room to unlock a hidden room. These gets you 3% more info for your database.

Next, use the door that is just a tad north from the Save Point. There is some great fighting in the room beyond (it's a great place to score some skill points). Press ◉ on the left side of the room to push a walkway into position for later; you reach the walkway by disembarking on the right side. Go up there and take the belts left, down a tad, then back around to reach a box with a Life Leech ring; this is a very useful item.

Consider reversing course for a moment to save the game again. Load D-Kill Rs, keep on the D-Charges, and use D-Frames to improve your HPs as much as possible.

The top of that room has a puzzle to open a door. To complete this, look at the symbol above the door. Destroy the green panels on the left that are shown in the symbol (middle-bottom, right-second row, middle-top, and so forth). Do the same for the brown panels (left and right-bottom, left and center-second row, etc.). This unlocks the Zohar Storage Room door. Don't go in until you are ready for a good fight!

INTRODUCTION

ARCHIVES

CHARACTERS

TACTICAL FILES

EQUIPMENT

THREAT ASSESSMENT

REGIONAL ANALYSIS

SEQUENTIAL DATA

E.S. LEVI

	900000
O:	MACHINE
:	???
P:	28000
:	40
	14000
TEM:	D-TYPE M
TEM:	NONE
RONG:	NONE
AK:	NONE
SORBED:	NONE
LL:	NONE

The E.S. Levi doesn't have many special tricks, but instead presents a cruel fight because it has amazing stats. The battle with the E.S. Levi contains the following hurdles: High HP, brutal damage, nice armor, revenge, counters, decent evasion, and three Anima Attacks over the course of the battle. The struggle is both predictable and crushing at the same time.

Between special attacks (which are only done around 80% health, 40%, and finally at 20%), the Levi relies on single target attacks, such as Acala's Moan, and area-of-effect blasts with Indra's Moan. The area-of-effect blasts are trivial, and are mopped up with Half Repairs. Critical Acala's Moans are not so trivial, so keep your health topped off constantly. This fight is going to go through Nano Repair DXs and Half Repairs; that is fine.

Occasionally, you'll have a mine planted on one of your E.S.s. Use a Down Repair to take these off before the three turn counter runs out. You cannot afford to have that happen in this fight. By the same token, use Down Repairs after important characters have been debuffed by the Levi.

Before long, you must face the Levi's first Anima Awakening. As long as you have kept health in good shape, the double attack that heralds the Awakening shouldn't kill off anyone outright. Heal that E.S. to full, then use charge to get everyone into a guarding position. Without charge, the Anima special attack will kill one of your people outright. It's worth "wasting" an entire round charging to make sure that his full output won't trash anybody (without charge, we're talking about 00k damage).

If you can apply that strategy and survive the Anima Awakening, the battle is going to be fine. The Vajra Armor that the Levi depends on afterward is powerful, but careful timing makes it almost worthless to him. To defeat it, have one character use a level one Anima Awakening special attack; this disrupts the armor by adding a weakness of one type to the Levi. It is essential that one of your E.S.s has D-Sensor so that you can see where the weakness appears, then try to start harping on that. If this isn't a main damage type for you, have no fear; the process can be repeated. Knock a couple of holes into the Levi's armor to see major exploitation in action.

The only issue is that if you do this too many times, the Levi will take a turn to recast Vajra Armor (this happens once the Levi has four weaknesses).

If you don't use this strategy, dealing damage and accruing Anima takes forever. Use the person who has your D-Anima equipped to do the brunt of the special attacks, as they are going to have the easiest time gaining back the Anima.

Watch for your E.S.s to get hit with Skin Down. Improved charge with D-Clean is wonderful against this because you can heal your E.S. to full while removing the Skin Down!

After 40% health, the Levi upgrades its speed, accuracy, and evasion. This doesn't make as huge as difference as it sounds, considering that you've already been facing an uphill battle and winning soundly.

Keep two characters charged to a high Anima level for the end of the fight. If the Levi manages to take out one of your people in the 20% Anima Awakening, respond with level three special attacks for a fast kill. He'll never get a chance to take advantage of his minor victory.

A door opens after the fight concludes. To the right of the old Save Point, there is the L-10 door that you passed earlier. This opens, revealing an elevator. Within the room itself, there is a point to disembark on the left side. Do so, and use the Zohar Elevator Startup Switch. For another treat, note that Jin learns Lightning Waltz by coming back into the boss room later and picking up the glowing sword that was left behind by the enemy. After doing that, retreat to save, then take the L-10 elevator.

Or, if you choose, use the elevator in the room to access the chapel (the lift is in full working order now and will remain functional for return trips as well). Though it takes a few minutes, your group can now comfortably head back to the Elsa if you have more questing to do for special items. With the levels and extra equipment gained during these fights, it's even easier to accomplish other goals (such as taking down Erde Kaiser Sigma).

L-10 SPECIALIST AREA

POINTS OF INTEREST	
1	L-10 SHELTER SWITCH
2	ROPEWAY CAR

ITEMS	
1	ETHER PACK M
2	MED KIT L
3	ETHER PACK L
4	SKILL UPGRADE C
5	5000G

ENEMIES	
1	CRUSTATA
2	GADREEL
3	PERUN
4	SETTANINAE
5	STRIBOG

The Gnosis in this area are all quite tough, use area-of-effect attacks for fast boost, then rely on characters with strong special attacks for high damage solutions. Break damage is a major issue, but it can be circumvented by either equipped items with a bonus to your characters' Break Limit, or by beating the fights with maximum speed. Another good trick is to Break the Settaninae outright (their Break Limit is awful).

Walk down the corridor, to the right side of the area. There is a room there with the L-10 Shelter Switch; use it to unlock the way into the heart of the L-10 area. Return to the midpoint in the corridor and use that side passage to reach the unlocked shelter. The fighting remains heavy, but it has been some time since you've been able to stretch your group's muscles in ground combat.

When the walkways begin, follow them until the path splits. The path on the left leads to a dead end room where there is a brief scene, and you can pick up 5000G from the containers there. The right side soon leads to a room with a **Save Point** and store.

The Ropeway Car there leads down to a lower section of the massive chamber. Through several tough fights with very high-tier Gnosis, you can make your way to a series of ruins at the bottom. For these tougher Gnosis, it's extremely useful to use potent Break attacks and keep the enemies out of combat; they have high health and require a few rounds of beating to put down, and letting them attack you means that your party might reach their Break Limit (not life-threatening, but very annoying). And with so many Save Points around, ether points are not much of an issue. This is the first area where you find elemental absorbs commonly. Having KOS-MOS or MOMO in your party, to use Hilbert Effect, makes these fights much easier.

ANCIENT RUINS

POINTS OF INTEREST	
1	POWER CIRCLES

ITEMS	
1	SARASVATI'S ROBE
2	GUSTAV NECK
3	LONG HORN
4	REVIVE L
5	VI EMPEROR
6	SKILL UPGRADE B
7	MED KIT DX
8	FIVE STONES
9	SKILL UPGRADE C
10	REJUVENATOR M

ENEMIES	
1	ARMAROS
2	AZAZEL
3	GADREEL
4	IBLIS
5	PERUN
6	RED TESTAMENT (BOSS)
7	RED TESTAMENT, SECOND FORM (BOSS)
8	RED TESTAMENT'S ALLY (BOSS)
9	STRIBOG
10	SVAROZIC
11	T-ELOS (BOSS)
12	ZARATHUSTRA (END GAME BOSS)

The ruins have many strange devices and Gnosis to observe. Along the initial hallway, there is a Power Circle; use this to switch the direction of the wall ahead. In the primary setting, your group can travel to the right. When toggled, you can choose this or to go to the left. This area is extremely well connected, but the issue in getting around lies in setting the walls so that your group can advance to the next row. Do this by setting the walls so that the approach from one side pushes the group forward, then back and take the long way around to reach that column from the appropriate side to advance. This sounds extremely complex until you actually do it in-game.

INTRODUCTION

ARCHIVES

CHARACTERS

TACTICAL FILES

EQUIPMENT

THREAT ASSESSMENT

REGIONAL ANALYSIS

SUPPLEMENTAL DATA

On the right side of the third row is a box with Sarasvati's Robe (a nice upgrade for Jin, and perhaps one of the first items to tempt damage-spec players away from his swimsuit). A Gustav Neck is on the left side of the same row.

After getting both of those, turn the highest Power Circle so that the route from the right side would send the group up to the door beyond. Retreat from there and go as far back as you can without toggling the Power Circles; your goal is to get to the second row in the center, hook right, and have that Power Circle positioned to push your group up to the third row.

The next region has quite a few fights, but a treasured **Save Point** is not far away; take the left at the first junction to reach this bastion of free ether points. On the right side is a box with a Long Horn suit of armor. Follow the main hallway up to the top, where everyone can move into a chamber of crystals. Move to the center of the room and watch the next two scenes.

When Shion awakens, destroy the rocks blocking the northern path. Take this path to the lone grave and blast that open to descend into the crypt. Watch the scene inside, and enjoy the action when Shion returns to her body. As soon as this scene ends, another battle begins.

HP:	56000
EP:	530
BL:	720
INFO:	MACHINE AND HUMAN
TGT:	???
EXP:	32000
SP:	40
G:	16000
N ITEM:	KAP-VEL
R ITEM:	NONE
S ITEM:	LIFE DEMON
STRONG:	FIRE
WEAK:	NONE
ABSORBED:	NONE
NULL:	POISON

This encounter with T-elos is a lot more decisive. Shion is placed into your main party for the start of the encounter, though she can be taken out of it at any time thereafter.

Early in the encounter, T-elos does very unimpressive damage (Echidna is decent on Break but is otherwise minor; Magdalene 16 is a long-range attack that is also weak). Even the area-of-effect Ether attacks that T-elos uses won't pose too much of a threat until she nears half health.

Use this early period to build up to your full Boost Limit, get T-elos' Break Gauge up to 70% or so, and to steal her *awesome* Life Demon ring. That is such a keeper.

T-ELOS (LATE GAME)

Nearing half health, T-elos gets her special attack ready. U-Teneritas hits a single target for very high damage and adds Break Points to their gauge as well. You might not want to have your lower HP characters in the group for this, as they might not survive the burst. Tougher characters, however, should be just fine and will be in great shape after healing.

Now that you are in the real meat of the battle, use your character's Master Skills for a serious increase to survivability or damage, depending on your playstyle. Using these before the halfway point is just wasting EPs, since they just get you to the tough bits faster then wear out of you.

Nearing one-third health, T-elos uses Heartbreaker, a major Break increaser. If you've been using enough Break throughout the fight, this is a great time to use Erde Kaiser Fury to try and get her past her limit (to interrupt her next special attack).

After T-elos is past her Break Limit, use all of the Boost that you've saved to level major special attacks against her. With careful timing, she might not get another attack in the entire fight!

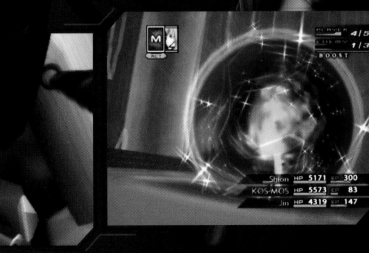

Advance past the door that appeared after T-elos fell. Notice that KOS-MOS now has her third special attack; it's very nice against single targets, especially in major encounters.

ZIGGY'S SIDE MISSION

Azazel and Armaros Gnosis in this area are the ones that possess the Sephirotic Canes (needed for Ziggy's final weapon, back on the Elsa). Collect 99 of these if you wish to complete that side mission.

Take the route to the right in the crystalline area, and use the **Save Point** that you soon find. Explore to the left from there, and look for the box with VI Emperor (useless if you have Shion's Miyuki Special already, but still fun to collect). Keep going left, past there, to reach a pink crystal; destroy that to open the way forward.

The next crystal area has more Gnosis, but it also has more treasure. Search the left side thoroughly for a Five Stone and a Skill Upgrade C. The right route is mostly vacant, with just a couple fights and a Rejuvenator M.

Both routes lead to another pink crystal; destroy that and walk up the long, green pathway that appears. Use the **Save Point** when you see it, then wave hello to the person up top. It's certainly someone you expected to see at this point.

THE RED TESTAMENT

RED TESTAMENT	
HP:	12000
EP:	355
BL:	150
INFO:	BIOLOGICAL
TGT:	???
EXP:	5000
SP:	40
G:	0
N ITEM:	UNION RING
R ITEM:	NONE
S ITEM:	WHITE SHIRT
STRONG:	NONE
WEAK:	NONE
ABSORBED:	NONE
NULL:	POISON, HEAT

RED TESTAMENT'S ALLY	
HP:	9000
EP:	256
BL:	80
INFO:	BIOLOGICAL (HUMAN)
TGT:	???
EXP:	5000
SP:	40
G:	0
N ITEM:	REJUVENATOR DX
R ITEM:	NONE
S ITEM:	RESEARCH UNIFORM
STRONG:	NONE
WEAK:	NONE
ABSORBED:	NONE
NULL:	POISON, HEAT

Get your stealing done against both targets at the beginning of the fight, as usual. Once you start to lay on the damage, this encounter won't last. Both targets are easy to Break, and neither have enough HPs to stand up to serious special attacks.

Indeed, this is only a warm up, for the real fight is yet to come. As soon as your battle ends, another begins.

RED TESTAMENT (SECOND FORM)

HP:	52000
EP:	999
BL:	780
INFO:	BIOLOGICAL
TGT:	???
EXP:	40000
SP:	40
G:	18000
N ITEM:	KAJIC RING
R ITEM:	NONE
S ITEM:	VELVET PANNIER
STRONG:	ICE, LIGHTNING
WEAK:	NONE
ABSORBED:	FIRE
NULL:	POISON, HEAT, SEAL ETHER, SEAL BOOST, REFLECT DAMAGE

Now this is a fight that can test your patience. The Red Testament isn't the absolute worst of all the encounters in the game, but he presents an ability that is clearly potent; this creep is immune to damage when he isn't past his Break Limit. That doesn't give you very large periods to do damage, but with preparation it isn't too bad.

Keep Safety or Best Ally (auto revive) on anyone with low total health or who is absolutely crucial to the fight. It's a single target spell so it takes a few rounds to get it put on your people, but even having it on just your healer is a good backup measure for wipe protection.

Erde Kaiser and Erde Kaiser Fury are extremely useful for getting in Break damage. Though the Red Testament is resistant to these forms of damage, the Break is worthwhile, and the results are better than physical attacks, especially in the later part of the encounter.

The key is to save up a large amount of Boost and use it in a solid rush. Because the Red Testament is strong to two major elements and weak to none, it's usually best to use Boosts during his Break vulnerability to have your highest damage dealer get many attacks (as opposed to using special attacks).

Ether is going to be very important in this fight. Toward the later stages, the Red Testament is going to use Abyss Walker and go immune to physical damage. Beyond that, the entire fight is about Break damage and ether attacks, so something has to give. Keep your best healers, breakers, and ether attackers in here for a good win. Shion, Ziggy, and MOMO get the job done!

There isn't much else to the fight. If you have someone with high health, like Ziggy, it won't be too dangerous. The Red Testament can do wicked Break damage and harm many people at once during the later portion of the fight. However, high HP characters survive long enough to use Revive/ Seven Moons and keep going.

Retreat to the last **Save Point** and save your game again, after the fighting is over. Examine the White Shirt that you stole, and give yourself a bit of a debate about using it. Though dangerous to rely on, this piece of armor has great potential for damage. If you use Shion purely as a healer, this isn't worthwhile. However, those who use Shion for damage dealing get a lot out of the ludicrous critical rate that the White Shirt provides.

Enter your equipment screen and remove all items that are useful for getting more experience, skill points, money, and so forth. The next fight is a make or break struggle over the fate of the entire universe; you don't need to fret over getting a few more bucks. Instead, stack on every combat-enhancer you can find. Have one person (e.g. Ziggy) decked out with as many HPs as possible. They should stay in your group the *entire* battle as a way of preventing full wipes. Prepare MOMO and Shion for healing and Ether Attack duties.

INTRODUCTION
ARCHIVES
CHARACTERS
TACTICAL FILES
EQUIPMENT
THREAT ASSESSMENT
REGIONAL ANALYSIS
SUPPLEMENTAL DATA

VECTOR

6

ZARATHUSTRA

HP:	70000
EP:	999
BL:	999
INFO:	MACHINE
TGT:	???
EXP:	0
SP:	0
G:	0
N ITEM:	NONE
R ITEM:	NONE
S ITEM:	NONE
STRONG:	FIRE, ICE, LIGHTNING, BEAM
WEAK:	NONE
ABSORBED:	NONE
NULL:	POISON, HEAT, SEAL ETHER, SEAL BOOST, REFLECT DAMAGE

Zarathustra is a machine with some real power. Though it takes less time to blast through it, compared to the Red Testament, you have to be more careful in this encounter. Zarathustra is able to combine some attacks extremely well, and a party without the right configuration may suffer for it.

First off, notice that area-of-effect attacks are common from this divine machine. Get used to that, as much of this battle revolves around keeping your whole party going while under assault. Debuffs are also thrown out, so it's wise to have a couple of people with Refresh.

As early as 80% health, Zarathustra builds energy in its core and uses the first Embryon attack. These area-of-effect onslaughts will Break parties instantly, for most configurations. By the time you recover, it's an uphill battle to get everyone's health back in line. This is why it's so useful to have one person with massive HPs.

For the rest of the fight, elemental shifting will take place. Physical attacks were useful at first, but now you are in the chaos phase of Zarathustra's cycle. Rely on fire and beam attacks to do the brunt of your damage, and Boost frequently to keep damage rolling in while preventing enemy attacks. It's not like you need to worry about getting a finishing strike here, especially considering that the fight is worth no experience.

STAGE OF FIGHT	WHAT TO USE
STARTING	PHYSICAL
CHAOS	FIRE, BEAM
ORDER	PHYSICAL, ICE, LIGHTNING

Use Mind Down to keep Zarathustra taking high damage from your ether attacks, and rely on anything that raises ether attack for your casters. By the middle of the fight, you should have two casters on the line. Shion and MOMO are always solid choices.

By the middle of the fight, Zarathustra restores its arms and enters its Order Mode. If one of your casters is low on ether points, either get them killed off and use a Seven Moons, or replace them with a physical character for this stage.

When Zarathustra enters its final phase, combining Chaos and Order, you should leap at the chance to finish it off. Use all Boost for your highest damage dealer, and attack again and again to end the battle.

Circuitus is near the end, and it's a crushing area-of-effect attack if you can't stop Zarathustra in time. This takes three rounds to cast. On round one chaos and order start to resonate. On round two chaos and order become one. Then, everything blows up during round three. Have Best Ally or Safety on any low health members of your party; this attack is quite damaging.

If things are getting tight, rely on Erde Kaiser (of whatever type is appropriate for the current stage of battle) to reach Zarathustra's Break Limit quickly. Ether cost is such a trivial issue in this battle, because you can pull out all the stops and use Ether Packs, Seven Moons to Revive casters, and so forth.

The final battle is challenging, but it's not going to keep you thwarted for long. If your group does run into any trouble, try even more item use during the fight (some players have a real tendency to save things for later, but there is no *later* for this fight). Also, collect a couple of final weapons for your characters. Some of them, like Shion's, are so easy to get that it's a matter of taking a few minutes to get +40 attack power!

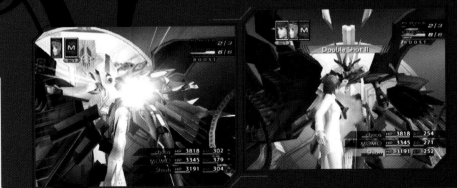

If you decide to level build, for fun or an easier victory, consider doing it with your E.S.s (even as far back as Abel's Ark). Fast E.S. battles bring in experience and money at an amazing rate.

With the machine put in its place, you are left to watch the ending movies. Stick around for these (or skip them if you get too impatient) and save the game. Doing so allows you to collect Allen's Swimsuit and Flawless (an alternative outfit for chaos).

When you try to load this file, the items are awarded and the group is taken back to the Elsa, where you can continue to seek better equipment, finish peripheral missions, level your characters, and so forth.

Congratulations for playing through Xenosaga III. This was certainly a great addition to the series, and you've faced some of the toughest elements in the game. If you haven't faced Omega Id and Erde Kaiser Sigma, work up to giving those brutes a try. Read through the Supplemental Data chapter and find out what else is out there in the world of Xenosaga.

INTRODUCTION

CHARACTERS

TACTICAL FILES

COMBAT TECHNIQUES

REGIONAL ANALYSIS

SUPPLEMENTAL DATA

SUPPLEMENTAL DATA

This chapter is dedicated to grabbing all of the odds and ends of the game, and bringing them together in one place. Side missions, optional tasks, collection quests, and everything else that is not directly required to make progress in the game is discussed here.

EXTRA GAME FUNCTIONS

When you load Xenosaga III, use the Data option instead of loading if you want to learn more about Xenosaga I and II. This area also lets you use your save information to see the models of characters, craft, and monsters that you have encountered.

All movies and scenes from the game are also accessible from here, once you have viewed them in-game. Show your friends some of the coolest moments of the game from here!

Then, after beating the game, you can even watch Xenosaga III movies with certain costume changes. By shifting the movies to Swimsuit Mode, you get to see the scenes with everyone wearing their Swimsuit (provided that you have discovered those characters' Swimsuits already). Sadly, characters outside of the main party will still be normally clothed. With characters like Sellers in the game, that is probably for the best.

DO YOU HAVE CLEARED DATA FROM XENOSAGA II?

If so, use this when starting your new game in Xenosaga III. Though this doesn't immensely change the progression of the game, you do receive a special outfit for Shion that is completely unavailable otherwise. This Vector Uniform has a very nice Break Limit for an early item, so that gives it merit even beyond the fun of having outfit selections right from the start.

SIDE QUESTS ON FIFTH JERUSALEM

There are a few side items to explore while Shion is visiting Fifth Jerusalem. This is one spot in the game that has very little leeway because it will not appear in the EVS, and you aren't going to be on Fifth Jerusalem for too long. So, you should try these out early on, if you are interested in doing them at all.

HONEY TEDDY

- Enter Café Steam and talk to Oksana
- Ask to look at the Secret Menu, then leave
- Walk to the park and speak with Isakios; keep talking until Isakios mentions the password
- Go to the Möbius Hotel and start the event to meet chaos; do so, attend the CAT Testing Grounds Event, then speak to Isakios again before returning to the hotel
- Go back to Café Stream and speak with Oksana; say Double Whammy!
- Speak to Kesar and Collect the Honey Teddy (even if you blow up his food, leave and return for the Honey Teddy)

DIVE TEDDY

- Inside the Hotel Möbius, speak with Hermie (near the elevators)
- Go to the Park and talk to Dario and Paula
- Hermie Shows Up; talk to everyone again to get the Dive Teddy

JUST A LITTLE SOMETHING

- Use the console on the east wall of the Möbius Hotel (Receive 10G)

MINOR EVENTS ON MILTIA

There are some events in the game that won't get you a huge amount of treasure or change the course of destiny, but they are still interesting. These are recorded here, for those who want to find everything there is to find. All of these must be started before the Third Descent Operation begins; this changes the cityscape to the point where many of the mini-quests are no longer possible.

DEATH PRESCRIPTION DRUG QUEST

- Speak with Erin and Julia, on Miltia of the Past (before the war), in the 3rd City Block
- Speak with Lodge in the 4th City Block
- Speak to Andy, by the open space area
- Speak with Lodge in the 4th City Block a second time
- Speak with Andy Again and receive Prescription Copy
- Save your game, then return to Lodge
- Select the Fourth Answer (reload to see the First, Second, and Third Options)

- Select the Third Option first to correctly answer the question.
- Speak to Lodge, Erin, and Julia Again
- Speak to the man standing by Andy's seat
- Upon landing on Michtam, speak with AWAMORI and choose to read the Letter
- Check the Online Shop for new items for purchase afterward

INTRODUCTION
ARCHIVES
CHARACTERS
TACTICAL FILES
EQUIPMENT
THREAT ASSESSMENT
REGIONAL ANALYSIS
SUPPLEMENTAL DATA

THE RED BALLOON

- Destroy the door to the Glass Building on the Eastern District of Miltia and climb the steps inside

- Speak to Colin, on top of the building, and use a trap to catch the cat nearby

- Grab the balloon as soon as possible once the trap stuns the cat

- Grab the balloon and talk to Colin again

- Leave the area to reset things, then return, if you miss the balloon

- Speak to Colin and watch the balloon scenes several times, receive Strawberry Ice Cream as a reward

- Note that Colin's text after the Third Descent Operation changes based on how much interaction you had with him here

ICE CREAM TRUCK QUEST

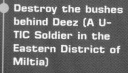

- Look for the Haramiya Ice Cream Truck in the Eastern District of Miltia

- Talk to Haramiya (he is inside the truck)

- Examine the Red Button on the side of the Truck

- You can leave the shutters open, half-closed, or fully closed

- The final position of the shutters determines what happens to Haramiya during the Third Descent Operation

- Closing the shutters fully will save Haramiya and Nina and gets you a DX Ice Cream

CHALLENGER COUPONS

- Purchase Coupons from the Terminal in the Eastern District of Miltia (near the store)

- Speak to Scott, Aizen Magus, and Bailey for the hints to winning

- Don't read the following answers if you want to figure the numbers out on your own! (Sixty-Eight, Thirty-Seven, and Twelve)

- Return to the console later, near the time of the Third Descent Operation (or afterward, via EVS); this gets you 80,000G

TAMPERING WITH THE FOUNTAIN

- Destroy the bushes behind Deez (A U-TIC Soldier in the Eastern District of Miltia)

- Enter the tunnel

- Examine the Fountain Control and choose all patterns

- Take the Skill Upgrade C from the floor of the area when you leave

FINAL WEAPON MISSIONS

INTRODUCTION

ARCHIVES

CHARACTERS

TACTICAL FILES

EQUIPMENT

THREAT ASSESSMENT

REGIONAL ANALYSIS

SUPPLEMENTAL DATA

After completing Abel's Ark, a number of end-game missions become available for your characters. The vast majority of these are meant to give everyone a final weapon, though there are quite a few accessories that are given as secondary rewards. Even if you don't use all of your characters frequently, these missions are fun and are well worth your time. The secondary accessories that are given are sometimes even more powerful than the weapons themselves, so you won't want to miss anything!

CHAOS

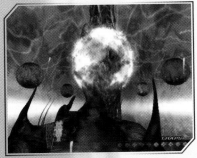

Go into the Elsa's Lounge and talk to ADONIS; the droid gives you the Grief Stone, saying that it has been acting oddly since you went to Abel's Ark (it's resonating with the Ark).

Go to the four spheres that you defeated in Abel's Ark. Walk/fly to the end of spheres and use the Grief Stone on the glowing areas near the boss fights that you once survived. When all four are absorbed into the Grief Stone, fly to the center of the spire. The Universe and God Breath will be acquired. These items are chaos' final weapon and a ring that halves energy costs while providing useful points to the character in addition.

JIN

Go to the men's quarters, on the main deck of the Elsa. Talk to the droid, PANACHE, in the bathroom. He says that he knows how to create a legendary sword, but he'll need some ingredients. Purchase a VB-Crimson from the store (and leave it unequipped), then get the Prayer Beads from Miltia if you haven't already. This requires you to go down to Miltia and walk around the macro map on the right side of the city. There is a business district with a chest sitting right out in the open. Use code 5150 to enter the district and collect the Prayer Beads.

Give these items to PANACHE, and in return he'll forge the VB-Dawn for Jin. He'll also give you the impressive Nine Stones accessory.

JR.

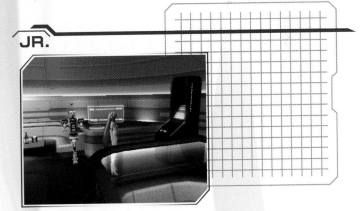

Jr.'s Vaquero is certainly nice, but you need to beat the fifth world of Hakox to get it. This takes some time and mental investment, but you probably wanted to snag Ziggy's Swimsuit from world four anyway, so this isn't more than another hour's work really.

KOS-MOS

Her KWP-XX is a final weapon, and it can be purchased at the store for 300,000G. Also, her D Unit V1 armor can be grabbed at the store as well; this costs 50,000G and changes KOS-MOS's appearance.

MOMO

Enter the women's quarters on the Elsa, and talk to KAMIKAZE. That droid will inform the ladies of your group that the little dog from the Durandal has run off. The pooch has charged into the EVS and is somewhere about the Durandal in the UMN. Follow little Alby!

Talk to the dog on the Docks of the Durandal, somewhat on the left side of the map; Alby will rush off to the train and leave for the Park. Head there and take the escalator up from the Park's front area to find the dog again. Alby goes farther into the Park, and is discovered a third time on the right side of the Park. When you meet Alby that time the dog is taken home, and you receive Heaven's Door. While you talk to KAMIKAZE again, you also receive the Moon Bridge. Speak to VALENCIA in the Elsa to use Heaven's Door.

SHION

On of the first things that happens after you are back on the Elsa, when Abel's Ark has been beaten, is that Miyuki contacts the party.

She offers to make Shion's ultimate weapon, but she needs some help doing it. Though she has a Geocrystal that she pinched from Vector, she needs another as well.

If you remember the Floating Landmass, there were Geocrystals there. By destroying all of the Geocrystals and searching the debris, you find a Rough Geocrystal (this is often done when you first clear that area, so it's likely that you already have that item by the late stage of the game). Otherwise, return to the Floating Landmass in the EVS and get it now.

Walk close to the UMN Terminal near the Save Point once you have the Rough Geocrystal. Miyuki will give you Brisingamen, a useful item, and tell you to refine the Rough Geocrstal. Go into the women's quarters and talk to Bunnie Bob to get the Rough Geocrystal refined. Talk to Miyuki a final time, and she'll send you the Miyuki Special!

ZIGGY

Ziggy's final weapon is the slowest to get, and it might very well be the last of all the weapons you go for. CABRILLO, on the main deck of the Elsa, is happy to make a Gnosis Nail for Ziggy. However, she wants you to get her 99 Sephirotic Canes to exchange for it. You might be suddenly thinking (what the heck are Sephirotic Canes; I've never seen them). Indeed, you probably haven't. These items are found only on Azazel and Armaros Gnosis, and those are seen in the final two maps before the end bosses of the game.

If you want to collect all 99 of the Sephirotic Canes, plant yourself at one of the final Save Points and keep blasting those tough Gnosis. Reset the encounters as needed, and repeat, repeat, repeat. The good news is that you can do this after beating the game if you get impatient.

SWIMSUIT CHALLENGE

CHARACTER	SWIMSUIT LOCATION	ACTION REQUIRED
ALLEN	N/A	BEAT THE GAME, SAVE THE CLEARED DATA, LOAD THE CLEARED DATA
CHAOS	ARCADIAN RESOURCE DUNGEON	SEARCH CRYPT IN FLOATING LANDMASS AREA, BEAT AREA, RETURN IN EVS; USE CONSOLE AT TEMPLE ENTRANCE TO FIND HIDDEN DUNGEON
JIN	LABYRINTHOS, MARGULIS' ROOM	OPEN BOX
JR.	MILTIA WORLD MAP, RIGHT SIDE	OPEN BOX
KOS-MOS	ELSA, E.S. BAY	COMPLETE SEGMENT ADDRESSES, ACCESS SEGMENT ADDRESS MENU TO CONFIRM, TALK TO THEODORE
MOMO	DABRYE MINE, ENTRANCE	FINISH MAI ENCOUNTER, RETURN TO ENTRANCE, PLAY CRANE GAME SEVERAL TIMES
SHION	PEDEA ISLAND, WEST SIDE	RETURN TO ISLAND VIA EVS AND SEARCH BY THE WESTERN BUILDING
ZIGGY	N/A	CLEAR ADVANCED HAKOX LEVELS

The Swimsuits in the game look quite different, and many of them are really cool. These items, especially if gained as early as possible, offer a very high Luck stat in exchange for trivial defense. For random encounters and even for many of the boss fights, this increase in damage output is enough

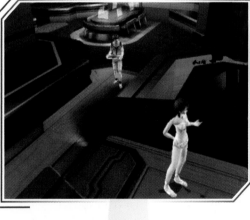

to make the Swimsuits quite viable. Think about it as 30% more criticals gained from using a single item!

ADDITIONAL OUTFITS			
CHARACTER	CLOTHING NAME	CLOTHING LOCATION	ACTION REQUIRED
CHAOS	FLAWLESS	N/A	CLEAR XENOSAGA III AND LOAD GAME WITH FINAL SAVE
KOS-MOS	D UNIT V1	STORE	BUY IT
SHION	WHITE SHIRT	RED TESTAMENT ENCOUNTER	STEAL FROM RED TESTAMENT
SHION	RESEARCH UNIFORM	RED TESTAMENT ENCOUNTER	STEAL FROM RED TESTAMENT'S ALLY.
SHION	VECTOR UNIFORM	N/A	USE XENOSAGA II CLEARED GAME SAVE TO START XENOSAGA III

INTRODUCTION

ARCHIVES

CHARACTERS

TACTICAL FILES

EQUIPMENT

THREAT ASSESSMENT

REGIONAL ANALYSIS

SUPPLEMENTAL DATA

ARCADIAN RESOURCE DUNGEON

	POINTS OF INTEREST
1	COMMUNICATION CRYSTALS
2	ELEVATOR TERMINALS
3	LIGHT BRIDGE TERMINALS
4	AMPLIFICATION PANEL
5	WHITE DOOR (PUZZLE CLEAR)

	ITEMS
1	2000G
2	SKILL UPGRADE A
3	MED KIT L
4	100G
5	200G
6	DRAUPNIR
7	ANGEL'S EXPERIENCE
8	SKILL UPGRADE D
9	CHAOS' SWIMSUIT

You are probably wondering what this is. If you've already been playing the game a fair bit, think back to when you grabbed the Arcadian Resource, at the end of the Floating Landmass area. The plot throws you forward past a few things, and you might not have had access to the EVS for a time. Once you do get that access, return to the Floating Landmass and use the terminal at the entrance of the temple; this wasn't functional before because it requires the Arcadian Resource. Once used, this unlocks an elevator that goes down instead of up!

What you see below is an optional dungeon (without fighting, so it can be done at any level), that leads to chaos' Swimsuit and a few bonus items. This isn't a quick place to defeat, as there are a few levels of puzzles along the way.

You are forced to take two groups through this dungeon at the same time. It's a leapfrog scenario, where one group must advance to a communication crystal before the other group is able to act, then things continue to switch off from there, with one group enabling the other to progress by moving blocks into position, or bridges, or by removing obstacles.

FIRST AREA: MOVING BLOCKS

Advance with Shion's party to the first elevator and use that to go up a level. On the right side is a communication crystal; switch to the second party with that one. Have your second group move to the left and access the terminal there to send a lift up to the others. Next, move north and around the area until you reach another communication crystal.

Shion's group can now take the left route around the upper tier. The second path to the right leads to a terminal (use that to send an elevator down). Use another terminal that is up and left from there, then backtrack to the first passage on the right. Access that communication crystal now.

The second group has its next communication crystal on the right side of the dungeon, but you need to move to the center of the map first. The lifts that Shion's group lowered make it possible to walk farther than before. Use the terminal over there and note that crystal's position, but don't use it until you've fully explored the walkways. There is a box with 2000G. Right, from there, is another terminal to use. With that done, weave back to the top of the map and to the far right. The platform that came down is waiting to take you upstairs. Leave the area by the only means available.

This switches everything back to Shion's group automatically. Use the nearby terminal again (it has regained power), and retreat to use the lift that has appeared to take you up a floor.

SECOND AREA: ENERGY BRIDGES

Have the secondary group use the southern terminal and cross the bridge that appears. Then, access the communication crystal to switch groups. Have Shion's group use the north bridge from the central area, then shut off the power from the other side. Hit the crystal when that is done.

Now, the alternate group can cross from the left side of the entry (the bridge isn't blocked anymore). Take that route and hit the amplification panel before returning to where you were. Shion's group can then take the left path from the central pillar and open another amplification panel. Have Shion use the southern terminal nearby as well (you may need to shut down a bridge from the central pillar to accomplish this).

Let Jr.'s group use that bridge, after switching parties, and turn on the amplification panel to the south. This opens the way for them to leave the level by turning on only one more terminal. Cross that last bridge and hit the final terminal before walking up the steps.

Have Shion turn off her southern bridge, cross to the center, and use the bridge on the right to make your way across the entire map (it's linear from there). You reach an elevator that takes everyone up to the next floor.

THIRD AREA: COLORED DOORS

This time the puzzle is fairly easy, and it's forgiving as well. If you get into trouble, use the communication crystals to restart the area. From the beginning, use the pink door, then move south with the blue doors (twice), and green. Trash the container at the bottom, then communicate with the second group to have them push around to the central terminal. Use that to give power to the lifts, and go after the other containers in the area, if you wish.

Your main goal is to reach the white door at the top of the map. Using that completes the puzzle for both groups and brings you the box with Draupnir (a very nice item).

The group reunites and heads to the top of the optional dungeon. There, you receive Angel's Experience, a Skill Upgrade D, and chaos' Swimsuit. These are fitting rewards for such a lengthy puzzle challenge!

DATABASE UPDATES

UPDATE FILE	REGION	ACTION REQUIRED
01	VECTOR S-LINE DIVISION, SECTOR 3	SEARCH CONTAINERS AFTER OPENING THE GREEN PATH
02	PEDEA ISLAND, DARK PROFESSOR'S BASEMENT	SEARCH FOR ENTRANCE TO HIDDEN LAIR, RIDE SECRET LIFT DOWN TO BASEMENT AND SEARCH
03	ELSA	COMPILE ALL FEDERAL REPORTS AND USE EACH ONE AT SCOTT'S TERMINAL, ON THE ELSA
04	ARCHON CATHEDRAL, OUTSIDE	SHOOT MAIN STATUE TO REVEAL
05	ISOLATED RESEARCH FACILITY, DATA ROOM	USE ALL DATA TERMINALS AND SEARCH HIDDEN ROOM
06	MILTIA, FOREST PATH	SEARCH THE PATH WHILE ESCORTING VIRGIL UP THE PATH
07	DABRYE MINE, ELSA'S CAVE	OPEN TREASURE BOX IN CAVE
08	MILTIA, EAST SIDE	BREAK INTO BUILDING ON RIGHT SIDE AND SEARCH
09	MILTIA, HOSPITAL	SEARCH THE ROOMS ON THE SECOND FLOOR
10	LABYRINTHOS, FIRST FLOOR	SEARCH MARGULIS' ROOM
11	MERKABAH, SPECIAL E.S. AREA	RETURN TO THE MERKABAH IN THE EVS, UNLOCK E.S. ROUTE TO CORE, SEARCH THERE
12	DURANDAL, BRIDGE ENTRANCE	OPEN TREASURE BOX
13	ABEL'S ARK, PINK SPHERE	OPEN TREASURE BOX
14	FLOATING LANDMASS, TEMPLE LEVEL TWO	SEARCH PUZZLE AREA FOR BOXES

Database Updates are done throughout the game, so you cannot finish your database until very late into Xenosaga III. Collect every Update File while going through the game; this way you can receive your reward as soon as the game automatic update occurs.

With your database at 100%, open the Database Screen to confirm, then travel to the E.S. Bay of the Elsa. Talk to Guinness, and receive the legendary Kibisis. This stunning item provides +3 Boost, 1500 HPs, and 300 EPs. Wow!

FEDERAL REPORTS

FEDERAL REPORT	REGION	ACTION REQUIRED
1	MILTIA, WEST SIDE	DESTROY A CONSOLE
2	MILTIA, NORTH SIDE	DESTROY A CONSOLE
3	MILTIA, EAST SIDE	SEARCH U-TIC TRANSPORT
4	MILTIA, WEST SIDE	DESTROY A CONTAINER (LEFT SIDE, BELOW STAIRS)
5	MILTIA, EAST SIDE	TALK TO DYING SOLDIER
6	MILTIA, WEST SIDE	SEARCH TRASHCAN BY VENDING MACHINES
7	MILTIA, TRANSPORT GATE EXIT	SEARCH THE LEFT CORNER
8	MILTIA, TRANSPORT GATE EXIT	LOOK ON THE RIGHT SIDE

Special Item:
Acquired Federal Report 06 !

Collect the eight Federal Reports while traveling on Miltia. Reports 1 and 2 are available as soon as you can explore the city, while the rest of the Federal Reports are found after the Third Descent Operation begins. Note that you can miss some of these during your playthrough and come back later, in the EVS, to finish the mission.

When you have all of the Federal Reports, give them to Loria (2nd Floor, Hospital Area) for Decoder 07. Then, return to the Elsa and use all eight Federal Reports with Scott's computer, in the Professor's area.
This gives you Update File 03.

INTRODUCTION
ARCHIVES
CHARACTERS
TACTICAL FILES
EQUIPMENT
THREAT ASSESSMENT
REGIONAL ANALYSIS
SUPPLEMENTAL DATA

SEGMENT ADDRESSES

To get an extra prize after you have unlocked all of the Segment Addresses, finish the last Segment Address, access the Segment Address Database, and let the system confirm that you are done with the work. Return to the Elsa and speak with Theodore, in the E.S. Bay. He'll give you **KOS-MOS's Swimsuit**.

SEGMENT ADDRESS #	DOOR LOCATION	DECODER LOCATION	OBTAIN BY	TREASURE INSIDE
01	DABRYE MINE, HIDDEN ROOM	FLOATING LANDMASS, PUZZLE LEVEL ONE	TREASURE BOX	WITCH'S EYE
02	ABEL'S ARK, GREEN SPHERE	HAKOX MINI-GAME	DEFEAT BEGINNER LEVEL	G-IGNIS III
03	PEDEA ISLAND	DARK PROFESSOR'S LAIR, BASEMENT	DEFEAT ERDE KAISER SIGMA	ERDE KAISER SIGMA DEVICE
04	CAT TESTING GROUNDS, GNOSIS STORAGE AREA	CAT TESTING GROUNDS, LOUNGE AREA	TREASURE BOX	KWP-XI
05	LABYRINTHOS, AREA 13	HOSPITAL, 4TH FLOOR	TREASURE BOX	ERDE KAISER FURY DEVICE
06	DURANDAL, PARK	CAT TESTING GROUNDS, WEAPON'S DEVELOPMENT AREA	DEFEAT OMEGA ID	ERDE KAISER DARK DEVICE
07	HOSPITAL, 2ND FLOOR	HOSPITAL, 2ND FLOOR	DELIVER ALL FEDERAL REPORTS TO LORIA	RING OF COERCION
08	S-LINE DIVISION, SECTOR ONE	PEDEA ISLAND	TREASURE BOX	TEARS RIVER
09	ELSA, PROFESSOR'S AREA	CAT TESTING GROUNDS, END BOSS	DEFEAT BOSS	ERDE KAISER DEVICE
10	CAT TESTING GROUNDS, DOCKS	MERKABAH, TOP OF SHAFT	TREASURE BOX	KAP-NAR
11	MERKABAH, HONEYCOMB	DABYRIE MINE, BOSS	DEFEAT BOSS	SWEET PAIN
12	FLOATING LANDMASS, BEDROCK LAYER	MERKABAH, HONEYCOMB	TREASURE BOX	GUARDIAN WEAPON
13	ABEL'S ARK, BLUE SPHERE	LABYRINTHOS, AREA 13	TREASURE BOX	DRAGON'S EYE
14	ELSA, E.S. BAY	ABEL'S ARK, BLUE SPHERE	TREASURE BOX	IRON MAIDEN
15	LABYRINTHOS, FRONT AREA	DABRYE MINE, ENTRANCE	TALK TO MAI ABOUT HER FATHER	HINOKA KAGURA

WHAT HAPPENED TO TETHLLA MAGUS?

After the encounter with Mai and Leupold is over, you get to really see why this young woman is so upset with U-TIC. Keep that in mind when you are exploring the Hospital later in the game. Though you won't be able to find or save Tethlla Magus, you can at least learn what happened to him and set Mai's mind at ease.

The data about Tethlla Magus and what was done with him is learned by using the computer consoles in the hospital. Search the upper floors and record this data, then return to the entrance of the Dabrye mine (either during the main game or in the EVS at a future point). Talk to Mai, and she'll get some peace. She'll also reward you with Decoder 15.

OMEGA ID AND THE WEAPON DEVELOPMENT AREA

After defeating Citrine, use the Weapon Development Area Key she drops in the CAT Testing Grounds. Area 06, reached by train, has a locked door that you couldn't pass the last time you were in that region. Use the key on the nearby terminal to open the way, then use another computer inside the area to start an E.S. fight against Omega Universitas. That fight is quite simple, and you should use it to accrue extra Anima for the real encounter ahead.

After Omega Universitas falls, the group immediately goes into the fight with Omega Id. It is very useful to have a full spread of Repair items for your E.S.s, the best possible gear in the game for your craft, and some level-building won't hurt either. Omega Id offers the longest fight in the entire game, and frankly, it's the hardest as well. Though predictable and deceptively easy to understand, Id is able to exploit even trivial flaws in both strategy and tactics.

Omega Id has a Counter, Revenge, does high melee damage, and isn't shy about taking hits either. The normal sets of hits from Id deal substantial damage to any target, so you can't afford to get into the fight without your best gear.

Consider adding Revenge and Counter abilities to any of your E.S.s (as the vast majority of Id's attacks are short-range). In addition, any of your close-range E.S.s must have D-Kill R and D-Kill C to avoid the frequent reprisals that Omega Id unleashes. You just can't afford to take 10-20K damage right before a round where Omega is going to score a critical. In addition, put one D-Sensor on an E.S. or else you'll regret this loss the entire match.

Hopefully, your party is able to sustain at least 55-60k of burst damage with each of your E.S.s. This makes it safer when Omega Id uses its area-of-effect Destructive Wave; criticals from that attack in the later fight can do quite a bit of damage. Also, even when your E.S.s charge in response to Waves of the Berserker, Id is able to deal heavy damage to a single target. That ability heralds Demon Lord, and it is used twice during the late fight (pain, pain, pain).

Id has a wandering elemental immunity. There will always been one weak element, and there will always be one that does no damage at all. This changes every round, so it is essential that you take a good look before starting your attacks. When one E.S. has primary weaponry that will be useless that round, Charge, use Repair Kits on other E.S.s, or look at secondary attacks or special attacks to deal a different damage type.

After falling below 80% health, Id will start to check your Anima levels each round. On rounds when more than one of your mechs has level one or above Anima on their Gauge, there is a good chance that Id will gain 150,000 health, go into a full guard mode, and ruin your day. To avoid this, use all Anima at the beginning of the fight. Then, each time any E.S. gets up to level one Anima, use Anima Awakening. When there is a risk of having two craft get up to level one in the same round, have the second E.S. simply Charge. It's never worth having Id gain 150k of health.

When you do see Waves of the Berserker, top off all health and consider using Charge to do so (it prevents the risk of a string of criticals automatically taking down a full HP E.S.). Even when Charge won't absolutely top off someone's health, it does so much by halving incoming damage next turn that worrying about a few-thousand HPs is silly.

Toward the end of the fight, be very wary of Waves of the Berserker; Id can do two Demon Lords in the same round! Full health and having every E.S. Charge is all that you can do. It's usually close, but enough to keep your party safe.

Use Half Repairs to counter the Destructive Waves, enhanced charges to make up for normal hits, and go for the Nano Repair DX or Full Repairs as needed. This fight costs some money, but that is the way of things if you want to take on the toughest mech fights in the game. You receive the Decoder 06 and the Emperor's Bracelet for winning. This is one of the greatest tests of an E.S. pilot, and your patience deserves the acknowledgement.

Because Decoder 06 gets you the Dark Erde Kaiser ability, the battle against Erde Kaiser Sigma is going to be much easier!

THE BATTLE WITH ERDE KAISER SIGMA

It is possible to defeat Erde Kaiser Sigma before collecting the three other Erde Kaiser types (Erde Kaiser, Erde Kaiser Fury, and Dark Erde Kaiser). However, having all three of these turns the fight into a festival of simplicity in your favor, so it is highly suggested that you look into the Segment Address section and go about finding the three Golden Doors that are accessible before taking on this encounter.

Once you are ready, form a party that has very intense ether attack. Most of this battle isn't very physical, save for the first few turns. Thus, ether is the way to go. MOMO, Shion, and chaos get the job done nicely. If you are seriously worried about failing due to damage, take MOMO, Shion, and Ziggy (with Ziggy loaded up on health so that he can't die before getting a chance to use Seven Moons or Revive items on the others).

Then, use the EVS to visit Pedea Island. Search along the right side of the water line until you find a path up onto small cliff. Destroy the rocks around there and look for the Dark Professor's hideout. Inside, you get to  speak with a Coconut Monkey. This Monkey has you watch a video from the Dark Professor, then gives you the ability to challenge Erde Kaiser Sigma; even if you lose, the party won't die, and you can always do the challenge again by speaking to the Monkey (who stays on the rock outside).

Erde Kaiser Sigma uses varying Kaiser Shields to prevent damage. For the first few rounds of the fight, gain any extra Boost by just beating on the big robot with physical attacks. Soon, however, it will shift into one of its Shield Modes. This is where the Erde Kaiser abilities come in; they allow you to take down the shields. See the following table.

ERDE KAISER SIGMA SHIELDS	
SHIELD MODE	**IDEAL RESPONSE**
BEGINNING OF BATTLE	PHYSICAL ATTACKS
KAISER SHIELD ONE	WEAK TO LIGHTNING, USE ERDE KAISER TO BREAK
KAISER SHIELD TWO	WEAK TO ICE, USE ERDE KAISER FURY TO BREAK
KAISER SHIELD THREE	WEAK TO FIRE, USE DARK ERDE KAISER

INTRODUCTION
ARCHIVES
CHARACTERS
TACTICAL FILES
EQUIPMENT
THREAT ASSESSMENT
REGIONAL ANALYSIS
SUPPLEMENTAL DATA

After bringing down the first shield, slam Sigma with Beam attacks (until the new shield rises, the robot will be weak to Beam attacks). You can even Boost you best ether attack/critical character so that they have as many attacks as possible with heavy beam strikes.

On the next possible action after losing a shield, Erde Kaiser Sigma puts up a different shield (this is why you need all three Erde Kaiser types to have such a good time here). However, the third time Sigma loses a shield, it loses all of its defenses entirely. Now, any damage that isn't physical will do a tremendous amount.

Save up some Boost until Sigma starts to "build power." Then, use Boost after Boost to blow the robot apart with Dark Erde Kaiser and other elemental attacks.

For winning, you receive the Gustav Wrist and **Decoder 03**. Head down into the Dark Professor's lair afterward, and use the Decoder on the golden door in his secret basement. The Erde Kaiser Sigma Device is there, to teach your characters Erde Kaiser Sigma!

Valencia, back on the Elsa (in the E.S. Bay) restores Heaven's Door for you once this is done as well. You need to have the Moon Bridge already (see MOMO's Final Weapon quest), but that is very quick either way. Talk to Valencia, get the Heaven's Door, and watch what it does. Classic item!

HAKOX

Hakox takes a number of hours to beat, as it isn't a simple mini game. You are likely going to need practice, and there are a few levels in there that truly challenge a person's mind and reflexes.

Not only do you receive a number of Skill Upgrades (to give you free skill points and compensate you for some of your time spent), but there are a few item rewards that are only found in Hakox. To complete the Segment Address list in the game, you *have* to at least finish the first world of Hakox (it's just ten stages, and most of them are easy tutorials).

The next huge reward comes when you finish the expert world, when Ziggy receives his Swimsuit. The fifth world grants Jr. his Vaquero pistol (the best weapon in the game for him). Beating those stages also unlocks the sixth world of Hakox.

If you complete the very final world of Hakox, everything is unlocked. You receive Evangelist, are able to use builder mode, and can toy around with your own levels after that point.

Also sprach Zarathustra

OFFICIAL STRATEGY GUIDE

BradyGAMES® Publishing

An Imprint of DK Publishing, Inc.
800 East 96th Street, Third Floor
Indianapolis, Indiana 46240

ISBN: 0-7440-0830-1

Printing Code: The rightmost double-digit number is the year of the book's printing; the rightmost single-digit number is the number of the book's printing. For example, 06-1 shows that the first printing of the book occurred in 2006.

09 08 07 06   4 3 2 1

Manufactured in the United States of America.

BRADYGAMES STAFF

Publisher
David Waybright

Editor-In-Chief
H. Leigh Davis

Director of Marketing
Steve Escalante

Creative Director
Robin Lasek

Licensing Manager
Mike Degler

CREDITS

Development Editor
Chris Hausermann

Screenshot Editor
Michael Owen

Book Designer
Tim Amrhein

Production Designer
Wil Cruz

SPECIAL THANKS TO THE FOLLOWING INDIVIDUALS:

BANDAI NAMCO GAMES INC.

Shinichiro Okamoto

Shinsuke Mori

Takashi Akiyama

Rachel Lee

Mikio Nagura

Jonathan Khersis

Austin Keys

NAMCO BANDAI GAMES AMERICA INC.

Shaun Woo

Brian Schorr

Tara Samuels

Minako Takahashi

Ryan Chennault

Merwin Del Rosario